Death

After cutting his teeth artist... the surreal Billy and the Conquerors and the Portsmouth Sinfonia, the author's leadership of the legendary Alan Clayson and the Argonauts in the late 1970s thrust him to 'a premier position on rock's Lunatic Fringe' (*Melody Maker*). The most representative example of his output on disc is the album, *What a Difference a Decade Made*. Since its release in 1985, Clayson's cult following has continued to grow as has demand for his production talents in the recording studio. His compositions have been covered by such diverse acts as Dave Berry, in whose Cruisers Clayson played keyboards in the mid-1980s, and, via a songwriting collaboration with former Yardbird Jim McCarty, Jane Relf (ex-Renaissance). In 1991, he returned to stage centre with Poacher's Pocket, the latest edition of the Argonauts and as a solo attraction of 'alternative' cabaret persuasion. Described by *The Western Morning News* as 'the A. J. P. Taylor of pop', he has written articles for such disparate journals as *Record Collector*, *Mediaeval World*, *The Times Educational Supplement*, *The Beat Goes On* and, while still a teenager, the notorious *Schoolkids Oz*. He has also been engaged to conduct numerous courses and lectures throughout Britain – and, more recently, the United States – concerning popular music and composition. *Death Discs* is his sixth book.

By the same author

CALL UP THE GROUPS:
The Golden Age of British Beat, 1962–67

BACK IN THE HIGH LIFE:
A Biography of Steve Winwood

ONLY THE LONELY:
The Life and Artistic Legacy of Roy Orbison

THE QUIET ONE:
A Life of George Harrison

RINGO STARR:
Straight Man or Joker?

DEATH DISCS

Ashes to smashes

an account
of fatality
in the popular
song

BY

ALAN CLAYSON

LONDON
VICTOR GOLLANCZ LTD
1992

To Alice Aetheria and Inese

First published in Great Britain 1992
by Victor Gollancz Ltd
14 Henrietta Street, London WC2E 8QJ

A Gollancz Paperback Original

Copyright © Alan Clayson 1992

The right of Alan Clayson to be identified as author of this
work has been asserted by him in accordance with the
Copyright Designs and Patents Act 1988.

A catalogue record of this book is available
from the British Library

ISBN 0 575 05475 1

Typeset by CentraCet, Cambridge
and printed and bound in Great Britain
by Cox & Wyman Ltd, Reading

Contents

Roll of Honour

Those whom this page commemorates are numbered among those who endured hardness in assisting me with the completion of this book. Let those who come after see to it that their names be not forgotten.

ROGER BARNES ALAN BARWISE DAVE BERRY
STUART BOOTH KATHRYN BOOTH ROB BRADFORD
BRUCE BRAND TERRY CLARKE HARRY CLAYSON
INESE CLAYSON JACK CLAYSON RON COOPER
PETE COX DON CRAINE KEVIN DELANEY
PETER DOGGETT IAN DRUMMOND MARY EMMOTT
TIM FAGAN SARAH FAGAN ROSS FERGUSSON
PETE FRAME ANN FREER GEOFF GODDARD
ERIC GOULDEN KEITH GRANT HELEN GUMMER
DAWN HARVEY GIULIA HETHERINGTON
BARRY HICKS PENNY HICKS LEE HORNSBY
MALCOLM HORNSBY DAVE HUMPHREYS
GARRY JONES GRAHAM LARKBEY BRIAN LEAFE
SPENCER LEIGH DAVE MAGGS HELEN MAGGS
STEVE MAGGS JIM MCCARTY COLIN MILES
STEVE MORRIS JILL MYHILL MARK PAYTRESS
CHRIS PHIPPS ANTONIA POMMERS IAN PREECE
VIV REDMAN EVAN REYNOLDS LYN REYNOLDS
NICK ROBERTS MIKE ROBINSON MARY LU ST CLAIR
CHARLES SALT DEBORAH SALT JIM SIMPSON
ELLIOTT STEIN ANN STONEHOUSE

LORD DAVID SUTCH   MIKE SWEENEY
JOHN TOBLER   JOHN TOWNSEND   PAUL TUCKER
LESLEY WESTON   SIMON WESTON   FRAN WOOD

Special mention must be made of Faith Brooker for instigating this project and seeing it through – even though she knew me of old.

*'You can be a
king or a street sweeper
but everybody dances to the
Grim Reaper'*

– LAST WORDS OF ROBERT ALTON HARRIS BEFORE
SUFFERING DEATH IN THE GAS CHAMBER IN SAN
QUENTIN GAOL, CALIFORNIA, 21 APRIL 1992

Prologue

'Don't Go Down in the Mine, Dad'

At first glance, this might appear to be one of those books designed quite deliberately to be junk. You know – the kind of tome you dip into occasionally, read in the bath, or that you bought to make an Art Statement by displaying it on your bookshelf between, say, *Heidi* and *The Conquest of Wessex in the Sixth Century*. Your record rack might likewise be a careful juxtaposition of, perhaps, LL Cool J's *Walking with a Panther*, *Session with the Dave Clark Five* and Ligeti's *Mass for Belsen*.

However, while researching the book, I found some days that morning had become evening and I hadn't even stopped to eat, such is the depth and breadth of the subject herein. Even the most respectable people will slow down their cars more than is necessary to stare at messy road accidents or settle down to a soothing half hour in an armchair with a tabloid and its latest revelations about a torso found in a pile of dead leaves. Morbid fascination is a longstanding human phenomenon – along with its response – black humour.

Irish maintenance staff at an Edmonton crematorium used to amuse one another by setting tunes and dancing jigs to some of the epitaphs. A particular favourite was 'Ohhhhhh, a light has from our household gone/A voice we loved is stilled/A place is vacant in our home/Which never can be filled', sung to a cross between 'Macnamara's band' and 'Delaney's Donkey'. Although death and horror have, to a lesser degree than love, been the natural ingredients of many popular songs, it is interesting to note just how frequently the Grim Reaper has made the charts, and the vast number of artists who have released what might be construed as 'death discs'. One of pop's hardiest forms, it is also, perhaps, the most comic – though much of the humour is unconscious, notably in the kitsch melodramas of the early 1960s.

While the recording industry is peculiar to the twentieth century, it has exploited instincts and traditions from time immemorial. From the cradle our heads and those of our forefathers have been filled with play rhymes about the most awful occurrences – mutilation of disabled rodents ('Three Blind Mice'), fractured skulls ('Jack and Jill'), ('Humpty Dumpty'*), water vertebrates drowning on dry land ('Once I Caught a Fish Alive'), assassination and conspiracy in the animal kingdom ('Who Killed Cock Robin?'), bereavement ('Go Tell Aunt Nancy Her Old Grey Goose Is Dead') and – geese again – mass extermination ('Christmas Is Coming').

'Oranges and Lemons' concludes with a chopper to chop off your head – and Bob Dylan's 'postcards of the hanging' (in 1965's 'Desolation Row') wouldn't have been that far-fetched an item of merchandise in days when pieces of rope from the previous execution were sold (by enterprising if unscrupulous chandlers) to folk in holiday mood who had gathered at Newgate to watch a felon get his neck stretched. Their faces would brighten with pleasure if the condemned chap started raving or put up a struggle as the noose was slipped over his head – and,

---

* In 1964, it was rocked-up (as 'Humpity Dumpty') by Gene Vincent, and given a ska treatment by Georgie Fame and the Blue Flames.

just for effect, the hangman would grin horribly and roll his eyes like a true showbusiness professional.

From the eighteenth century, such occasions boosted turnover of the 'murder ballads' which emanated from publishers in London's murky Seven Dials district to be hawked in the city's thoroughfares and ale houses. Unlike those in 'news ballads'*, a subject didn't have to be up to date either because, interviewed by Henry Mayhew for his *London Labour and the London Poor*, a 'street patterer' elucidated, 'There's nothing beats a stunning good murder after all. "The Murder of Sarah Holmes in Lincoln" has been in work twenty years.'

Another murder ballad, 'The Five Pirates of the Flowery Land', moved three thousand copies in an hour – an eighteenth-century equivalent of going straight in at No. 1. Though its final total of ninety thousand generated a tidy sum for the publisher, its versifier had been paid only an outright shilling – thus demonstrating that the sharp practice associated with sections of today's music business is nothing new. Long inbred too was a sense of hyperbole. It was sometimes suggested that a first-person-narrative ballad had been written by the suspected murderer himself. Though technically in contempt of court, these strategies were generally safe from prosecution – but it didn't help the cause of the men charged with murdering William Weare in 1823 when, even before the jury had been selected, a penny broadsheet went the rounds containing these lines: 'They cut his throat from ear to ear/The brains they battered in/

* Of which 'The Meeting at Peterloo' was typical. It was penned after troops were called in to break up a Parliamentary reform gathering at Manchester's St Peter's Field on 19 August 1819. They panicked and opened fire on the mob.

His name was Mister William Weare/He dwelt in Lyon's Inn'.

As always, accuracy was outweighed by commercial considerations. The printer of the Weare song was able to live off the profits for three years before resuming trade with a sheet headlined 'WE ARE ALIVE AGAIN', leaving so narrow a gap between the first two words that it looked as if Weare had risen from his tomb. So many were taken in by this printed pig-in-a-poke that it brought the word 'catchpenny' into our language.

Weare might not have survived into the next century but ballad pedlars did – and it was in 1910 that Lawrence Wright, huckster in a Seven Dials outdoor market, was so captivated by a Robert Donnelly number entitled 'Don't Go Down in the Mine, Dad' that he risked a fiver to buy all rights to it. Initially, few bothered with this moribund opus about a little boy who, dreaming of 'the pit all afire', begs his father not to go to work on the coal face. Dad shrugs it off as juvenile imaginings but, about to descend the shaft, he 'could not banish his fears', and decides to go back home. Sure as fate, before the day was out, a blaze down below took the lives of twenty of his workmates.

Lawrence Wright got a miracle too when nearly one hundred and fifty men died in a Whitehaven pit disaster. And with the 1912 coal strike following almost immediately, his investment acquired sufficient topicality to sell a million copies within three weeks, allowing him to establish a music publishing company that eventually moved uptown to the West End's Denmark Street. Later on, other music firms would congregate round here, thus fuelling the argument that 'Don't Go Down in the Mine, Dad' was the cornerstone upon which Britain's outpost of Tin Pan Alley was built. When recorded in 1910 by

14

Mr Stanley Kirkby on the Zonophone label – matrix number 342 – at 78 r.p.m., it was the first manifestation of a collision between ancient tradition and a new medium. 'Don't Go Down in the Mine, Dad' was nothing less than the first death disc.

Chapter One

The End of the Beginning

Before World War I, popular music usually meant orchestral pieces not far removed from light classics – and *bel canto* vocalists who could set auditoriums a-tremble with genteel eloquence and nicety of intonation. Such an exquisite was Stanley Kirkby whose sonorous tenor swelled throughout 'Comrades', released while the populace were still euphoric about the Relief of Mafeking and looking forward to a final showdown with Germany. As one of our chaps on campaign in the Transvaal, Stanley was attacked whilst asleep by an enemy lancer – whether Boer or 'native' is unclear – 'but my comrade sprang to save me and received it in his heart'.

Kirkby's unnamed 'darling old comrade' had much in common with the lad who galloped through the turmoil of battle to save his wounded lifelong pal from certain death in the heart-wrenching 'Two Little Boys', written in 1903 by Theodore F. Morse and Edward Madden. During those musical evenings that preceded the wireless, a child would be led forth, glistening with embarrassment, to the centre of the front parlour to pipe 'Two Little Boys'* in an uncertain treble.

On the Winner label with Stanley Kirkby, Robert

---

* That might have been the case closed on the song but for its discovery by Rolf Harris when it became the oldest composition to top the British charts.

Carr warbled 'Cheer Up Mollie (Patriotic Song)', sentimental nonsense about a tin-helmeted soldier off to the front, heartening his missus (as she buckles on his rifle for him) with such eternal verities as 'it's men that must go out to fight, dear, and women must just wait and pray . . . some (men) will count with the missing and slain . . . and if we don't meet on this earth, dear . . . just wait for the roll call up yonder and join me in God's land of peace'. 'Goodbye Dolly Gray', 'It's A Long Way To Tipperary'*, 'Are We Down Hearted' and like products kept mum too about the cause being less noble than first imagined – and, sung from a woman's perspective, so did 'We Don't Want to Lose You (Your King and Country Need You)' and 'I'll Make a Man of You' ('if you'll only take the (King's) shilling') as the face and pointing finger of Lord Kitchener loomed from recruiting posters.

When the war wasn't over by Christmas, as rashly predicted, we danced to different tunes. Professional composers, if not quite so optimistic, weren't beyond veiling the floricultural likes of 'The Rose of No Man's Land' and the evergreen 'Roses of Picardy'† with romance, while, in Passchendaele, the sun was actually obscured by smoke at the height of summer – thereby lending the 'Roses of Picardy' lyric 'till the shadows veil their skies' an unintentional allusion by writer Fred Weatherby. From the trenches came the involved realism

---

* During a mid-1960s craze for olde-tyme whimsy, both of these items were recorded by Warren Mitchell as BBC television's loud-mouthed, ignorant Cockney vulgarian Alf Garnett on Songs of World War I. 'Goodbye Dolly Gray' was also the A-side of a 1967 single by the Mojos.

† In the same year as the Mojos' 'Goodbye Dolly Gray', Vince Hill had more luck with his Top Twenty revival of 'Roses of Picardy'.

of 'Hanging on the Old Barbed Wire', 'Hush! Here Comes a Whizzbang', 'I Want to Go Home', 'The Bells of Hell', 'The Battle of the Somme', 'There's a Long Long Trail a-Winding', 'Far Far From Wipers', 'Adieu la Vie' and, to the melody of 'What a Friend We Have in Jesus', 'When This Lousy War is Over'.

Long after it *was* over, a 1958 radio programme, *The Long, Long Trail*, strung together related sketches using war songs as links. This was in turn adapted with a more coherent plot for the West End theatre, and then for one of the most inspired anti-war movies ever made, *Oh! What a Lovely War*, directed by Richard Attenborough.

World War II, on the other hand, was a conflict unremarkable for incisive ditties of death as we had learned from the last global bust-up that war wasn't as much fun as it was cracked up to be. What was the point of either telling lies or rubbing in how ghastly it was? Civilians cowering in air-raid shelters knew that already. Indeed, some of them were middle-aged veterans with missing limbs, from Mons, Ypres or Passchendaele. Better to look on the bright side with 'The King Is Still in London', Bud Flanagan's 'Who Do You Think You Are Kidding, Mr Hitler' and 'We'll Meet Again' by 'Forces Sweetheart' Vera Lynn. You could risk a comment on wartime shortages, e.g., 'When Can I Have a Banana Again' and Elsie and Doris Waters' 'Please Leave My Butter Alone', as long as you made a joke of it. When the Yanks came over, they brought with the chewing gum, Lucky Strikes and hand-painted ties, their own brand of uplifting music.

If the Americans had vaudeville, we had the music hall – so called because every artiste was expected to make use of the pit orchestra if only for a rumble of timpani as a rabbit was produced from a magician's top hat. Usually the bill would contain an entirely musical act that, before the advent of television, would live off the same repertoire for years. With exceptions such as Noël Coward's much-covered 'Miss Otis Regrets' proving the rule, death was not generally considered suitable for even the second house at the Glasgow Empire. However, singing comedian Billy Merson did not risk offence with his perennial and nonsensical 'Wreck of the Dover Express', in which 'I wrote a farewell to my darling and poisoned meself with the ink' was a typical line. Because it concerned lethal vengeance on a foreigner, you could also get away with 'The Spaniard that Blighted My Life', the Merson composition that, in 1913, launched Al Jolson* as a showbusiness ubiquity.

It was also recorded by Stanley Holloway; but an opus much more synonymous with this British comedy actor was the mid-1930s 'Albert' quartet. The first of these, in 1934, was 'The Lion and Albert', which became more of a parlour room party piece than 'Two Little Boys'. On a day trip to Blackpool, this 'grand little lad' and his parents, Mr and Mrs Ramsbottom, were ravenous for stimulation as 'there was no wrecks and nobody drownded . . . nothing to laugh at at all'. Bathed in tedium, they decided to visit the zoo where Albert poked a sleeping lion in the ear with an ornamental stick. Irritated, the beast dragged the boy through the cage bars 'and swallowed the little lad whole'. Put as prosaically as this, those who've never heard 'The Lion and Albert' might be forgiven for wondering how such a nasty story could possibly be entertaining. The answer lies in the vexed and excessive pragmatism of the parents as their only child is eaten ('and after we've paid to come

* Who remade it in 1946 as a duet with Bing Crosby.

in!') and the blunt composure of secondary characters such as the animal keeper ('are you sure it's your boy he's eaten?').

After a three year rest, Stanley resurrected the family for 'Albert and the 'Eadsman'. As the lad's birthday treat, the three go to the Tower of London where they catch sight of a ghostly executioner and a headless Lady Jane Grey. The axeman turns his attention to Albert who successfully routs his attacker by pushing a slice of toast in his face.*

This episode had been introduced by a leitmotif on the ivories from another Holloway release – sung rather than recited – from this period that described another Tudor queen, Anne Boleyn, who haunted that selfsame tourist trap at midnight 'With Her Head Tucked Underneath Her Arm', courtesy of her husband, Henry VIII whose spectral feasts were queered by her grudgeful presence. Drunken sentries mistook her burden for a football, thus allowing Stanley to drop in a topical quip ('they think it's Alec James† instead of poor old Anne Boleyn').

Mixing song and monologue, the prolific Holloway also left us with definitive versions of 'Ain't it Grand to Be Blooming Well Dead' – a sardonic serenade from a coffin en route to an East End grave, anticipating Jacques Brel's 'Funeral Tango' by decades. His finest moment was, perhaps, 'Sweeney Todd', an idiosyncratic account – accompanied by full orchestra instead of solitary piano – of Fleet Street's demon barber. Their throats slit, customers were gutted by the widow next door, and

---

* The last 'Albert' record was 'Jubilee Sovereign', irrelevant here as it centres merely on the child swallowing same.
† Arsenal soccer XI's centre-forward during the late 1930s.

their flesh baked into the meat pies sold in her shop. Business was brisk – because 'dead men can't talk with a mouthful of soap' – until that Saturday night when Bow Street Runners apprehended Todd who was hanged in chains at Tyburn – but he was called from the tomb by Old Nick who made use of his professional skills ('Wake up, Sweeney, I want a shave!').

How Satan might have employed US funnymen Moran and Mack is open to speculation. In the late 1920s, they shifted millions of records as 'The Two Black Crows'. Because they were black themselves, they could discuss 'coons' and mock the Uncle Tom American negro caricature with impunity for much the same reasons as modern 'alternative' comediennes are able to crack sexist jokes. I'd prefer not to venture an opinion but refer you instead to 1928's 'Two Black Crows in Hades' as a sample of their 'humor'.

It was more like 'hum*our*' on 'Grandfather's Clock' – the one that 'stopped when the old man died' – by the Radio Revellers, vocal sound-effects specialists. This opus revealed the sunny side of Henry Clay Work who also composed the mordant 'The Ship That Never Returned'.*

Slave work 'hollers' were the root of songs such as steel drivin' 'John Henry', so happy in his job that he wished to die with 'that hammer in my hand'†, and lazy 'Railroad Bill' (who would 'kill anyone that done me harm' until 'the Butcher (death) cut him down'). More

---

* Work was also responsible for the Civil War singalong, 'Marching Through Georgia'.
† Lyrically, 'John Henry' was a close relation of 'The Dying Hogger', a mechanic who requested that the undertaker 'put into my cold, still hand a monkey and an old oil can'.

purposely comical, 'Stack O' Lee' was a black gunfighting gambler, a 'bad man' hanged to 'set your spirit free' after a fracas in a saloon in either Memphis, New Orleans or St Louis, depending on the version.

As 'Stagger Lee', it was US No. 1 for Lloyd Price in 1959. This was some achievement for a negro vocalist with a traditional song – albeit one rejuvenated with a rock 'n' roll beat. Best-selling records in the States, you understand, used to be assigned to one of three tabulations – popular, country-and-western (formerly 'hillbilly') and 'sepia' (or 'rhythm-and-blues' as it became). This meant that you could top, say, the 'sepia' chart without figuring at all in the parallel dimension of pop, unless your disc picked up enough plays on pop radio and consequent sales in commensurate chart return shops. Only on rare occasions could you score in all three.

In the decades that preceded rock 'n' roll, a white North American radio listener might tune in by accident to muffled bursts of what segregationalists heard as 'the screaming idiotic words and savage music' on some faraway negro-run station. No white presenter would ever programme 'Hangman Blues' by Blind Lemon Jefferson or Mattie Delaney's 'Tallahatchie River Blues' (in which her 'daddy', i.e., lover, had drowned in a 1927 flood disaster). Even more *verboten* were 'Death Letter' from Son House and Bukka White's 'Fixin' to Die'*.

Among other 'sepia' platters that did not baulk at suicide were St Louis Jimmy's 'I'm Going Down to the River (and Drown Myself)' and 1950's 'Empty Life' with singing pianist Mercy Dee lost 'in a world of shadows. It almost drives me insane'. Its slow-paced arrangement

* Revived on Bob Dylan's début album in 1962.

was interchangeable with that of the Texas-born blues-man's previous single, 'Danger Zone' where, twitching with barely controllable emotion, he calms down sufficiently to gently censure his woman for promiscuity but issues a 'final warning' that 'any move may prove dangerous and cause crepe to be hanging on your door'.

Perhaps Mercy had been too morally generous for his own health's sake, and was going the way of singer Lonnie Johnson, his brain so pulped by paresis of advanced syphilis in sweetly sinister 'Careless Love'* that he commits murder. A misspent youth might also be why Howlin' Wolf and Sonny Terry were, respectively, 'Goin' Down Slow' ('I've had my fun (now I'm paying for it')). No doubt Wolf's foolish past provoked frank exchanges between him and the wife whose nagging made him 'soon rather be dead, sleeping six feet in the ground' than remain married to her in 'How Many More Years!'.

The blues also pulled no punches about World War II. No 'When Can I Have a Banana Again', Arthur 'Big Boy' Crudup's 'Cool Disposition' mingled universal suffering ('this war is *awful*/it upset so many homes') and personal tragedy ('I want to kill somebody because my baby's got another man'). In 1952, the stalemate in Korea inspired his 'I'm Gonna Dig Myself a Hole' – and 'when I come out, there won't be no wars around'. Howlin' Wolf attacked armed discord between nations in 'Killing Floor' – which was unearthed by the brassy Electric Flag in 1968 just as Elvis Presley had covered Arthur Crudup's 'That's Alright Mama' and 'My Baby

* Sanitised in a 1962 C & W treatment by Ray Charles. 'Careless Love' was a precursor of the Coasters' contagious 'Poison Ivy' (1959), resuscitated during the 1960s beat boom by the Dave Clark Five, the Rolling Stones and the Paramounts.

23

Left Me' in the mid-1950s. It would be pleasant to think that Wolf at least got the royalties due to him, for Crudup, like many other blues artists with a lackadaisical regard for business, died still awaiting a fat cheque, in his case for his services to the King.

Arthur's three-score-years-and-ten were blamelessly uneventful when compared to such as Peetie Wheatstraw, toast of Louisville's red-light quarter, who named himself at various times 'The Devil's Son-in-Law' and 'The High Sheriff of Hell'. Plenty of blues musicians were killed in stabbings, shootings and brawls while among those incarcerated for instigating the same were Bukka White, Son House – and Leadbelly (Huddie Ledbetter) who was inside a Louisiana gaol when folk music archivist John A. Lomax, searching out prison songs, was stunned by the range of the guitar-picking convict's seemingly boundless repertoire, embracing everything from the most low-down blues – his 'devil's ditties' – to country square dance and children's play rhymes like 'The Grey Goose' (preacher defies the scriptures by shooting a goose on a Sunday but finds it impossible to eat). Though British folk scholar Cecil Sharp claimed to have discovered a Kentucky version in 1917, Ledbetter was attributed with the composition of 'Black Girl', crazily roaming the pine forest surrounding the railway line where her husband, an engine driver, perished horribly in a crash ('his head was found in the driving wheel but his body has never been found').

Robert Johnson was tormented too – by an inferno of devils, phantoms and ectoplasmic monsters. The most obsessed of his rural exorcisms in this vein – 'Hellhound on My Trail' and the Faustian 'Me and the Devil Blues' – were both taped on the same day (20 June 1937). I've given him less space than I have Leadbelly because of the nature of this discussion but I ought to say that there are those – such as pop critic Charles Shaar Murray – who reckon Johnson was one of the greatest men ever to have walked the planet. I wouldn't go quite that far, but I would urge anyone making a serious study of the blues to go first and last to Robert Johnson.

The blues ain't finished yet, not by a long chalk. With its blending of cowboy pessimism and Victorian broadness of gesture, what else is C & W if not white trash blues?

And, lifting its tune from 'The Ship that Never Returned', Vernon Dalhart's 'Wreck of the Old '97' was, in 1924, the first C & W million-seller. It sprang from a spectacular derailment that occurred in Danville, Virginia in 1903 when driver Steve Grady, thrashing the engine to make up lost time, was 'scalded to death by steam' through the failure of air-brakes with the train's consequent plunge over a precipice ('you can see what a jump he made'). To the same clickety-clack locomotive rhythm, the opus was first recorded by Henry Whittiler, one of its reputed composers. Nevertheless, most of Dalhart's other hits* were written by Kansas-born Carson Robison who began his recording career in 1920 as a whistler before switching to vocals. He and his accompanying Hill Billies were forever on the radio in Britain from 1932 until the outbreak of war.

* While disaster epics were Dalhart's stylistic trademark, hard on his heels in 1924 came Virginia's Ernest ('Pop') Van Stoneman with the traditional 'The Sinking of the Titanic'. Later versions of 'Wreck of the Old '97' have ranged from a suitably ramshackle beat-group arrangement by the Downliners Sect to Johnny Cash's race through it during a recorded concert before inmates of San Quentin penitentiary in 1968.

Just as John A. Lomax collected blues songs in order to preserve them, so the John Edwards Memorial Foundation collected western folk songs from field tapings and the voices of practitioners crackling from obscure 78 r.p.m., and even cylinder recordings. Among works thus gathered was Jack Webb's 'The Night Guard' concerning a fatal goring by a rogue steer, its small-hours creepiness made more so by a vocal delivery utterly devoid of emotion. Billie Maxwell takes more of an interest in the chilling 'Haunted Hunter', possibly because it was actually her – as a trapper – who, travelling alone in 'the sickly moonlight' of the mountains, encountered a grey walker who left no footprints in the snow. Worse, the very sight of him left her to be found blinded, her hair whitened with shock.

Billie co-wrote 'Haunted Hunter' but Victor Records advertised in vain for the composer of the release in the 1920s of 'Haywire Mac' McClintock's 'Sam Bass', a ballad of a notorious bandit whose activities triggered the founding of the Texas Rangers. He was, romanticised in the song as a Robin Hood-type figure who came to a bad end only by the treachery of Jim, one of his sidekicks. Presumably, Sam's illegal doings were deemed ethical because Mac declares, 'what a scorching Jim will get, when Gabriel blows his horn'. On the look-out for more souls to damn, Satan bit off more than he could chew when he ran into some drunken cowpokes who lassoed and branded him in Powder River Jack's 'Tying a Knot in the Devil's Tail'.

Swerving off the trail and upwards into them thar hills, we hear the sobbing of small lives shattered by the tragedies outlined in 'Put My Little Shoes Away', 'Wreck on the Highway', 'The Death of Little Kathy Fiscus' – and in 1923, 'You Will Never Miss Your

Mother Until She is Gone' in what even his recording manager described as the 'pluperfect awful' singing of Atlanta's Fiddlin' John Carson. He was certainly no Slim Whitman who could slide, in the space of a bar, from light baritone to a note-perfect but alarming yodelled falsetto. Like Fiddlin' John, Slim regretted taking his mum for granted, on receiving a 'Letter Edged in Black' informing him of her death. With a melody not dissimilar to 'Red River Valley', he'd already borne 'That Silver Haired Daddy of Mine'* 'vainly fighting the battle of time' as his son tortured himself by recalling 'all the heartaches I've caused you to bear'.

Should you make your excuses and leave the heavy atmosphere round Slim's place, you might wish you'd stayed if you'd come within earshot of the forced laughter at the weak jokes in the semi-instrumental 'I Laughed So Hard I Nearly Died†' from the Rex Cole Mountaineers.

There are worse ways to go but, however it happens, righteous cowfolk are destined for 'the faraway ranch of the boss in the sky' after Billy Hill's 'Last Round Up', a C & W 'standard' whether covered by the unsung Singing Mountaineers on Regal Zonophone or by the Sons of the Pioneers, elected to Nashville's Country Music Hall of Fame in 1980. Tex Ritter along with Cowboy Copas, Jimmie Rodgers, Gene Autry, Hank Williams and

---

* Also a big hit in 1939 for 'Oklahoma Yodelling Cowboy', Gene Autry. As an arbiter of his fame, the most common folk instrument in the South during the 1930s was a make of guitar etched with the image of Autry on a rearing horse.
† Or, away from C & W, for a moment, 'Laugh? I Thought I'd Die' from the soundtrack of 1960s television series *The Addams Family* (more recently turned into a full-length film). Amazingly, in 1974, a middle-aged Briton actually did die laughing whilst watching an episode of BBC 1's *The Goodies*.

other icons were among those who found themselves similarly immortalised in 'I Dreamed of a Hillbilly Heaven', penned by Eddie Dean, a rather elderly Autry protégé.

Another dozing with a stetson over his eyes was Jules Allen, a genuine cowpuncher of the 1890s. His 'Cowboy's Dream' personified the Lord as the proprietor of ranchland so boundless in acreage that it 'always makes room for the sinners'. Though the tune coincided in every particular with that of the quasi-traditional 'My Bonnie', the libretto was, reputedly, the property of a Mr Coffee, father of a captain of the Texas Rangers.* It came to be accepted as a bona-fide hymn when, herding steers the long miles along the Chisholm Trail from Texas to Missouri, a trail boss would call a halt on Sundays and assemble his hard-bitten underlings to blast up praise to the Lord, asking His blessing and guidance on the task in hand – then it'd be back to the heat, flies, stink and, for the greenhorns, the burning agony of saddle-sores.

In the Old West, death was not so terrible. If nothing else, it meant a surcease from toil for ordinary working people whose hardships were presumed to pre-empt future punishment. Some believed that, in the hereafter, those who'd had it easy when alive were made to do all the work. That was much the situation in 'Poor Man's Heaven', a duet by Bud Billings and Carson Robison. Their vivid vision also extended to feathered beds, strawberry pie ('twenty feet high'), whipped cream ('they bring it in a truck'), lakes of beer, breakfast in bed and, crucially, ownership of their own homes.

* But deemed 'traditional' when it appeared on a 1959 album by the Sons of the Pioneers.

Aptly plagiarising the melody of 'There's a Tavern in the Town', 'Take Ma Boots Off When I Die', a *risqué* western swing novelty by Robison's backing Hill Billies, had a fornicating poker-player who'd 'shot my way from Texas to Rio Grande' assuming that he'd be in the clear before the Lord ('when they hand me out my wings') as, to balance his sins, he'd inherited the widow and sixteen children of the wife-beater and wanted killer that he'd gunned down.

Hillbilly banjo and Jew's harp solos had no place in Gene Autry's John Wayne-esque incantation of 'A Cowboy's Prayer' to an unobtrusive bank of strings. Gene wraps it up with the most concrete details of an idealised redneck funeral – 'darkened shades . . . smell of flowers . . . the sound of "Taps"* . . . the tread of footsteps in the front yard'. He wants the ceremony brief and to the point, and his epitaph a simple 'Here Lies a Man'†.

Johnny Bond was the main 'feed' on Autry's long-standing California radio series *Melody Ranch*. He was also the composer of near on five hundred published C & W songs of which the remorseful 'Conversation With a Gun' for Tex Ritter‡ was a characteristically solemn monologue. Confined to a wheelchair through over-confidence at a shoot-out, a former pistolero transfers a bitter and sardonic guilt to his now rusting weapon,

---

* Nothing to do with running water but an elegant evensong hymn beginning 'Day is done, gone the sun . . . ', suitable indeed for funerals but heard most often nowadays at Remembrance Day ceremonies and at the close of Scout and Guide campfire entertainments.
† A similar sentence was chipped on the headstone of the black ex-heavyweight boxing champion, Sonny Liston.
‡ Who was taken by an apoplectic fit on 2 January 1974 at a Nashville jailhouse whilst attempting to arrange bail for one of his backing musicians.

inanimate slayer of desperadoes like Lightning Dan, Utah Pete and 'a rustler known as Lou'.

The source of Cowboy Copas' sorrow in deceptively bouncy 'Tragic Romance' was mistaken identity when he espied his intended in the arms of another, 'huggin' and kissin' like true lovers can'. Rather than wait for an explanation, he packs his belongings and quits town. Years later, he is seated in a restaurant, chatting with a complete stranger about intimate matters. In an incredible coincidence, this chap reveals himself to be the brother of the girl (who'd since died of a broken heart) – and it was he that she was embracing with effusive but sisterly affection 'on that fatal night'.

If you've any tears left after that unlikely tale, weep them for Tessie and her condemned boyfriend on her last visit to 'Birmingham Jail' by Bud and Joe Billings ('Singing with Guitars and Violin' elucidates the label of Zonophone 5647). Rather than record another duet with the illustrious Carson Robison, Bud teamed up with his brother again for 'The Engineer's Child' in which a lachrymose violin transports us to the apparent deathbed of a railway employee's daughter. He drags himself off to work, perhaps forfeiting a chance to witness the infant's last moments. His anticipation of grief dissolves, however, when she recovers – as indicated by the green light placed by her mother in the window of their trackside home as his train hurtles by. He thanks the Lord that it wasn't red.

Maybe the greatest death song of this century was 'Riders in the Sky',* covered by numerous acts includ-

* Also known as 'Ghost Riders in the Sky'.

ing the Sons of the Pioneers*. Topping the US hit parade for eleven weeks in 1949 and on instant replay for hours at a stretch when I rediscovered it twenty years later, the best version of this Stan Jones composition was certainly that of Vaughn Monroe and his Orchestra – though 'Orchestra' is rather a misnomer as, based loosely on a strain from 'When Johnny Comes Marching Home Again', it utilises only the galloping propulsion of acoustic guitar and, suspended outside the implied key, a three-note *ostinato* on unison trumpets. Over this sparse instrumentation, husky Monroe is augmented by a male chorus. The narrative concerns an old cowpoke cantering towards an empty horizon in the requisite inclement weather. Resting on a ridge, he is astonished to see a spectral stampede of heifers forever a fraction out of reach of pursuing herders whose once exuberant 'yippee-i-ays!' have long decayed to an ethereal drift on the wind. One unhappy horseman hails the open-mouthed watcher, and advises him, 'Cowboy, change your ways today' otherwise he too will be 'trying to catch the Devil's herd' for all eternity.

'Riders in the Sky' was an early instance of the incorporation of a western theme into mainstream pop – and as such was popular with pre-teens and others disenfranchised by the lovey-dovey couplets prevalent on most pop offerings. Also a fixture on the BBC Light Programme's *Children's Favourites*, Doris Day's 'The Deadwood Stage' (from the 1953 film, *Calamity Jane*) rained 'injun arrows thicker than porcupine quills', and, as well as its thrilling 'whip-crack-away' chorus, introduced a character who had on his gun 'more than twenty-seven notches'.

* Through whose ranks Roy Rogers 'King of the Cowboys' passed.

Despite the underlying soppiness of a disagreeable boy-girl romance, the Kingston Trio's 'Tom Dooley' was a dilution of the nineteenth-century North Carolina hill ballad 'Tom Dula'. It was something else too: the first death hit of the post-Elvis era. With smooth harmonies and dazzling smiles, these acoustic troubadours made palatable for *Children's Favourites* the saga of Tom's knifing of his faithless Laura, his arrest (by Sheriff Jim Grayson) and consignment to a cell before being hanged next morning.* The way the Trio told it, Dooley's fate seemed no more terrifying than having to report to the headmaster's study for the cane.

'Tom Dooley' was covered in Britain by Johnny Worth and Bill Adams and the Coronets, but only Lonnie Donegan's version was up to the Trio's fighting weight in the Top Ten. With his stage name borrowed from Lonnie Johnson, Donegan was, more than Tommy Steele, a UK 'answer' to Presley in his vivacious processing of black music for a white audience. Backed by his Skiffle Group, he headed his country's equivalent of North America's 'rockabilly' throughout its late 1950s prime.

Skiffle became more homogenously British when Donegan – amid much vilification from purists – scored his third No. 1 with a rewrite of the Liverpool lay, 'My Old Man's a Fireman on the Elder-Dempster Line'. However, in the beginning, he'd delved deep into folksy Americana – blues, spirituals, hillbilly, you name it. Following his lead, certain of his discoveries were also

* The true story was that Dula was executed at 2.17 p.m., on 1 May 1868 for the murder of Laura Foster of Wilkes County in 1866. She was suffocated with a handkerchief stuffed down her throat, and Dula's lover, Anne Kelton, was believed to have actually stabbed her. Kelton was never brought to trial.

featured by his myriad disciple groups – and thus a portfolio of skiffle 'standards' emerged.

Contained within were all the good old good ones like 'Wreck of the Old '97', 'Stack O' Lee', 'Railroad Bill', 'John Henry', Leadbelly's 'Ella Speed' ('first degree murder with a Colt 41'), 'Black Girl' and 'The Ballad of Jesse James'*. There were also liberal dashes of religion in 'Oh Mary Don't You Weep' (because 'Pharaoh's army got drownded' chasing the Israelites over the Red Sea) plus more Old Testament hellfire in 'Well Well Well'†, 'I'll Fly Away' ('to the bright, celestial shore'), 'Come Down Gabriel' and 'Rock O' My Soul' ('in the bosom of Abraham').

Such material was not exclusive to British skiffle. Arising from the commercial success of the Kingston Trio, combos in the same wholesome mould such as the Highwaymen, New York's Journeymen‡ and the Brothers Four sought their place in the sun to the adulterating degree of inserting morose show tunes like 'Nothing More to Look Foward to' (from the Broadway musical *Kwamina*) into LPs and concert sets. Also representative of the idiom, however, were Tom Paxton's 'Rambling Boy' ('dead and gone' but continuing to ramble in heaven), 'John Hardy'§ (a 'desperate little

* Its central theme was the murder in 1882 of the mid-western outlaw shot in the back by a 'dirty little coward'. Levon Helm of the Band contributed to *The Legend of Jesse James*, a 1980 concept album.
† Rendered as 'In My Time of Dyin'' when recorded by Bob Dylan in 1962.
‡ Who shared the Kingston Trio's manager. Their personnel included Scott McKenzie – future 'San Francisco (Be Sure to Wear Flowers in Your Hair)' hitmaker – and John Phillips, later of the Mamas and the Papas.
§ In 1965, this became 'The Story of John Hardy', a maracca-driven A-side by the Sir Douglas Quintet. Authorship was claimed by Doug Sahm, the group's leader.

man' from West Virginia who went to the gallows), 'Clementine' (which underwent a finger-snapping 'jazz' treatment by Bobby Darin in 1960) and 'Ballad Of Moreton Bay' (starvation and torture in a nineteenth-century penal colony in Australia). Even with amended lyrics* – often reducing barbed invective to nursery rhyme level – and the artists' fresh-faced presentation, there grew a feeling among the stuffier clergy and parent-teachers associations that this trend was somehow subversive. The danger, however, passed without fuss. Besides, a new moral pestilence had arrived with the Twist – and the consequent breakdown of western civilisation – not long after skiffle lost its flavour on the bedpost overnight.

Though the form was dead, its content survived in folk clubs and among left-wing collegians. Some artists back-pedalled to harmless old chestnuts like 'Barbara Allen' and 'Rogues of Lynn'† but there was a greater tendency to give 'em self-composed items on more contemporary catastrophes than Steve Grady's jump in the Old '97 (albeit in much the same tradition). On receiving their degrees in 1962, the Highwaymen regrouped for an album that contained guitarist Dave Fisher's 'Mighty Day' which noted a recent flood in Galveston in which Texas homesteaders wouldn't believe it was happening 'till death was in their face' after the waters of the Gulf of Mexico crashed through

* Such as those to 'Clementine' with the removal of original lines like 'roses and other posies fertilised by Clementine' and 'though in life, I used to hug her, now she's dead, I'll draw the line'.
† Also known as 'When We Were Under the King', it concerned the respective dooms of a miller, a weaver and a tailor (e.g., 'the Devil got his claw on the little tailor . . . '). The contrasting arrangements of this piece by Poacher's Pocket and the Clancy Brother and Tommy Makem are recommended.

the sea wall. On the same LP, the quintet harked back to 23 October 1958 for Peggy Seeger and husband Ewan MacColl's 'Ballad of Spring Hill'*. 'When the Earth is restless, miners die', it ran – and seventy-four of them did just that while trapped underground for eight days, obliged to sustain themselves until rescue with 'songs and hope' and, more pragmatically, coal, bark from the supporting timbers and whatever else a starving, frightened man could keep in his stomach.

After the last cadaver was brought up, the mine was sealed off, never to be worked again – a fact unembroidered in the song. Peggy and Ewan expected you to draw your own conclusions – but in 1948's 'Plane Wreck at Los Gatos', Dust Bowl balladeer Woody Guthrie protested that Mexican migrant workers – 'just deportees' to a local newscaster – had already 'died in your valleys . . . plains . . . trees . . . bushes . . . both sides of the river, we died just the same' before expiring when their 'sky plane caught fire' over a canyon. In its preachy approach, it was a taste of things to come. Soon the hit parade would include entries that would cover just about every aspect of mortality – and fatality.

* Recorded as 'Spring Hill Mining Disaster' by the Brothers Four in 1964.

Chapter Two

Teen Angel

Some lorry drivers think they can do what they like. Beneath bruised skies, one of these carrion of the road – later charged with involuntary manslaughter – hurtles way past the speed limit through a housing estate of raw red brick. One hand is on the wheel; the other conveys a pork pie to and from his mouth. Without looking, he jerks out of a side turning. With a braking scream, a girl on a motorcycle vanishes beneath his double wheels. A bike bearing a spotty youth appears next. He's been riding behind – the better to study her famous rear taut against a denim mini-skirt. However, a few press-ups in the undergrowth are not to be. Instead, the evening climaxes with her writhing in the dirt of Cement Street, life puddling out of her, and him standing by, in helpless horror. Curtains draw back in nearby windows. Someone rings for an ambulance, and the lorry driver climbs back into the cab to find his cigarettes. Surrounded by flashing blue lights and dull watchfulness, she's pronounced dead, and the boy – at first a detached spectator like everyone else – wonders what his mother will say when the police come round.

What a great idea for a song – but it needs some unabashed romanticism. Let's make 'em hopelessly in love and about to be married. How about the very next day? Perhaps they could be eloping because one set of parents disapprove. Don't put any trace of sex in it because it's only 1950-something and it might not get on the radio. The end's too ugly as it stands. Brighten it up a bit. Brighten it up a lot. See, it has to be like a pre-Raphaelite painting – birds twittering, not a leaf stirring, a touch of mist on the sunset horizon of an endless blue summer. We'll have him kneeling with his crash helmet on the tarmac beside her. Like, he can't prevent one crystal tear falling on to her unblemished face. Cradled in his arms, she will gaze up at him, as beautiful in death as she had been in life.

From the late 1950s until well into the next decade, the record business was as abundant as it would ever be with ditties of this persuasion – vulgar, ridiculously sentimental, frequently corny but nearly always completely sincere. In those dangerous years before the Pill, the lovers were always 'good kids' who never gave in to nature's baser urges. Only a 'cheap' girl didn't 'save herself' for her future husband. Above undignified gropings, she and her 'steady' were the type to be reassured by clean-cut Pat Boone's stolid compliance to middle-aged dictums. Indeed, their Bible might have been *Twixt Twelve And Twenty*, Boone's manual for wholesome boys and girls. It preached that your parents' word was law: get your hair cut, don't talk dirty, go to Church, stick to a secure job with Eldorado as a bonus in your pay packet. Revelling in his wedded state, Pat further paraded his dearth of private vices by baulking at kissing leading ladies in his films. Well, you never knew where these things might lead.

Pat Boone's tacit chaperoning was compounded by the taming of Elvis Presley, a recently demobbed sergeant. His sanitisation was epitomised by Italianesque ballads and infrequent self-mocking rockers which humoured the teenagers who had made him. With this capitulation to showbusiness proper, the grubbing music industry sought to isolate what it perceived as the King of Western Bop's more palatable, all-American aspects. These would form the model on which to groom legions of smooth-running ciphers.

The hit parades of North America – and, by implication, everywhere else – were soon constipated with twee, insipidly handsome boys-next-door; all hair-spray, doe-eyes and bashful half-smiles. Their forenames matched – and so did the piffle they were required to perform; much of it emanating from songwriting 'factories' like New York's Brill Building, where such stars-in-embryo as Carole King and Neil Sedaka won their spurs.

If Jimmy, Johnny and, especially, Bobby faltered after a brace of *Hot 100* entries, queuing round the block would be any number of substitutes, like stock Broadway chorus girls hoping to be thrust into an abrupt starring role. To keep the part, they'd have to parrot Pat Boone values and, with the gentlest humour, answer enquiries from teen magazines about preferred foodstuffs, favourite colours and the age at which they hoped to marry.

On vinyl, the latter aspiration was usually nipped in the bud when couples were suddenly and brutally parted at the whim of the Grim Reaper. This is typified in *the* set work for students of the genre, Jeff Barry and Ben Raleigh's 'Tell Laura I Love Her', straight off the Brill Building assembly line. In summer 1960 – probably the optimum moment in this golden aeon of death discs – it swept into international Top Tens, either in its original form by Ray Peterson* or via a plenitude of indigenous

---

* Among polio victim Peterson's earlier singles were a stab at Little Willie John's 'Fever' and 'The Wonder of You' (later a million-seller

38

covers.* The lyrical thrust is that Laura's Tommy (the first-person narrator) wants to give her everything; namely, 'flowers, presents but most of all a wedding ring'. In hopes of affording these, he enters a stock-car race for a cash prize but dies in a subsequent smash-up – but not before relaying (via his mother and, later, from a world unseen) the sentiments of the title to his beloved.

It was the girl's turn in Mark Dinning's 'Teen Angel' – which spent a fortnight at No. 1 in the States in March 1960. This involved an ill-judged try by a sixteen-year-old at negotiating a railway crossing in her car. Presumably to the hissing of a punctured radiator, her musing swain observes that her hand – the only part of her left unmutilated – still wears his high-school ring. It remains on her finger to the grave.

The lady actually got to walk down the aisle in 'Darling Jane', a John D. Loudermilk B-side concerning a honeymoon drowning. Laughable though it seems now with its convoluted rhyming and offhand angst, it was not unlikely that 'Darling Jane' may have sparked off Roy Orbison's abundantly superior 'Leah'. Also published by Nashville's Acuff-Rose, 'Leah's floating marimbas, pattering tenor drums, ghostly choir and drawn-out *morento* of Hawaiian guitar encapsulates both

---

for Elvis Presley). His version of 'Tell Laura I Love Her' wasn't issued in Britain after an extract was played on a BBC news programme to illustrate the furore in the US 'Bible Belt' by those who considered it un-Christian. Profits from 'Laura' financed the establishment of Dune, Ray's own label. However, after a series of flops, he transferred to MGM and attempted to rise anew as a C & W entertainer.
* One was by Welshman David Spencer who, prudently renaming himself Ricky Valance (to remind consumers of the recently deceased Ritchie Valens), had a clear run in Britain despite the BBC refusing airplay in view of a spate of recent British motor-racing fatalities.

the sub-aqua dissipation of sound waves, and the ambivalence of the pearl diver's nightmare. Ultimately Roy's vocal outpouring in the keening one-word chorus intimates that yearning for lost Leah is too deep for satisfactory verbal articulation.*

He might have been handsomer than Orbison but fellow Texan Johnny Preston was an unexciting vocalist whose chart strikes depended chiefly on a wise choice of material. In that vintage year of 1960, he came up trumps with 'Running Bear', the tragic account of a Red Indian who is fatally attracted to Little White Dove, a spinster of an enemy tribe. Though she reciprocates his devotion, their love – like that of Romeo and Juliet – can never be.

Evoking images of tomahawk-wielding redskins dancing round a campfire in the approved fashion to a pulsating tom-tom, 'Running Bear'† had been composed and produced by the Big Bopper, who reaped no earthly harvest from the work, having perished in the same aeroplane crash as Buddy Holly.‡

The Everly Brothers had known Buddy well enough to be his pallbearers. That fame had cost so dear was a sobering thought. The manner of Holly's exit from this vale of sorrow might have given John D. Loudermilk's demo of 'Ebony Eyes' – about a 'plane crash, for gawd's sake' – the piquancy that caused Don and Phil to record it as a chart-topping 1961 single. A much-parodied saga,

---

* 'Leah' would be in the set at Orbison's last concert.
† Roy Orbison reworked aspects of 'Running Bear' for 'Indian Wedding' (B-side of 1964's 'It's Over'). This matter-of-fact tale of how the newly wed Yellow Hand and White Sand were united in death also featured a glance back at 'Leah' in the high-pitched construction of Yellow Hand's 'wedding song'.
‡ Or, 'Buddy Holley' as his memorial plaque read.

the high altitude turbulence affecting Flight 1203 puts the tin lid on the nuptials of a soldier whose weekend pass hasn't allowed sufficient time for him to go home for the ceremony. A compassionate chaplain, therefore, grants permission for the intended bride (the 'beautiful Ebony Eyes') to wing her way to camp. Alas, neither she nor any of the other passengers make it, and the lad is advised by the airport loudspeaker to 'report to the chapel across the street'. After catharsis and a dull ache, he anchors himself to the notion that she'll be the 'first angel I'll recognise' when he too passes through the pearly gates.

A less cheery vision was awaiting Frank J. Wilson and the Cavaliers when their manager was the only fatality on a tour bus that veered off the freeway. I'm not saying there's anything in it but, *precisely* at that moment (well, that month), the combo's only death disc, 1964's 'Last Kiss', had just entered the *Hot 100*. Weird, eh?

Across the Atlantic, did Twinkle's 'Terry' also contain a self-fulfilling prophecy? 'Terry' was about a biker who, irked by his girl's infidelity, zoomed off to a lonely end of mangled chrome, blood-splattered kerbstones and the oscillations of an ambulance siren. A decade after it peaked at No. 4 in the UK charts, Twinkle's ex-boyfriend, Michael Hannah – whom she'd left for her future husband a year before – was killed in the Paris Air Show disaster in 1974.

'Terry' had caught, if not the mood, then *a* mood of 1964. As well as upsetting the BBC, it also suffered an initial banning on ITV's epoch-making *Ready Steady Go* not only for its death content but because it didn't conform to the specifications of the Mod-dominated Beat Boom*. In the following week's *TV Times*, a reader's

---

* From Kingston-upon-Thames, Twinkle (Lynn Ripley) was in fact

letter suggested a special edition entitled *Ready* Teddy *Go* to cater for Rockers – for there was no doubt about Terry's identity. His uniform was blue jeans, motorbike boots, grease-stained T-shirt and a real or imitation black leather windcheater. A glacier of brilliantine, his duck-tailed cockade was in direct line of descent from that of the 1950s Teddy Boys, as was his taste in music. I can't listen to Twinkle's hit without being transported to the gormless menace, hard-faced coquettishness and donkey-jacketed virility of some backdated funfair in the sticks where the last chip shop closes at 10.30 p.m.

If Twinkle merely mourned, a lifetime's sleepless contrition traceable to the Big Break-Up afflicted the sultry Shangri-Las in that more celebrated teenage morality play, 'Leader of the Pack' which apotheosed what might have been Terry's North American blood brother. He too rode a vehicle that wasn't as stable as his love – but if Terry's story was in Ealing monochrome, that of the Leader was full Cecil B. de Mille technicolor.

A charismatic 'fast' boy, Jimmy is despised by Betty's parents for coming 'from the wrong side of town'. To her schoolfriends, it seems inconceivable that someone like him could possibly twist his eternity ring on to the digit of a 'nice' girl like Betty. 'Is she really going out with him?', they ask incredulously over a deceptively casual spoken introit. This is an interesting question because she is and she isn't. As the production builds from loaded conversation to panicked shriek ('Look out! Look out! Look out!'), it turns out that after meeting him at the candy store, though he might have come on

---

more a metropolitan dolly-bird in her John Lennon cap – and kinky boots. 'I never wear anything except boots' ran one press release.

initially as the rough, untamed outsider, he is a regular guy underneath (if something of a sad sack)*, and he and Betty fall for each other. Nevertheless, her father orders her to terminate the relationship. Obediently, she tells Jimmy 'we're through'. He sort of smiles, guns his machine and shoots off into the neon night to wind up just like poor old Terry, albeit amid the extra drama of record producer George 'Shadow' Morton's liberally applied collage of snarling engines, squealing rubber, clashes of metal, *et al* – get the picture? A mighty sickening one it is too – and so we leave Betty in the final deflated bars, oblivious to playground stares as she weeps, haunted down the years by Jimmy, asleep in Eden's bed.

'I don't know – what do you think?', was the attitude that pervaded the release by Red Bird Records – whose office was in the Brill Building – of the ludicrously tragic single. Such a lurid display of emotion could either be on the deletion rack within three weeks or sell millions. Infiltrating North America's crowded airwaves, to Red Bird's relief, the Shangri-Las took the States by storm, topping both the *Billboard* and *Cashbox* lists. Over in Blighty, the record flagged at No. 11 but, reissued and slightly edited, it was to claw its way to No. 3 in 1972, and enjoy a second Top Ten coming four years later.

Whoever said the Shangri-Las wouldn't last? One of the outstanding girl groups of the 1960s, they were two pairs of Brooklyn sisters, Mary and Betty Weiss and the twins Mary Ann and Margie Glaser. By 1964, they were the Bon-Bons whose best-remembered 45 was the

---

* For whom James Dean was an obvious role model – as he would be for the person who boasted of being 'too fast to live/too young to die' in Chris Spedding's 'Motorbikin'' (1975).

opportunist novelty record 'What's Wrong with Ringo?', pressed as the Beatle drummer recovered from a fever provoked by tonsilitis. Under Morton's aegis, they adopted a new name and scored a smash with his 'Remember (Walking in the Sand)', and then reached a commercial zenith in 1965 with 'Leader of the Pack' (which Morton wrote with Jeff Barry and another Brill mainstay, Ellie Greenwich). During the downward spiral that followed, the girls and their investors explored the 'Pack' theme from new angles like alchemists endlessly conducting the same experiment in the wrongheaded expectation of turning base metal into gold.

As 1965 drew to a close, they introduced another surly lout with Brooding Intensity that parents wouldn't have in the house in 'Out in the Street'. Next up was a revival of 'Give Us Your Blessings', Ray Peterson's *Hot 100* swansong from 1963, featuring one more pair whose courtship is marred by Ma and Pa's hostility. So Mary and Jimmy (him again) run away in his car but fail to notice a detour sign. Their consequent double death and the hook-line plea reminds the parents how unfeeling they have been. However, in 1966's desolate monologue, 'I Can Never Go Home Anymore', it's the daughter who's wracked with guilt because her mother's low opinion of her boyfriend forces her to leave home. Mum dies of loneliness, her judgement about the chap's unsuitability proves correct and, to a backwash of lush violins and incorporeal chorale, the single fades to the oppressive mawkishness of Betty Weiss crying for the parent who is no more. A Primal Scream or what?

The generally unsuccessful post-'Leader of the Pack' recording career stretched into 1967 after the Shangri-Las saw out the Red Bird contract with 'He Cried'/ 'Dressed in Black' – and 'Past Present and Future', recited with intense world-weariness. Well, what do you expect from women who have borne the demise of several suitors and a mother since 1964? The Shangri-Las were, purportedly, a wild bunch on the road as demonstrated by some unpleasantness with a rifle at one cultural backwater. Moreover, during the promotion of 'Past Present and Future', it was noted that the outfit had become a trio but no one would elucidate on the whereabouts of Betty. Neither would she be present when the reformed Shangri-Las surfaced later in nostalgia revues of the late 1970s.

The incorrigible old Mods and Rockers who attended these events were unlikely to see the words 'Nervous Norvus' on any bill. Yet, it could be argued that the gentleman with this nomenclature was the veritable father of the modern death disc. His grisly 'Transfusion', issued in 1956 was warbled in the nonchalant light tenor of one who, by then, had sung on over three thousand commissioned demonstration recordings at seven dollars apiece (two at a knockdown eleven dollars) in his studio in Oakwood, California.

One morning when business was slack, Norvus*, formerly a trucker, amused himself by taping one of his own songs, accompanied by a lone acoustic guitar and what amounted to a nascent drum machine. It probably hadn't a hope of official release, being a description of a speed-crazed, jive-talking driver who was the cause of innumerable accidents. While the blood spilt from this maniac's wounds and 'a solid mess of contusion' is being

* Issued by an Indiana company of no great merit, his début single, 'Gambling Fury'/'Golden Yellow Moon' had been credited to 'Singing' Jimmy Drake – his real name. The cream of Norvus-Drake's 1950s recordings were unified on 1985's *Nervous Norvus* (Big Beat NED 12), seven years after the artist expired at the age of sixty-six.

replenished, he aggravates blood bank personnel with empty promises never to speed again, and flippant remarks such as 'put a gallon in me, Alan', 'pour the crimson in me, Jimson', and 'Hey Daddio, make that Type O, huh'.

Surprisingly, a quartet called the Four Jokers liked 'Transfusion' enough to release, via Diamond Records, an uptempo swing arrangement with boogie-woogie piano and Nervous on backing vocals. Encouraged by this syndication, the composer began hawking his own more basic version round Los Angeles. Eventually, a tape landed on the desk of radio disc jockey Red Blanchard who, after superimposing skidding and collision noises, passed it on to Dot Records who unleashed it on the masses as it stood. An immediate air ban on the grounds of bad taste did no harm at all, and in a matter of weeks 'Transfusion' – classic rock's *Springtime for Hitler* – was lodged in the national Top Ten.

The spring of 1956 was the Nervous Norvus moment never to return. Nevertheless, before the US public decided it couldn't take any more, he clocked up a lesser hit – but a hit all the same – with the follow-up, 'Ape Call', but only its B-side, 'Wild Dogs of Kentucky', may be deemed relevant to this discussion.

An excuse given in one verse for the 'Transfusion' character's constant hurry is that he's 'got to make a date with that chick of mine'*. If as riven with recklessness as 'Transfusion', Jan and Dean's 'Dead Man's Curve' is bereft of any such romantic interest. Cruising in his Stingray late one night, a rider is challenged to a race by

* Faced with a similar problem, Gene Vincent exhibited an infinitely more commendable respect for the Highway Code in 1960's 'Why Don't You People Learn To Drive'.

cocksure stranger at the wheel of a shiny new XKE Jaguar. With a green traffic light as starting signal, it's to be no ordinary drag race but one that embraces a notoriously hazardous bend round which the Jaguar owner loses control and is carried from the resulting wreckage feet first. A celestial harp *arpeggio* bridges the second chorus and a passage in which the other bloke explains to a doctor what happened, adding that he'll never forget the horrible sight' as the chorus re-enters to fade along with the now standard screeching radials and buzzing carburettor sound effects.

Though he didn't go the same way as Frank Wilson's manager or Michael Hannah, 'Dead Man's Curve' mirrored in fiction an actual event in April 1966 that almost took Jan's life. A portent of this might have occurred a few months earlier during the shooting of *Easy Come Easy Go*, he and Dean's only major film, when a runaway railway carriage injured seventeen members of the cast – notably Jan, whose fractured leg was still in plaster on the duo's *Filet of Soul* (*sic*) album cover. This mishap was trifling compared to the outcome of the twenty-five-year-old singer's ill-starred journey in a Corvette to an appointment before the draft board in April 1966.

Certain folk will do anything to stay out of the army. Jan crunched into a parked lorry at seventy miles per hour. Three people died and Jan was found slumped across the front seat with his brain exposed. Severely paralysed, he was obliged to relearn speech and bodily co-ordination, and was still undergoing surgery as well as therapy years later.

The climax of 1978's *Dead Man's Curve*, a celluloid biography of Jan and Dean, was a mock-up of their troubled 'comeback' performance in 1973 at the Hollywood Palladium. Occasional stage appearances since have been better received – paradoxically, their 1985 album of new material did brisker business in the foyers than compilations containing remakes of old smashes that included a depressingly limp 'Dead Man's Curve'.

Prideful daredevilry wasn't restricted to men – as instanced by Noël Harrison's 'A Young Girl of Sixteen' a kind of contemporary Rake's Progress written from a different set of hormones, in which the subject surrenders her soul as she lies on the side of the road. The sex of the accident casualty is not stressed in 'D.O.A.' by Bloodrock which details the said unfortunate's final thoughts as they ebb away in the ambulance rushing vainly to hospital.

Although careless drivers could be said to have brought their fate upon themselves, actual suicide was not often spelt out on vinyl until the sixties really started swinging. There were, none the less, plenty of borderline cases. Off-the-cuff examples are the metaphorical 'Last Leaf' by the Cascades (about to be blown off the branch by spooky studio-manufactured wind) and, both recorded by Marty Wilde, morose 'Misery's Child' and 'Danny' Wilde's arch-rival, Cliff Richard, also had a crack at 'Danny' which, reflecting the main character's dejection, began as the title song of Elvis Presley's 1958 gangster film before it was changed to *King Creole*. While an instrumental snatch was heard in the last reel of the movie, Presley's recording of 'Danny' was shelved until after his death in 1977, thus opening the floodgates for numerous cover versions. Gene Bua had first grabs in the States but, in 1960, Conway Twitty's treatment shifted a million. Because he'd already had a hit with 'Danny Boy', it was rechristened 'Lonely Blue Boy' (and Twitty's backing combo became the Lonely Blue Boys).

Then there was Jess Conrad's asinine 'Why Am I Living?' in which snatches of kindergarten babble (ooo dadda yip-yip/oh dadda shandu/doo la-la jambin/shoo-laaaaaa' *ad nauseam*) underlined gems of crackerbarrel pensiveness like 'you're on your own till you die' and 'there ain't no answer' but when there is, Jess'll 'love to live . . . to love'. Just as woeful is 'Carlos Dominguez' ('an unhappy man') by the Countrymen, remarkable as the first UK act to cover a Paul Simon opus. When 'Carlos Dominguez' came out in Britain it was a month prior to the rendition by its creator (as 'Jerry Landis') in May 1964. As savoury a morsel of information is that Twinkle revived 1962's 'The End of the World' from Skeeter Davis, another almost-but-not-quite suicide ditty – as was John D. Loudermilk's 'Torture' (for Kris Jensen).

Of the discs that came closest to saying it out loud, the most effective was Jody Reynolds' 'Endless Sleep' – which provided Marty Wilde with his first hit. Following a lovers' spat, the girl is endeavouring to drown herself (and tempting her lad, siren-like, to join her). Nevertheless, even though the sea 'seems to say, "I took your baby from you away"' (grammar!), she is saved before the disc whirls its own little life away.

It was Pat Boone of all people who dared to go all the way with 'Moody River'. As the sudden conclusion of a mild misunderstanding between the parties, Pat's paramour throws herself into the murky depths, not forgetting to place on the bank a symbolic glove and a shame-smitten note rationalising her behaviour. Arriving on the scene too late, Pat gazes into the waves – caused, perhaps, by a deep sigh from the river floor – but sees only his own 'lonely, lonely face', poor soul.

During the early- to mid-1960s, Tin Pan Alley had an

even nastier turn than Pat when it was confronted by self-contained British beat groups with internal sources of new material and their own publishing companies. Nevertheless, if, say, the Poets' 'I'll Cry with the Moon' was near the knuckle, few composers besmirched pop's most unpretentiously optimistic period by touching on anything that hinted at suicide. The most conspicuous exception was by Manchester's Toggery Five. Runners-up to the Bo Street Runners in *Ready Steady Go*'s national beat contest, they rather blunted the impact of this near-victory by choosing 'I'm Gonna Jump' as a first single. Driven to this extreme strategy by the object of his desire's 'making out with other guys', the adenoidal admirer announces with a sort of despairing triumph that he intends to 'jump in the river, yeah, you know, I'm gonna diiiiiie!' over a plodding accompaniment layered with unearthly 'aaaaaah's'. It was hardly the meat of the Light Programme, and, after a sprinkling of plugs on Radio Luxembourg, that was that for the Toggery Five.

Jobbing tunesmiths of the old regime, however, played it safer by furnishing the likes of Manfred Mann with 'There's No Living Without Your Loving' ('this old world ain't spinning anywhere') and Them with 'I'm Gonna Dress in Black', a *tour de force* which, if it hadn't been hidden on a B-side, might have done for this Belfast outfit what Geoff Stevens' 'The Crying Game' did for Dave Berry. Enhancing Dave's wounded baritone on this enduring 1964 melancholia are tearful *legatos* achieved by session guitarist Big Jim Sullivan with a volume pedal, the precursor of the wah-wah.

As the decade wore on, pop's under-used brain was jolted into reluctant action by elements such as the Beatles' Aeolian cadences – and, though it meant sweating a little over lyrics, Bob Dylan's rapid-fire stream-of-consciousness literariness in which he sang stridently through his nose about less wistful topics than happy boys and girls with marriage in mind.

Even if obscured by surreal imagery and psychedelic clutter, suicide was the theme of 1969's 'Halo in My Hair' (in which 'the world can carry on') by the Bulldog Breed. Much less agreeably indirect was the austere 'My Days Are Numbered' (after 'I woke up and found no one beside me') by Blood, Sweat and Tears (who chuck in a backwards guitar solo by their ztaK evetS).

Came the 1970s, and Bryan Ferry was holding the deed at arm's length in Roxy Music's 'Strictly Confidential' as trivialities – 'will it be sunny then, I wonder?' – interfere with his gathering of final thoughts on paper as a false dawn (where 'there is no light') creeps nearer. In artistic debt to Roxy Music, Deaf School projected their Enrico Cadillac Jnr into a hotel suite to consider 'What a Way to End It All' as he, perhaps, prepared a bullet for a brief but eventful flight. At the less affluent tail-end of the social carnival, a would-be suicide on a scorching summer's day feels 'like some bad story in yesterday's news' as, to a solitary guitar, Nick Lowe contemplates a close-miked and funereal-paced 'Endless Sleep' (nothing to do with Jody Reynolds) on what he called the 'dead side' (as opposed to the 'live' one) of a 1977 EP.

To some, self-slaughter represents the ultimate selfishness. How about thinking of other people for a change? What about the sorrow of the bereaved? To my knowledge, no one's ever come up with a number dealing with the other victims of a suicide – but there are plenty covering those wringing their hands over more inadvertent deaths. With the promptness of a vulture, an 'answer' disc to 'Tell Laura I Love Her' reared up in

1960 in Marilyn Michaels' desperate 'Tell Tommy I Miss Him'* which instals our grieving heroine in the chapel in apparent spiritual communication with Tommy.

I wonder if Tommy ran into John Leyton's old flame up there? There's every chance that they showed up at heaven's door at roughly the same time – for, in 1961, John was roaming the moor to the wraithful wailings from Beyond of 'the girl I lost a year ago'. My younger sister had 'Johnny Remember Me' on instant replay on our Dansette record player for weeks on end. Under pressure she might tell you that this evocative sound-picture was the greatest death record ever made – and, if in a perverse mood, I might agree. It was certainly the most exhilarating – and how could anyone with lyrical appreciation not derive pleasure from the lines about Johnny hearing her 'singing in the sighing of the wind blowing in the tree tops'. If he wasn't particularly enamoured with pop whilst in charge of the record department of Liverpool's North End Music Stores, twenty-seven-year-old Brian Epstein's instinct for a smash was demonstrated amply by his bold requisitioning of 250 copies of 'Johnny Remember Me' when rival dealers, influenced by the unanimous 'miss' verdict on BBC television's *Juke Box Jury*, didn't order any.

One of Brian's prospective clients, John Lennon, loathed its galloping 'Ghost Riders in the Sky' propulsion but there were enough buyers with 6s 8d to spend who begged to differ over what was to be lauded as *the* hit song of 1961. Its technological donkey work was courtesy of console boffin Joe Meek who many – I for one – would rate higher than any other producer (including

---

* Also recorded by Laura Lee (1960) and Skeeter Davis (1961).

Phil Spector) for inventiveness and originality. Though his innovations altered recording procedures forever, he functioned in his cramped RGM Sound studio which, located down London's busy Holloway Road, was littered with what looked to Geoff Goddard 'like odds and ends he'd picked up from a junk shop, wired it all up and made something of it. He didn't have the capital for much else.'

If Meek was the mind of RGM Sound and the likes of John Leyton and the Tornadoes the flesh and blood, its soul was surely Goddard, the in-house songwriter and general factotum. Presently 'nobody of any importance' in the University of Reading's catering department, Geoff remembers composing 'Johnny Remember Me' in a conscious attempt to follow up Leyton's also-ran stab at 'Tell Laura I Love Her', a flop that had, nevertheless, enhanced the media representation of Leyton as a lonely heart. While Ricky Valance's success also helped acclimatise the public – and the BBC – to death in the popular song, Geoff was still obliged to tinker with the phrase 'the girl I loved who died', settling for the more ambiguous 'girl I loved and lost' (i.e., maybe the relationship rather than her life was over) to allow 'Johnny Remember Me' the best possible chance.

Other than music press coverage, the new 45 received additional publicity from an article in *Psychic News* in the light of Geoff's claim that his muse 'had resulted from my interest in spiritualism'. After an unfruitful Saturday hunched in a fretful cloud of cigarette smoke over a front-room piano and a Grundig reel-to-reel, 'I got out of bed on Sunday (and) just started playing the opening chords and spoke words into the microphone. They weren't sort of "you/blue" – they didn't rhyme. The song just sort of "came out", if you know what I mean.'

Into the bargain, during one of the twice-weekly seances held at RGM Sound, contact was made with Buddy Holly who, consulted about 'Johnny Remember Me', answered via the tumbler, 'See you in the charts!'

At the session a few weeks earlier, to a backing track by the Outlaws* and pianist Goddard, Leyton's voice – plus the 'Wuthering Heights' responses of session singer Lisa Grey – were drenched in characteristic RGM bathroom echo. Known chiefly for his role as 'Ginger' in the BBC Children's Hour serial, *Biggles*, John was no Roy Orbison as a vocalist but he was a blond, rugged hunk who, with Meek's inspired knob-twiddling, could be made to sound the part. The disc was launched in the inappropriate setting of a department store opening on the *Harpers West One*, television series when Leyton as the management's celebrity guest, pop star 'Johnny St Cyr', was prevailed upon to mime his latest single†.

Other pertinent John Leyton recordings from the pen of Geoff Goddard included the richly orchestrated 'Son This Is She' (youth is advised by late father – as 'a voice from above' – about a new girlfriend) and 1962's 'Lone Rider' (ghostly motorcyclist cautions living bikers against taking 'risks for kicks').

The Lone Rider obviously hadn't managed to get round to Terry. In 'Swamp Legend' by the Countrymen, after an apt preface of gurgling noises, a young

* An instrumental quartet that then included bass guitarist Chas Hodges, later half of gorblimey chartbusters Chas and Dave.
† 'Johnny Remember Me' has since been exhumed by Showaddywaddy (1974); as part of the 1985 hit 'I Feel Love' medley by Bronski Beat and Marc Almond, and by the Phantom Chords (with the Damned's Dave Vanian) in 1990. Incidentally, its story line was repeated vaguely and in a less storm-tossed fashion by Geoff Goddard in 'On Lover's Hill' for Mike Sarne in 1962.

man is incited by a sweetheart beckoning 'from another world' to join her up there as soon as he can.

Some long for reunion at any price. Most of the needle time evoked on the final section of Jimmy Cross' repulsively amusing 'I Want My Baby Back' features a monologue with a stark undertow of howling wind, a spade knocking hollowly on wood and a lid creaking. The singer and his lover are reunited (*à la* Edgar Allan Poe) in the departed one's coffin from which Cross is heard lilting a muffled last chorus. This ghastly situation evidently came about, after he was driving her home from a Beatles concert. With no brakes, his car cannot avoid a head-on collision with – it's that man again – 'the leader of the pack' (just after his fall from the charts with the Shangri-Las). Crawling from the debris, Jimmy's most immediate concern is the girl's welfare but 'over there was my baby . . . and over there . . . and way over there'. Life without her then becomes so intolerable that he elects to 'get her back one way or another' because he insists, he digs her so much. Get it?

Me? Forgive my xenophobia but I prefer the British version by the Downliners Sect from the 1965 'concept' EP *The Sect Sing Sick Songs*. Almost as hitless as the Toggery Five, this Surrey outfit still outlasted the Yardbirds, the Spencer Davis Group, Them and many other more fêted rhythm-and-blues contemporaries. With a grace-saving and over-developed sense of humour, the Sect had a less tactiturn approach to the afterlife than the 'I'm Gonna Jump' quintet – as well as the commercial wisdom to bury on a B-side the self-referential 'In*secti*cide', a showcase for wailing mouth-organ and crushed-note piano with vocalist Don Craine's perfunctory lyrics about committing insecticide if his baby leaves him.

On their 'I Want My Baby Back', who could begrudge

them changing 'Beatles concert' to 'Downliners Sect concert' where the girl, soon to be cut off in blooming youth, had been 'screaming and tearing her hair out'. Also on *The Sect Sing Sick Songs* is 'Now She's Dead' which could be the 'I Want My Baby Back' geezer in the interim between the auto calamity and the reunion. On this piece, the Sect snipe at the Bachelors, a smarmy Irish trio who they detested, via a plummy, off-key chorus that splashes vivid hues on to a mordant soliloquy of a 'girlfriend six feet underground'. Unable to yet accept her demise, the boy still inadvertently telephones her old number.

This compulsory extended-play acquisition for any death disc connoisseur worthy of the name closes with 'Midnight Hour' – not the Wilson Pickett standard, but a slow twelve bar blues with a spectral vocal undercurrent framing a domestic incident in which a lady is battered to death with a chair, and her unsuspected killer's pangs of conscience keep him awake in the witching hour.

The silver age of the death record in the later 1960s spawned a plethora of small intensities such as 'Michelangelo' in 1967 by 23rd Turnoff. Placing the great Renaissance painter and decorator at the 'end of life's game', they reason that because 'the love of my life never came to the Church', he devoted his energies totally to art. However, the big record that year was Bobbie Gentry's 'Ode to Billy Joe'. To six violins, a couple of cellos and her own guitar, this University of Los Angeles philosophy graduate assumes the personality of a member of a family from the Deep South seated at an evening meal. She drops into the ensuing conversation the fate of a local boy, Billy Joe MacAllister, who threw both a mysterious bundle and himself off the Tallahatchie Bridge* over the Mississippi. Interrupted by requests to, say, 'pass the biscuits, please', the news is treated with the same butterfly attention paid to any other snippet of banal chit-chat round the dining table.

Thus Bobbie Gentry helped usher in a new phase of death discs that, unlike 'Transfusion' or the histrionic 'Leader of the Pack', did not slap it on with a trowel. To the inch, it let enough out to indicate the gravity of the issue without using crass sound effects, dwelling on detail or sensationalising the tragedy. Laura, Jimmy, Terry, Betty and all the rest of them started playing it cool as in 'Jimmy' by Tim Hollier and, also from 1968, the more immortal 'Honey' from Bobby Goldsboro. As a rhythm guitarist, Goldsboro had spent a three year pop apprenticeship from 1962 in Roy Orbison's employ. 'See the Funny Little Clown', earned Bobby his first gold disc, but it would be the non-original 'Honey' that would be his *magnum opus*. Dripping from the workman-like pen of Robert Russell, it was open to several interpretations (the British journal *Disc*'s theory was that the 'angels' who spirited 'Honey' away were initiates of California's dreaded motorcycle fraternity, the *Hell's* Angels. Hmmm . . .). In any event, when the rather insipid female in the song pops off, Goldsboro – as a spouse, father or someone else with an emotional attachment to her – takes it in his stride – and, off-stage, he had every cause to be a happy man. As well as slicing to No. 1 in the States, 'Honey' catapulted him into the British Top Ten where he was blocked at No. 2 by Gary Puckett and the wretched 'Young Girl'. When repromoted in 1975, 'Honey' once again stalled in second position, frustrated on this occasion by the Bay

* Which collapsed on 20 June 1972.

City Rollers. None the less, both ascents testify to the record's evergreen status. Whatever you or I might feel about it, three million Bobby Goldsboro fans can't be wrong.

A similar veneer of maturity now gleamed from the Brill Building – from where came Cynthia Weil and Barry Mann's prototypical 'Angelica'. Without fuss, an inattentive husband eases his remorse as a widower by buying flowers for the grave of Angelica for whom 'too many springs had passed'. Debating the merits of various recordings of 'Angelica', the ones most likely to win out are those of the sophisticated Sandpipers (1966) and Scott Walker (1967). Sinatra might think twice about covering 'I Want My Baby Back', but 'Angelica' – along with 'September of My Years', Jacques Brel's 'If You Go Away' *et al* – was the stuff of 'quality' entertainers like himself, Tony Bennett, Perry Como, Jack Jones – all the Las Vegas shower – whose flop singles are often excused as being 'too good for the charts'.

Like its fictional victims, the good, honest trash contained in records like 'Tell Laura I Love Her' and 'Terry' is no more. Now and then, however, the corpse has twitched without warning. At the heart of the 'Burial Waltz' (1969) by New York's burlesque poetry-rock outragers, the Fugs, was another tale of two lovers meeting beyond-the-tomb, though a more subtle effort than that outlined by Jimmy Cross. Within the swirling reconstruction of a Viennese ballroom orchestra, and mention of fetishes and phalluses, it boils down to 'bury me in an apple orchard/that I might touch your lips again' – less 'I Want My Baby Back' than a more tender 'On Ilkla Moor Bah't 'At'.

At the opposite end of the pop spectrum, winsome boy-girl quartet, the Brotherhood of Man, scored its biggest smash in 1977 with 'Angelo', a Mexican shepherd boy who captures the heart of a rich landowner's daughter. Daddy frowns at the liaison and they run away. Indeed, they run and run and run. Finally, the barrier of the sea prevents them from running any further. Comprehending that their love is doomed, they choose to die on the sand. The cause of death is unstated but it was probably fatigue.

Whatever may have happened to Angelo and his girlfriend, a disclosure about an old friend from the 1960s cropped up in 1988. Do you remember the late 'Leah'? Well, with his previous occupation invoking painful memories, her beau turned to a different water-centred pastime. As the titular 'Windsurfer' on Roy Orbison's *Mystery Girl* album, he surged across the waves to swooping Leah-esque Hawaiian guitar with an apposite Beach Boys tinge to the backing vocals. An indifferent sportsman and unlucky in love, he 'practised in his dreams' until the hour when his loneliness carried him away on the tide to oblivion; his bellying sail a smudge on the horizon.

Chapter Three

Baby's Sleeping in the Graveyard

It's around three o'clock in the morning, and the polished door of the hospital chapel is slightly ajar. A young husband is on his knees in the front pew, searching within himself for an appropriate prayer. The aisles are deep in sinister darkness; the only sounds audible are a faint hum from the central-heating system and the boots of some half-awake night porter clacking about echoing corridors. Amid the white statuettes and unlit candles, the man supplicates the Almighty to take his own life in exchange for that of his 'sweet wife' and forthcoming son who are in the throes of a difficult labour that the doctor, 'with his head bowed low', has estimated will mean the death of one or the other. There seems to be no answer, so, with the night and his own desolation weighing on him, he rises to his feet with the aid of a chair. A moment later, his heart feels lighter – but then 'my legs gave way and suddenly I began to fall'. From nowhere, medical help arrives in time to hear his breathing slacken and see the shadow of death cross the curiously ecstatic face of one who knows that through his sacrifice, 'somehow they're both going to be all right'.

That was the crux of 'The Deal' by Pat Campbell. To the restrained whine of a holy organ, this monologue is delivered in the first person by the father – or, to be strictly accurate, the father's ghost. Campbell's placid tone is at odds with both the despair in the delivery room and his fatal seizure. Unintentionally funny, it's surely one of the most kitsch singles ever released. Homely in content and committed in execution, this sort of thing attracted a similar audience to that of Pat Boone. I regret having to keep on about him but, to the old and square, Pat was a clean, nicely spoken contrast to that obnoxious Presley. As well as polite and embarrassed retreads for the pop charts of 'sepia' hits like 'Ain't That a Shame' and 'Long Tall Sally', Boone himself ventured into 'The Deal' territory with a patronising treatment of father-in-law Red Foley's 'Steal Away'. This spiritual focused on a baby's funeral that was conducted by a folksy negro minister with a 'manner grandly awkward and a countenance grotesque'. Direct from *Uncle Tom's Cabin*, he referred to the coffin-bound child as a 'pretty bit of clay (that) done gone away'* in an age when the BBC's *Singing Together* schools programmes handbook raised hardly a liberal eyebrow with its directives to sing 'mah' for 'me' and 'dat' for 'that' on the few 'coon songs' included.

Infant mortality crops up only sporadically in pop. Well, it rather brings the party down, doesn't it? In plainer language than that used in the Book of Genesis, Bob Dylan slips Abraham's aborted sacrifice of Isaac in the land of Moriah into the first verse of 'Highway 61 Revisited' (1965), and Cream bawled the traditional 'Mother's Lament' to a boozy piano as a calculated anti-climax to the over-amplified intellectual flash of *Disraeli Gears*.

'Some went to war, some never came home' was a crucial phrase in 'Sons of' by Belgium's Jacques Brel. Both a

* A more palatable version was released by Lonnie Donegan in 1962.

figurehead and *éminence grise* of modern songwriting, as well as being the perpetrator of the death disc *par excellence*, Brel was to leave his mark on the output of such diverse wordsmiths as Mort Shuman (an early and lifelong disciple), the Kinks' Ray Davies, Leonard Cohen, Judy Collins, David Bowie, the Sensational Alex Harvey Band and – also the foremost interpreter of his work – Scott Walker.

In Walker's 1967 version of 'My Death', he'd gloomed that, Heaven or Hades, 'there is nothing much to do'. Therefore, 'let's not talk about the passing time' but eat, drink and be merry in the sphere of our sorrow, stick around for our friends, and hope to be taken when indulging in sexual congress. As is common with Brel compositions, the lyrical determination of 'My Death' was warped in translation. Does death wait, for instance, like 'an old roué' or 'a patient girl who knows the score' (to rhyme with 'swinging door')? It hinges upon the gender and leanings of the singer. Elly Stone (in *Jacques Brel Is Alive and Well and Living in Paris*) and David Bowie gave in to the bloke while Scott Walker chose the more socially acceptable partner for 'My Death' on both his first solo LP and for a performance on the *Billy Cotton Band Show* in 1967.

The singing of this canticle to existentialism on an uncool BBC television variety show summed up Walker's vocational dilemma. The advent of psychedelia made this *Jackie* pin-up seem too youthful and long-haired for regular watchers of the programme; yet he didn't cut much ice with a hip younger audience either.

A most unlikely duo to have been influenced by Brel were Ken Howard and Alan Blaikley, erstwhile managers and songwriters to Dave Dee, Dozy, Beaky, Mick and Tich. Yet, if pieces like 'Bend It' and 'Zabadak!

caused po-faced critics to dismiss them as sellers of superficiality, there was a shock in store for those few who heard *Few and Far Between* by Jean Musy for whom they had supplied an English libretto several worlds from 'Zabadak!', though sung by Dave Dee. Overlooked in 1975, *Few and Far Between* was as mournful as a seagull's cry, particularly after 'Remorse' chases 'Radiance' into 'Child in the Rain' – which I interpret as being about a couple whose emotional bonds loosen following the loss of a child whose baleful presence encircles a house in the midst of Yuletide celebrations.

Yeah, well, Alice Cooper observes in 'Dead Babies' that 'little Betty's sleeping in the graveyard'; her death from a domestic accident traceable to her father being almost permanently away, and her mother frequenting a bar every night. Neither bothered with a sitter on the understanding that Betty would never wake up and annoy the neighbours.

At Wembley's Empire Pool in 1972, Cooper was supported by Roxy Music, then on the verge of a chart breakthrough. A year later, their electronics wizard Brian Eno was replaced by Curved Air's Edwin Jobson. On the rebound, Eno knocked out a solo album, *Here Come the Warm Jets*. A highlight of this catchy sample of avant-gardening was the two-chord trundle, 'Baby's on Fire' which decorates the title image with so much negative symbolism ('Juanita and Juan . . . selling second-hand tobacco') that it could be about anything – or nothing.*

As far as I'm concerned, the same applies to Yoko Ono's 'Don't Worry Kyoko (Mummy's Only Looking

* Eno thought highly enough of 'Baby's on Fire' to include it on two subsequent in-concert albums, *June 1, 1974* and *801 Live* (1976).

for her Hand in the Snow)'. It might have been an exaggerated commemoration of her third husband (and fellow member of the mutable Plastic Ono Band) John Lennon missing a bend and rolling over a hired Austin Maxi somewhere in the Scottish highlands. Only one passenger, John's son, escaped uninjured; Yoko, John and Yoko's daughter needed stitches. However, 'Don't Worry Kyoko' is largely a means whereby the world of Art's Screaming Lord Sutch was able to show off a vocal flexibility that interjected screeches, wails and nanny-goat vibrato into the proceedings. Lennon found the opus as potent as his 'teenage self had found Little Richard's "Tutti Frutti"' but when it stretched into its twentieth cacophonous, headache-inducing minute at a Plastic Ono *Supergroup* spot during a charity knees-up at the Strand Lyceum, he and the other backing musicians were seen to exchange nervous glances.

When the Beatles' Apple Corps opened for business in 1968, it brought to the public many maverick artistic enterprises in this vein including a shy-making album trilogy of John and the second Mrs Lennon's self-obsessed soul-baring (as in 1969's *Life With the Lions*, which was built round one of Ono's miscarriages).

Pete Seeger demonstrated that he had at least leafed through the relevant passages of the Book of Ecclesiastes when he sang of 'A time to be born, a time to die' as well as the bits in between on 1962's 'Turn! Turn! Turn! (To Everything There is a Season)'*. Not so jingle-jangly joyous was 'The Three Bells' from the Browns – Arkansas siblings Maxine, Bonnie and Jim. Its hero – if that is

* Composing royalties from the Byrds' 1965 arrangement of 'Turn! Turn! Turn!' gave Seeger's bank balance a welcome shot in the arm.

the word – Jimmy Brown was an Average Joe like
Solomon Grundy in that he came and went with his
birth, marriage and funeral the most exciting events in a
quiet life during which, I suspect, he never stepped
beyond the valley cradling his home village. The song
was conceived in 1945 by French composer Jean Villard
and, as such, was nationally successful for Les Compagnons de la Chanson. In 1948, two English lyricists
independently came up with radically opposing notions
of 'Les Trois Cloches'. Dick Manning's was the cheerful
'While the Angelus Was Ringing'* which went no
further than the wedding day but Bert Reisfield's more
downbeat 'The Three Bells' gripped the public harder.
As well as a version by Les Compagnons de la Chanson
trailing the Browns into the 1959 UK hit parade, a
rendering by Brian Poole and the Tremeloes clawed its
way into the Top Twenty six years later.

Sticking as closely to the Browns' arrangement as
Poole did, Roy Orbison had a go in 1973. Roy's history
up to that point – first wife and two sons killed in
separate accidents in the mid-1960s – makes you wonder
how he found the mental detachment to record a number
so close to the bone. Who could prevent a knotted
stomach, a lump in the throat, even tears when the third
bell leads into that 'rainy morning, dark and grey' when
'little Jimmy Brown had passed away'. Otherwise, all
you can do is get the giggles as you might when listening
to 'The Deal'.

Because his years hadn't been as rife with profound
personal tragedy as Orbison's, the mordancy is not as

* The most renowned recordings of 'While the Angelus Was Ringing' were those of Allan Jones (not the editor of *Melody Maker*) and
Josef Locke.

unbearable in the 'All My Trials' portion – even 'you know your daddy is bound to die' – of Elvis Presley's 'American Trilogy'. Paul McCartney also made an 'unplugged' revival of the quasi-traditional 'All My Trials' – known also as 'All My Sorrows'. In 1990 it was a throwback to days when it slowed things down between more extrovert offerings from skiffle groups like the pre-Beatle Quarry Men who were warily magnifying their volume with electric amplifiers. If there was no 'live' attraction down the ping-pong youth club, you might smooch instead to the Shadows' turn-of-the-decade harmonised cooing of its 'carefree lovers down country lanes/don't know my grief, can't feel my pain . . . all my trials, Lord, soon be over'.* The most telling line, however, is 'my love has gone, left me behind' which could imply a parting either from choice – or at death's behest.

An even gloomier retrospective was Charles Aznavour's 'Yesterday When I Was Young' where he's deploring his own wasted youth. Catching this diminutive *chansonier* at the London Palladium once, I had to agree with Bob Dylan's view that 'he just blew my brains out'.

Rather than end it all as dolefully, the sailor in Brel's 'Amsterdam' pops off 'full of beer, full of cries' in a tavern brawl, while Peter O'Toole-as-Miguel de Cervantes-as-Don Quixote, in *Man of la Mancha*, devotes the last period of his life to a quest of foolish grandeur in a world where 'evil brings profit and virtue nothing at all'. Eventually, he yields up the ghost, assisted by Sophia Loren and James Coco, but goes out with a bang, leaping

* 'All My Sorrows' reared up again on a 1968 album by the Nocturnes featuring New Seekers-in-waiting Eve Graham and Lyn Paul.

from his death bed – 'what is sickness to the body of a knight errant' – during the finale-medley of 'Dulcinea', the much-covered 'Impossible Dream (The Quest)', 'The Psalm' and the 1972 film musical's main theme.

One theatre season of *Man of la Mancha* had Jacques Brel in the title role. He was then, I suppose, at the apogee of his fame as a composer in English-speaking territories – though, in the process, the more acerbic of his lyrics had been emasculated as instanced by the Kingston Trio's 1964 rendition of 'Le Moribund'* – 'one who is dying' – as 'Seasons in the Sun'. Brightened up still further by the self-styled 'most popular poet in the world', Rod McKuen, it propelled Canadian Terry Jacks (ex-Poppy Family) to the top of the UK chart in 1974. With any what's-the-use-of-it-all ugliness removed, it came out as a run-of-the-mill sentimental lay about some dotard's happy memories – with ascending key changes to pep it up. A lot of Brel's output is too idiosyncratically Gallic to be translated accurately anyway. Jacks followed up with Brel's 'If You Go Away'† which became a 'Send in the Clowns'-type cabaret stand-by – but might not have done if certain of the original stanzas had been retained such as the one with something about 'the king who died because he never knew you'.

It would be difficult to imagine Van Morrison's lengthy and harrowing 'TB Sheets' becoming anyone's cabaret classic – the bleak resignation of an intimate

---

* 1973's 'Sunset' by Roxy Music had been a worthy if possibly unconscious approximation of the black lyrical thrust of 'Le Moribund'.

† Also released in watered-down form by the Kingston Trio. Terry Jacks was involved when, apparently, the Beach Boys taped a hitherto unissued version in 1972. Both were beaten hands down by Dusty Springfield's emotive cover.

beyond recovery from tuberculosis – or Steve Winwood's 'Midland Maniac', a tragic number with disconcerting breaks in tempo that echo the subject's elations and depressions prior to suicide.

Another weird shudder on the same Winwood album was Vivian Stanshall's text to 'Vacant Chair'. Though Stanshall was once a mainstay of the Bonzo Dog Doo-Dah Band, there are few quips in 'Vacant Chair'. Its original title was 'Oku Nsukun Oku'. This was a homily of Gaspar Lawar who Vivian telephoned a week after the death of a mutual friend, bass guitarist Dennis Cowan: 'I was lachrymose and self-pitying and he said in Nigerian, Only the dead weep for the dead. So I said to Gaspar, That's very cool of you. He said, No, just get on with life. So the sentiment of the lyric is: although people must die, most of grief and mourning is pity for yourself – but it's called "Vacant Chair" because there are funeral parlours that actually sell floral chairs called "vacant chairs".'

Awaiting the embalmer's attentions, a woman who 'treated me bad' is flat on the slab in the urban blues warhorse 'St James Infirmary' but, in the rustic heartlands of North America, bodies with greening abdomens were not refrigerated as easily. When he hanged himself, Jud Fry, the misunderstood 'dirty skunk, an ornery pig-stealer' in Rodgers and Hammerstein's *Oklahoma* musical of 1949, still had such a good-looking corpse – 'his fingernails have never been so clean' – that a neighbour expressed a flippant desire to preserve it for posterity 'but it's summer and we're running out of ice'.

A self-administered departure was Fry's way out of an unbearable life but 'Ol' Man Mose' (1964) was made of sterner stuff. According to the Swinging Blue Jeans, he lived in an isolated cabin, presumably to shield himself from the eyes of those inquisitive about his 'very funny nose' – until the prying narrator discovers that 'Ol' Mo' kicked the bucket'.

Approaching the topic of old age and impending demise with greater sensitivity, Scott Walker, whilst a Walker Brother, gave us the twee 'Old Folks' which assumed that rampant children on some forlorn housing estate would care enough to 'be still for a day (when) they take the old folks away'. As a solo act, he shook himself free of such wistfulness with the likes of old homosexual 'Big Louise', and 'Joe', a pensioner dwelling in a noisy seedy apartment block. While he 'sat a-dyin'', Joe reflects that, apart from the meals-on-wheels staff and a fat boy who had just moved to Sun City without saying goodbye, there's no one who knows him well enough 'to call me "Joe"' left alive. By Joe's side lies a postcard from Sun City, a 'desert place where old folks dry away'.

If Joe hadn't been the last of his family and contemporaries, he might have been sent off like the well-heeled gent in Scott's 'Funeral Tango'. Penned by the ubiquitous Brel, it's a kind of thinking man's 'Ain't It Grand to Be Blooming Well Dead'. The stiff in question's spirit guffaws mirthlessly at the hollow emotions and crocodile tears of 'phoney friends' and uncaring relations who have costed him down to his socks during a nosy grubbing through his belongings (which has also 'left my poor soul bare'). With an inheriting gleam in their eyes, they put on a solemn front and have 'even brought the kids who don't know who I am'.

Bereft of dreams but pensive at windows, Brel's 'Old Folks' – not the Walker Brothers' number – have little motivation beyond a simple daily routine between breakfast and sleeping side-by-flaccid-side. Two devoted

69

friends who used to be lovers, they are so near to the end that it's not worth getting the piano tuned or adopting another pet. Hobbies and pastimes are pointless now. Subconsciously they are both particularly disturbed by the ticking of their old silver clock that embodies an unspoken promise to each other, 'I'll wait for you' – as Twinkle's Terry might when she, bent and wizened, totters up to the threshold of paradise.

'Eleanor Rigby' was destined to die alone – but that was how she'd always lived. She expired in the church that was her only comfort, and was buried 'along with her name' with only Father MacKenzie, another lonely person who darns his own socks, in attendance. Old maids would make further appearances in the corporate and solo canon of the Beatles – especially through Paul McCartney who wrote the bulk of 'Lady Madonna' and all of 1971's 'Another Day'.

'Eleanor Rigby' was also the starting point for the group United States of America's 'Stranded in Time', a description of a couple so depressed at the onslaught of age that he sells the hall mirror while she 'tends to tell the time by pictures on the wall'.

Eleanor Rigby seemingly had no one to welcome her through the pearly gates, unlike the subjects of Paul Simon's 'Mother and Child Reunion' (1972). Simon dared to sing to a backing track that was his idea of reggae, then only just shaking off its dismissal by white collegians as 'skinhead music'. Its repetitive lyric featured a mother-as-angel preparing to welcome her boy to heaven as he completes 'the course of a lifetime's run'.

A supernatural get-together with an old love preys on Lonnie Donegan's mind in 1960's 'Beyond the Sunset', and on that of Fred Rose whose estate would benefit after Gene Vincent and Elvis Presley each recorded most remunerative versions of his 'Blue Eyes Crying in the Rain' – which assures an unnamed party that she and he will walk hand-in-hand once more 'in that land that knows no parting'.

Any contemplation of what lies beyond is absent from 'Green Green Grass of Home', an otherwise similarly inclined countrified ballad*. In the song, composer Curly Putman visualises a convict on his way to the gallows. It was not so much the fact that the song had been cut for mainstream pop consumers as the syrupy, string-soaked arrangement that Tom Jones took to the top of the charts in 1967 which, for years, blinded me to the notion that it was anything other than a sentimental journey of no more significance than, well, Doris Day's 'Sentimental Journey' or the World War II singalong, 'Home Town' – the one about 'those corny country cousins of mine'. Nevertheless, on closer inspection, it becomes obvious that, in the beefcake Welshman's plaintive speech before the play-out, the 'four grey walls that surround me', aren't in some dreadful bed-and-breakfast room – nor is the walk at daybreak (with 'a guard and a sad old padre') a trio of drunks holding each other up after a late chucking-out time on Saturday night.

Tom first listened to 'Green Green Grass of Home' on *Country Songs For City Folks*, an album by his idol Jerry Lee Lewis. Piety had been considered a regrettable eccentricity in olde-tyme rockers like Lewis and Little Richard, who were prone to intense bouts of loud apostolicism – because, for all their hollered arrogance, they were ingrained with superstitious terror of the eternal punishment of sin – and anxiety over whether God could take a joke.

* Recorded by Ferlin Husky and Porter Wagoner amongst others.

Thanks to unsolicited snippet coverage in an ITV commercial, 'Always Look on the Bright Side of Life' by Monty Python's Flying Circus was a 'sleeper' hit in 1991. Including a chorus about also looking on the bright side of *death*, it started as the contrastingly perky musical counterpoint to the crucifixion sequence in the *Life of Brian*. The movie could be regarded as a send-up of expensive and verbose Hollywood Biblical epics like *King of Kings*, *The Ten Commandments* and *Ben Hur*. The latter was provided with a typically grandiloquent soundtrack by Miklos Rozsa. The attendant album was, in its way, as morbid a death disc as the same year's 'Teen Angel', as the track titles suggest: 'The Burning Desert' – during which you can almost see the circling vultures – 'Naval Battle' (galley slaves trapped in a sinking ship), 'The Lepers' Search for Christ' and the appositely sombre 'Valley of the Dead'. A chariot race as fraught with danger as Jan and Dean's dash round 'Dead Man's Curve' concludes with Ben Hur's enemy getting what's coming to him – but not before he spits out the last of his blood and hate in the agonising 'Death of Messala'.

In confiscating Hur's land and gaoling his family but dying as he did, Messala might have been a candidate for a verse in born-again Little Richard's gospel-esque 'He Got What He Wanted (But He Lost What He Had)' from 1962 which castigated Samson who 'messed around and lost his hair', and Judas Iscariot who 'loved that filthy lucre'. Though Richard got hold of the wrong end of the stick, the stick still existed – and both of these disparate characters came to a sticky end.*

* 'He Got What He Wanted' was revived in 1964 by Freddie and the Dreamers. A song of like persuasion was 'The Preacher' by Jimmie

Newcastle's Animals went off on a devout tangent less pronounced than Little Richard's by slotting 'Bury My Body' between 'Story of Bo Diddley' and the gutbucket leering of John Lee Hooker's 'Dimples' on their LP début in 1964. Without the remotest hint that he might be mocking this negro spiritual, Eric Burdon trusts that, 'as my soul is going to live with God', Jesus can provide fresh wings if the initial pair malfunction. Perhaps Eric and the others recorded 'Bury My Body' to please their mothers.

Ten years later, another Geordie, Bryan Ferry, had his Roxy Music record 'Triptych' for *Country Life*. Triggered by an amodal 'mediaeval' riff, the former fine-art student sings less a set of lyrics than an impressionistic poem depicting the scene at Calvary.

On the same tack, we cannot go on without a wry look at *Jesus Christ Superstar*. After a flop with *Come Back Richard, Your Country Needs You*, creative collaborators Andrew Lloyd Webber and Tim Rice retold the story of Christ's final week in what was then a most audacious musical that provoked protests from all manner of religious organs. Issued well before its New York opening in 1971, its tunes were already familiar to an audience that trudged to its seats night after night as the show ran and ran; Tony and Grammy awards fell into its makers' laps, and a 1973 version was screened in a cinema near you.

After 1978's 'I Lost My Heart to a Starship Trooper' fizzled out, one of Lloyd Webber's wives, Sarah

---

Rodgers which tells of David and Goliath, and Daniel in the lions' den. I must also pass on that after Mr Acker Bilk came within an ace of a No. 1 with 'Stranger on the Shore' in 1961, a Manchester fan wrote to ask him if it was about Jesus.

Brightman, resumed a UK Top Ten career via a 1985 duet with boy soprano Paul Miles-Kingston. The item that did the trick 'Pie Jesu', was an excerpt from Lloyd Webber's *Requiem* (to his father). Back in the 1960s, Benjamin Britten's *War Requiem* contained a ditty of the same title but Andrew Lloyd Webber was less a Britten for the eighties than the rock era's answer to Sir Arthur Sullivan. You can take that how you like.

Chapter Four

A Little Dog Cried

Who's this? A man dressed in sheets takes in a stray dog. Soon afterwards, he is arrested and sentenced to be crucified. So the story goes in Jimmie Rodgers' 'A Little Dog Cried'* 'when his master died on a hill a long time ago'. This pathetic monologue was rooted in Victorian lore when canines had a prime position in metaphors of grief – as illustrated by painter William Archer who depicts a black one moping at the side of *The Empty Cradle*.

In the context of twentieth-century rock 'n' roll, Rodgers' doggerel was, as a concept *per se*, an exception. On disc, it was generally humans bewailing the passing of – often gallant – pets. An instance that springs to mind most readily is Red Foley's 'Old Shep', the hound who once rescued his young master from drowning in a swimming pool. Years flew by and the time came when the vet suggested that it would be merciful for Shep,

* The B-side of 'English Country Garden', Rodgers' biggest hit. In 1967, he was found slumped in his car with a fractured skull. While he managed a qualified recovery, he had no memory of how the injury occurred. Jimmie had the same name but was not the artist nicknamed 'The Singing Brakeman' – who was the first to be elected to Nashville's Country Music Hall of Fame. This accolade was well deserved as virtually every C & W trend that has emerged since his death on 26 May 1933 has been traceable to his influence. His final twelve songs were completed in a New York studio two days before a tubercular haemorrhage claimed him.

aged and infirm, to be destroyed. No longer a boy himself, the tearful owner 'picked up my gun and aimed it at Shep's faithful head . . . I wished they would shoot me instead'. I've never been certain if he (or the mysterious 'they') actually did it. Perhaps it's best not to know.*

Such a noxious decision was not forced upon Jim Reeves who, as a warrior returning from Korea, was guided away from an unstable dam (over which he would have walked out of habit) by 'Old Tige', a family dog with a reputation for bravery. As if it was the sort of thing Tige did every day, Reeves recalls offhandedly that 'he even saved me from the bull that gored my dad to death'. Once past the dangerous crossing, the dog vanished, presumably to pursue recreational activities in the undergrowth. However, on arrival home, Jim's mother told him – as a heavenly choir wells up in the background – that 'when you left, it broke his heart – Tige died three years ago'. It must be hoped that Tige had joined Shep 'where the good doggies go'.

In both traditional music and modern pop, dogs are the most common central characters in animal songs concerning death. Pre-empting the likes of 'Old Shep' by nearly half a millennium, 'My Dog and I' choruses that 'if death do come, as it may hap, my grave shall be under the tap, with folded arms there we may lie/ cheek to jowl, my dog and I'. In Edinburgh stands the statue of 'Greyfriars Bobby' who spent the fourteen years prior to his own death in 1872 by the unmarked grave of his master, having followed the funeral procession to the kirkyard at Greyfriars. Whatever the

* Elvis Presley released his shot at 'Old Shep' in 1957. Liverpudlian Clinton Ford recorded a surprisingly successful version two years later.

weather, however often the beadle chased him away, Bobby stayed at his post, infinitely patient and possibly possessed with a vague enchantment that his vigil was to be endless. The terrier became so much part of the scheme of things parochially that – as could only happen in Britain – the Lord Provost granted him the Freedom of the City – though Bobby chose to remain exactly where he was. With trumping euphonium, children's choir and canine pants as a percussive hook, the wee dog was immortalised on vinyl by local folk singer Doug Mann in 1978.

A possibly more reluctant loyal animal hero was General Custer's mount, 'Comanche', who, 'battle-scarred and torn', had been the only member of the Seventh Cavalry left breathing in the aftermath of the battle of Little Big Horn. Thus spake a single by Johnny Horton. It would be pleasant to think that this noble nag's wounds were not serious enough for euthanasia, and that his dotage was peaceful. In any case, his stuffed remains stand today in a Washington museum.

Both rider and ridden 'laughed themselves to death' in 'Ali Baba's Camel' by the Bonzo Dog Doo-Dah Band – and 'wherever you think Ali's gone, the camel's gone to h**l!' This item was unearthed from the 78 r.p.m. record collection of the unit's chief show-off Vivian Stanshall who would find enough common ground with mild-mannered Steve Winwood to become a popular and hilarious confidant within Traffic's fraternity. Their mascot was a white Alsatian named 'Mr Fantasy' after the title track of Traffic's first LP. In an evil hour, however, Mr Fantasy suffered a brainstorm and had to be put down.

There was nothing whatsoever the matter with the unfortunate marsupial who was roped-up in response to the strange and manifold last wishes of a dying man* in 'Tie Me Kangaroo Down Sport' (1960) by Down Under's Rolf Harris. This, the first of his hits, he promoted on the road (with a backing combo called – you guessed it – the Kangaroos) at teenage venues such as the Cubik in Rochdale and Manchester's Oasis. In his wake came a brief craze for the wobble board, prominent on the 45 – though exponents of the instrument could not easily join the Musicians Union; Harris himself was in Equity.

Rolf's treatment by proxy of the kangaroo paled beside the unfeeling behaviour of so-called 'Southern Gentleman' Sonny James towards an unwanted cat – the detailing of which crept into Britain's Top Thirty in 1956. Hardly a subscriber to the notion that pets are not just for Christmas, among Sonny's thwarted means of disposing of his puss were consecutive dumpings on a train, an ocean-bound liner (which sank) and a rocket to the moon. Still 'The Cat Came Back', and *in extremis*, its wicked master summoned a local posse to shoot it down.†

The New Christy Minstrels' stab at this vaudeville favourite appeared on the same 1965 album as jilted 'Julianne' who dwelt in a Kentucky mountain shack with only a dog for company before a passer-by peeping in noticed a shawl and rifle on the floor on which the 'hound dog lay a-dying' too – but of the human resident, there was no sign – nor ever would be, unless you count the ghost that some would swear they saw in later years. Local opinion blamed a 'hungry bear' for Julianne's disappearance.

* Such as 'tan me hide when I'm dead, Fred'. Lest we forget, there was a rival version of 'Tie Me Kangaroo Down Sport' by a Bobby Stevens.
† On April Fool's Day 1991, Radio Merseyside listeners were treated to a remarkable rendition of 'The Cat Came Back' by presenter Spencer Leigh and studio guests that included Ambrose Mogg, 'Elvis Presley' and 'Mark Knopfler'.

In a smaller world, spiders are predators of house flies. Such an encounter was described by North America's Monocles in 'Spider and the Fly'. Not the Rolling Stones number, this might be about an Oedipus complex, cannibalism or, as on the Move's 'Night of Fear', the perils of psychedelic drugs. You decide for yourself. See, an electric organ *vibrato* and throbbing tom-toms hover as an exultant *basso profundo* booms 'The fly! The fly is in the web!' Then, just like the man-fly mutant in the 1958 cult horror flick, *The Fly*, we hear a tiny, high-pitched voice bleating 'Help me! Help me!' Abruptly, the dialogue is interrupted by the ringing of an alarm clock. Johnny wakes up. His mother enters and asks if his sleep had been disturbed by a bad dream. So it has – but the nightmare continues for, under the sheets, the youth has changed into a giant spider (indicating that as well as absorbing *The Fly*, a Monocle had read Kafka's *Metamorphosis*). Worse, Johnny is famished and the closest source of satisfactory arachnid food is Mum, i.e., her actual flesh as opposed to her expertise as a cook.

Maybe it was a comment on how it would be if the tables were turned on those members of our species who don't think twice about crushing insects with the thumb – or serving up the severed limbs of livestock and poultry – such as the headless chicken in Eno's 'Dead Finks Don't Talk' of 1973. John D. Loudermilk's 'This Little Bird' – 'out of reach of human eye' – may have died naturally judging by its non-committal allegorical verses and a winsome minor key arrangement in 1965 by the Nashville Teens.*

Conversely, a mythical winged creature, 'Puff the

---

* Decca hedged its bets by issuing simultaneously both the Teens' and an apathetic Marianne Faithfull's pressings of 'This Little Bird', each with Andrew Loog Oldham in the producer's chair.

Magic Dragon' was condemned, like the Struldbrugs in *Gulliver's Travels*, never to quit this mortal coil*. Nevertheless, Puff was snuffed out psychologically by the desertion of a playmate.

More distressing in a physical sense was a pack of bloodhounds tearing apart cornered quarry in the traditional 'Cumberland Mountain Deer Hunt' as extrapolated by Uncle Dave Macon, an early fixture on the Grand Ole Opry, who punctuated this showstopper by plinking on the banjo imitations of baying hounds and view halloos. Don't ask me how.

As irregular a supporter of the anti-blood sports lobby was farmer's boy 'Tennessee' Ernie Ford whose 'Shotgun Boogie' of 1950 came to be regarded as nascent rockabilly – a strand of rock 'n' roll based on sparse, largely acoustic instrumentation and primeval rowdiness. It also glorified a brush hunter who slaughters rabbits, 'b'ar', squirrels ('tonight you'll be in the pot') with sadistic relish. Of the same kidney, his girlfriend shoots 'a big fat dove' for one of their candlelit dinners – but the romance is marred by her protective father who is not a man to enquire about a suitor's honourable intentions before firing on him. However, a constant heart, the lusty lad promises to return 'when your pappy runs out of shells'.

In one of the states adjacent to Tennessee roamed the 'Wild Dogs of Kentucky' as immortalised by Nervous Norvus.† Borrowing the tune of 'Julianne', he conjec-

---

* The original version was by Peter, Paul and Mary. Further indications of this piece's marshmallow nature were recordings by Nina and Frederick (on the EP *Sing for the Young in Heart*) and, in 1981, by Slim Whitman.

† With an unidentified canine vocalist duetting on the hook line. Pedants will wish to know that the British pressing was misprinted 'Wild Dog of Kentucky'.

tures that with 'their savage howls, the Devil's blood would freeze'. Clearly, these interjections intimate a grim and scrupulous enjoyment of a nightly task that, supervised by 'the shotgun man', would be incomplete unless 'coon is lying dead'.

You can manufacture a Davy Crockett cap from coonskin but if you're after an exotic carpet or bed-spread commensurate with such headwear and the stag's antlers upon which you might hang it, a voyage to the sun-scorched Punjab may be in order. On an evening verandah there, you might eavesdrop on a party of pith-helmeted, trophy-collecting huntsmen of the Raj justi-fying the 'ripping fun' of their manly jungle excursions with a 'kill or be killed' argument. Besides, with particu-lar reference to table manners – 'after they have eaten you, they never say their grace' – tigers would make 'beastly' domestic pets, biting and scratching if stroked. Such was the essence of 'Hunting Tigers out in Indiah' (to rhyme with 'yah!'), another revival of a 78 on the same Bonzo Dog Doo-Dah Band LP as 'Ali Baba's Camel'.

On the same plane of light comedy came Tom Lehrer's 'Hunting Song' in 1958 – about an idiot bagging 'two game wardens, seven hunters and a cow'. Yet most digs at mankind's abuse of his fellow creatures have been no fun at all, whether 'Gone' – referring to a culling of 'beautiful birds' – by Geronimo Black (a Mothers of Invention splinter group) to 'Little Woman', Dave Mason's reproachful tale of a poacher local to Traffic's cottage on the Berkshire Downs. As much a variation on 'Greensleeves' as those of Ralph Vaughan-Williams, it employed a shawm, recorder and a consort of viols. If these sounded archaic, they were musically sympathetic to the weapon used. Even in 1968, the partridge in the first verse was brought down with a bow-and-arrow, rather than the louder air-rifle and, therefore, less likely to attract gamekeepers.

Dave twice resigned from Traffic over 'musical differences' with Steve Winwood. The creator of 'Little Woman' might have also disagreed morally with his old colleagues when Steve, as part of the Cotswolds' landed gentry by the late 1970s, indulged new passions for beagling and deer stalking. 'That boy could kill anything', exclaimed Viv Stanshall. This may not have been true but the lyrics alone of Rex Barker and the Ricochets' 'Jeremy Is Innocent'* were unlikely to induce Winwood to mend his ways – even if it was. Over a riff lifted from Duane Eddy's 'Peter Gunn', its verses were merely alternate bars of a bawled 'Jeremy! Jeremy!' and, right on the beat, 'woof woof' and then a bang from a double-barrelled twelve-bore. It was designed to be irritating – especially to Jeremy and similar huntin'-fishin'-an'-shootin' aristocrats.

It was not a hit. 'Bride Eyes' (*sic*) by Art Garfunkel, however, was. An anthem of the animal rights movement, it was not intended for release as a single until the artiste was shown footage of long queues for *Watership Down* to which 'Bright Eyes' was the main soundtrack theme. I didn't *want* to like 'Bride Eyes' because doe-eyed Garfunkel is one of the myriad pop entertainers I love to hate. No doubt the fault for this prejudice is entirely mine. On principle, I didn't read *Watership Down* or watch the film – but I have seen some of its stars

---

* A Dead Badger production, a percentage of the royalties amassed by 'Jeremy Is Innocent' was donated to animal charities. In an earlier incarnation, the band were Ivor Biggun and the Red-Nosed Burglars who were ejaculated into the charts in 1978 with 'The Winker's Song (Misprint)'.

sightlessly staring and bloody in butchers' winders. As both a local musician and founder of the Reading Organisation for Animal Rights (ROAR), I felt that it was incumbent upon me to compose 'Only for a Moment', my perception of a battery-farm inmate's perspective.* This was recorded with a string *quintet* and mailed to an anti-vivisection body who were then selecting material for a 1983 *Artists for Animals* compilation LP. The verdict on my effort was something like: 'The number's OK but you're not. You're not famous or hip enough. We only have people like Paul Weller and Billy Bragg on *our* albums. Can't you get one of them to cover it?'

No, I couldn't. Instead, my original master was second track, side one on the Alan Clayson and the Argonauts' 1985 collection, *What a Difference a Decade Made* – with ten of its fourteen tracks concerned with death – which was released by Butt Records because I wanted to be on the same label as the Pretty Things. To date, it has shifted about six hundred copies worldwide.

A luckier act than mine, the Smiths, told it like it was more directly on the self-explanatory lead track of *Meat Is Murder* which topped the British album list in 1985. Rather than prissy 'Only for a Moment' violins, horrific electronic effects and cattle lowing heralded this account of the slaughter and consumption of frightened, bewildered brutes awaiting execution down at the abattoir.

Occasionally, the boot was on the other foot. Synthesisers were the whole of Morton Subotnick's *The Wild Bull*, inspired, it says here, by a Sumerian poem *circa*

* Two ex-Argonauts formed an outfit called Between Pictures. One of their 1982 B-sides, 'Down at the Factory', drank from much the same pool as 'Only for a Moment'.

1700 BC. In it, apparently, the said heifer kills this woman's husband – though you'd never guess it without reading the sleeve notes. Aurally veiled in stock trumpet fanfares, drum rolls and cries of 'Olay!', a snorting half-ton of heaving muscle similarly skewered Dave Dee, Dozy, Beaky, Mick and Tich's 'Don Juan', a strutting matador who, broken-hearted after catching his girl in the arms of another, decided not to fight back.

The horned, ring-nosed tool of Don Juan's suicide in this desperate recycle of the 'Legend of Xanadu' blueprint would have considered Tommy Steele's pacifist 'Little White Bull' (from the 1960 movie *Tommy the Toreador*) beneath contempt until the afternoon it cast aside adolescent folly and charged at the red cloth as though it meant business. Yet, attaining its majority too, 'El Toro El Goro (The Peace-Loving Bull)' was, related Sam the Sham and the Pharaohs, as bored at having 'to butt some flag-waving nut' as Jacques Brel's more curdled 'Los Toros' who on Sundays 'drop dead for us' – 'us' meaning grocery clerks who 'become Nero' and plain girls with bare midriffs and roses in their teeth, belying more mundane weekday occupations. A feathered spear dangling from its neck, a goaded bull in the swimming heat of summer might, indeed, 'dream of a hell where men and worn-out matadors still burn'.

So would the tortured bruin in the arena of the United States of America's 'American Metaphysical Circus' where, 'although he cannot sing, they can make him whistle Londonderry Air' – and what about the pale-eyed quadruped who was the principal ingredient of the goat's head soup depicted within the package containing the 1973 Rolling Stones' album of the same name?*

* Some Stones aficionados insist that this had cryptic connotations

84

A nasty picture of an arrowed fawn made the very front cover of the soundtrack album of *The Great Rock 'n' Roll Swindle*, a kind of subjective *Hard Day's Night* for the then-disintegrating Sex Pistols. It began with the working title of *Who Killed Bambi?* for which purpose what remained of the group taped a Costa del Islington pastiche of that name – rather like 'El Toro El Goro', oddly enough – with actor Ten Pole Tudor on barely decipherable, convoluted ranting, which, sodden with punk sloganeering and irksome repetition of the question, was far removed from Bambi, Thumper *et al*.

One of the few comprehensible phrases during this two-minute waste of time was 'never trust a hippy' – and they didn't come more untrustworthy than Scotland's Incredible String Band who had seen fit to kick off a 1969 album with merry 'Big Ted', about a farmyard boar whose soul had 'gone like snow on the water' after he was carted off to the butcher's to be, perhaps, reincarnated as a cow.

Of the same vintage, another type of afterlife was mentioned in 1970's 'Snowblind' by Judy Henske and her husband, former Lovin' Spoonful guitarist, Jerry Yester. A character called Fullbrook Sedgewynd trained a bear 'with little fear of Hades' via a system of rewards (of honey) to attack and devour Rosie and Nancy, two maidens who had spurned him.

The sexual symbolism of 'Fattening Frogs for Snakes' by Sonny Boy Williamson II (Rice Miller) was less unconscious. This repulsive old Mississippi legend's performances of the opus on a 1964 tour of Britain would

---

with an incident in Morocco in 1968 when a perturbed Brian Jones identified himself with a chalk-white goat about to be decapitated in order to feed some Jajouka musicians and their European visitors.

climax with him singing whilst blowing a harmonica with his nostrils.

A Caucasian equivalent of sorts was Burl Ives, still shambling round European auditoriums with a guitar in his seventieth year. His inevitable encore was the one about the gluttonous old lady who swallowed a fly* – followed by progressively bigger beings to catch it. Burl may have been Marvellous For His Age but I tend to judge musical recitals in absolute terms. Not quite my bag either was his self-composed 'Chivalrous Shark' that 'will eat neither woman nor child'.

This carnivorous fish's restraint compared favourably with human scavenging for deep sea consumables. The skipper of the nineteenth-century vessel in the Dubliners' 'Greenland Whale Fisheries' bit off more than he could chew when a harpooned whale 'capsized the boat and (we) lost five men' but what distressed him most was the creature's escape.

Whilst in a piscatorial mood, we ought to note 'Three Little Fishes' of 1939 by Kay Kyser and his Orchestra, a piece so infuriatingly catchy that, driven to distraction, a detainee in Kansas State Penitentiary bludgeoned his cell mate to death for humming, whistling and singing it incessantly. Spreading itself thinly enough to sell well without reaching the charts, a British version by the late Frankie Howerd would be a regular request on Saturday morning's *Children's Favourites*, aired by 'Uncle Mac' on the BBC Light Programme.

Phil Harris was one of those rare comedians who actually had hits with comedy records. During a post-

* An inversion of this idea was implicit in 'The Waltz That Carried Us Away And Then a Mosquito Came and Ate Up My Sweetheart', a John Fahey instrumental.

war fad for escapist horror flicks about outer-space 'things', he notched up his greatest smash with 'The Thing'. In 1950 too, Gene Autry made the big time with his seasonal 'Frosty the Snowman' – who became, I imagine, a puddle in the garden during the unusually warm January of 1951.

Scraping the barrel of non-human case studies an impoverished Captain Beefheart and his Magic Band procrastinate over taking a hammer to a 'China Pig' in 1969, and the Beach Boys 'just can't hold the tears back' over 'Betsy', a rusty old banger, maybe one oil change away from the Surfaris' 'Hot Rod Graveyard'. Estranged from the surf by the later 1960s, the Boys – more like Ancient Mariners these days – addressed themselves to ecological issues such as that stressed in Al Jardine's 'Don't Go Near the Water' (because it's suffused with industrial waste and sewage). Though pre-empted obscurely by Cream's 'pity for a falling leaf' in 1967's 'World Of Pain', Brian Wilson and Co. also railed against air pollution in 'A Day in the Life of a Tree'; its 'slow death' stressed by the group's manager, Jack Reiley's wheezy, groaning lead vocal.

Chapter Five

One Hell of a Band

A death in pop sells records. Before they had a chance to dry their tears, music industry moguls would be obliged to meet the demand kindled by tragedy and rush-release the product while the corpse was still warm. On 16 August 1977, record-store windows bloomed with the King's splendour. The ending of Elvis's days stoked up a hit parade renaissance of his 'decent' music. His final record date at Graceland the previous October had spawned 'Way Down'/'Pledging My Love', a minor hit in the time left to him, but a No. 1 after he'd gone. For the rest of 1977 he was never off Top Forty radio. On its playing lists were two new in-concert singles (including an 'Unchained Melody' pressed on tasteful white vinyl) with eight reissues for additional commercial ballast. Given a rubbishing the week before the sands ran out in an *NME* profile – which contained an unfortunate remark implying that he'd been dead for ages – his *Moody Blue* was racing towards the top of the album chart trailed by *its* retinue of swift repromotions. Shiftier manoeuvres were saved for later.*

It was a boom time for Presley's manager Colonel

---

* Such as 'Don't Cry at Christmas' by '?', a vocalist that Sun Records would neither deny or confirm was Presley. It had the required hot-potato-in-the-mouth singing as well as a narrative about a man incarcerated in gaol for the usual 'shot from a careless gun'. This likely story was coupled with a tedious instrumental by the same composer.

Tom Parker* who regarded his client's absence as no more a hindrance than back in 1958 when Elvis had been drafted into the US army for two years. Then there were rumours that Parker would be devoting himself professionally to Rick Nelson – who'd come into his own during Presley's patriotic chore – but these were nipped in the bud after Nelson hurtled downwards to eternity when an aircraft bearing him caught fire on New Year's Eve in 1985.

Though Elvis had shed the bulk of his artistic load by the late 1950s, he'd left such an indelible impression on the complacency of post-war pop that his own later capitulation to it was shrugged off by his countless fans as the prerogative of stardom. The myth of his omnipotence was such that adoration would be decades a-dwindling for devotees in a languid daze from the fixity of gazing – figuratively anyway – at the bolted gates of his mansion. For many, the haloed King still rules from the tomb.

On the monolith placed over him at Graceland, his chiselled middle name was misspelt. This was the tip of an iceberg of enough spurious ambiguity to hang a question mark over Presley's final repose. He'd been officially pronounced dead but humble folk clung to the fantasy that, alive and well, he'd been simply spirited away somewhere. For, however jumbled they become, all ingredients of survival myths represent a profound human impulse – not peculiar to pop – that holds facts too grievous to be borne at arm's length.

The likes of Glenn Miller, James Dean and Buddy Holly are also said to be lying comatose and horribly

* Who shelled out for a pew in the Elvis Presley Memorial Chapel adjacent to Presley's birthplace in Tupelo, Mississippi.

disfigured in remote sanatoriums – but the Tweedledum and Tweedledee of pop survival stories must be Presley and Jim Morrison of the Doors: prophet, poet and leper messiah. Among reported sightings are some in locations where you'd least expect to find them – shopping for groceries in a Dagenham Tesco's; moustachioed and crewcut in Detroit; opening a bank account in Toronto or, as 'Elvis' himself informed Spencer Leigh during a 1989 interview on Radio Merseyside, 'With some Aboriginal friends of mine, eating raw meat and fish.'

Splashed across the front page of one of the dafter tabloids in 1978 was a feature about a Mr and Mrs Parker – no relation to the Colonel – naming their only son Elvis Presley Parker on the understanding that here was the King reincarnated, ready to recover his domain on attaining man's estate. With dollars dancing before their eyes, there have been slightly less deluded adults claiming to be Elvis (like the one on Radio Merseyside) or Jim as Perkin Warbeck had claimed to be a Prince in the Tower.

Did you know that Morrison's birthday was 8 December, and that on that self-same day in 1980, John Lennon was assassinated? Exactly two years later, Marty Robbins died in Nashville aged fifty-seven. Five plus seven equals twelve. The twelfth Doors LP to be released in Britain was *An American Prayer*, a collection on which the quartet's living members added music to an extant tape of Morrison reciting poems, some with verses to do with death. Lennon's *twelfth* solo entry in the *Guinness Book of Hit Singles* was '(Just Like) Starting Over', his last prior to the cruel release of his spirit. Presley's *Flaming Star* – with a title-track lyric insisting that when a man sees one, 'his time has come' – entered the UK album list on the *fifth* day of the *seventh* month (making twelve again) two years to the month before Morrison – *just* like Elvis – suffered a fatal heart attack in a bathroom. Cue dimmers and creepy music.

The compilation of similar macabre coincidences can occupy many an idle hour – and there'll be plenty to chill you as you read on. The B-side of 'Way Down', for example, was 'Pledging My Love', first recorded by Memphis-born Johnny Ace whose worrying pastime of playing Russian roulette backfired during a round backstage at Houston's City Auditorium on Christmas Eve 1954. A few weeks later, 'Pledging My Love' was a US rhythm-and-blues No. 1. Since then, three versions of this song have been recorded by artists who afterwards passed away in peculiar circumstances. Jackie Wilson collapsed during a performance at the Latin Casino in New Jersey on 29 September 1975. Brain damaged, he regained consciousness only sporadically during a sojourn in the nearby Cherry Hill Medical Center where he died* without fuss nine years later in his climactic seven times seventh year. During a domestic dispute on All Fools' Day that year, Marvin Gaye was gunned down by his own father – and him a Church minister too.

Hounslow's Vince Taylor recorded 'Pledging My Love' as a 1959 B-side. A one-hit-wonder at home, he fared better in France, cutting up rough with a 100 per cent rock 'n' roll elixir that a loyal Gallic following would pay to hear regardless of passing fashion. However, during one unhinged evening at the Paris Olympia, he dismissed his backing combo and floated onstage in

---

* He'd been six feet under for two years when, to tie in with its use in an ITV commercial, Jackie's 1957 smash, 'Reet Petite', was reissued to rise quickly to No. 1. Two more dusted-off Wilson classics followed it into the Top Twenty. Much good did it do him.

atypical white vestments to preach a repent-ye-your-sins to a mystified and then furious *ye-ye* audience. From then on, it was a downward spiral as, assisted by a mind-bending drug intake, he returned to more orthodox performances which grew increasingly addled until he packed it in altogether in the mid-1980s. Not long after, he was beneath the cold, cold earth in Switzerland.

What's more, Vince was an acquaintance of singing composer Claude François who sidled into Britain's Top Forty with 1976's 'Tears on the Telephone'. Otherwise his deepest penetration into markets beyond French regions had been more oblique with the reflective 'Comme d'Habitude' which, with English lyrics by Paul Anka, was covered by acts as diverse as Frank Sinatra and the Sex Pistols. While this syndication enabled him to dwell in a sumptuous chateau near Fontainebleau, Claude's private life was blighted by divorce and chronic insomnia that had him gardening within the glare of arc lights until the grey of morning. Cut off in his prime by faulty electrical wiring on 11 March 1978, his demise was bewailed in microcosm as passionately as that of Elvis Presley, another of the many who recorded 'My Way'.

Presley could parrot entire passages of dialogue from the three films of James Dean, the rock 'n' roll rebel prototype who fled this vale of misery in his Silver Porsche Spyder at 86 m.p.h., on 30 September 1955 when it collided with another car.* An early manifes-

---

* Tragedy also struck the co-stars of Dean's *Rebel Without a Cause* (on general release a month after the accident). Sal Mineo was found stabbed to death outside his Hollywood apartment on 12 February 1976 while Natalie Wood drowned in 1981 after leaving the yacht on which her husband Robert Wagner and actor Christopher Walker were quarrelling.

ation of the worst aspects of pop idolatry, a dam then burst on a river of deed-poll James Deans, bedroom shrines, seances, and letters written to him years after the crash. Shards of twisted metal, allegedly from the Porsche, changed hands for huge sums, like relics of the True Cross.

As well as his movies, James' legacy to the world also embraced a single, 'Jungle Fever', that showcased his bongo-pattering. Its flip side was 'Dean's Lament'. Lamenting what? Had he an inkling of his own fate? After a recording star – even a peripheral one – has left his life, the music can never be the same. For the most zealous votaries, every lyric, every note implies portent that elevates pop ephemera to Holy Writ.

Matt Monro used to finish his set with one of his biggest smashes, 'Softly as I Leave You'. In Addenbrookes Hospital in January 1985, he would undergo an attempted liver transplant and a cancerous growth would be uncovered. He'd be discharged but would be back within two days to die quietly on 9th February.

Liverpool's Michael Holliday, the UK 'answer' to Bing Crosby, had been the chart victor when he and certain other singing Britons had fought over Marty Robbins' jogalong 'Story of My Life'. If that sort of immortality mattered to him, Holliday could die easy – but he didn't. Life should have been a bed of roses but he was plagued by mounting private difficulties. The Inland Revenue had him cornered with a final demand on past earnings, his hit parade days were spent*, and his wife was about to divorce him 'because I can't resist a pretty girl' – as he confided in a whisky-choked burr to the proprietor of London's Freddie Mills Nite Spot where, on 29 October

---

After 'Little Boy Lost' peaked at No. 50 in 1960.

1963, he'd just stunned 'em with an impromptu floor spot rendering of 'I Can't Believe You're in Love with Me'. Following Freddie's anxious 'I don't want you to do anything stupid, Mike', a pal drove him home. Soon after he was dropped off, Mike was hastened to the nearest hospital after banging his head on a brick wall - but this was merely the final nail in his coffin as the spirits he'd taken on board earlier had washed down a drugs overdose.

Sorrow would cross the Nite Spot's threshold again at around 1 a.m. on 25 July 1965 when, in a car parked in the alleyway to its rear, Mills himself died with a rifle next to him and a bullet wound above his right eye. The coroner concluded that it had been self-inflicted in view of 'showbusiness personality'* and ex-champion boxer Freddie's demoralised forbearance in the face of financial ruin, agonising headaches and his fast-dissolving celebrity. His widow and stepson were among the many who begged to differ, insisting that he'd been murdered by gangsters.

Similar circumstances and speculation surrounded the passing of James Sheppard of Shep and the Limeliters who'd been embroiled in litigation during which he'd been obliged to sing in the witness stand to demonstrate that the outfit's 1961 hit, 'Daddy's Home', was not a copy of a previous release, 'A Thousand Miles Away'. Police suggested that the motive was robbery when his body was found in a car on Long Island's Belt Parkway

---

* Among the Bournemouth pugilist's activities in this area was hosting BBC television's teenage magazine Six-Five Special, and a cabaret turn in his club. He also recorded a single, 'One For The Road', a medley of pub favourites such as 'Two Lovely Black Eyes' and 'I Belong To Glasgow'.

n 24 January 1970 – only weeks after he and the imeliters had re-formed for a nostalgia concert.

Foul play was suspected but no one was brought to ook when another group leader met a terrible end in a arked vehicle. Fresh from the US Top Ten with 1966's Fought the Law', Bobby Fuller left the other three of is Four to fend for themselves but, in going solo, also roke a contract with his record company. An appoint-nent was made on 18 July 1966 for the signatories to esolve the situation, but Bobby failed to arrive as he'd een detained in the mortuary. Apparently, gasoline had een poured into his mouth and ignited. The death ertificate read 'accidental'; the cops reckoned somehow nat it had been suicide. While these discrepancies were eing filed, the first shipment of *The Bobby Fuller Memor-l Album* was being loaded on to delivery vans.*

By so doing, the label treasured hopes that, because uller had been 'current' when he died, commercial blood ould be squeezed from such a retrospective. Well, Buddy Iolly had still been able to crack the Top Forty five eeks after his death when 'It Doesn't Matter Anymore'/ Raining In My Heart' clambered to the top in Britain† revive flagging interest in the Texan songwriter.

He couldn't say he hadn't been warned though, as, uring Holly's only tour of England with the Crickets, e Meek explained that a Tarot reading one evening at GM Sound had pointed categorically to 3 February as e date of the bespectacled Texan's death.‡ Sure

Containing the inauspicious line 'I guess my race is run', 'I Fought e Law' was a natural choice for an attendant 45. It was, however, vered in Britain by the She Trinity.
But no further than No. 13 in his native USA.
It would also be the date chosen by Meek to squeeze a fatal trigger his landlady and himself in 1967.

enough, on that night in 1959, Buddy and those low
on the bill of the Winter Dance Party Tour of the froze
upper mid-West states entertained about one thousan
customers at the Surf Ballroom, Clear Lake, Iow
United by artistic purpose and mutual respect, th
laugh-a-minute camaraderie on and off the boards ha
been typified by Holly bashing drums behind the B
Bopper – a kind of rock 'n' roll Max Miller – and the
them both joining Ritchie Valens, a younger singer,
form a vocal trio on the Coasters' dolefully comic 'Thr
Cool Cats'.

In order to get his clothes laundered and as a brea
from nights dozing upright in the tour bus with the roa
roaring in his ears, Holly had chartered a light aircra
to the next stop. The remaining two passenger sea
were raffled but the winners – fortunately for them
were each talked into surrendering them; the Bopp
pulled rank on Waylon Jennings*, the Crickets' ne
bass player, and seventeen-year-old Valens tossed a co
with the group's guitarist, Tommy Allsup, who calle
'tails' and lost. Moments after take-off in a modera
snow storm, the pilot misread the dial panel, and h
Beechcraft Bonanza ploughed into a frozen cornfield. F
and the three cool cats were rubbed out instantly.†

The morning after, British newspapers bristled wi
Holly, but in his own land journalists under the editori
lash tended to write him off as a has-been with Vale
and the Bopper being far hotter property. Our coloni
cousins had a point because Buddy's latest 45 was h

* Becoming a star of 'outlaw' country music in the 1970s, Jennin
composed and recorded 'Old Friend', a tribute to Holly.
† After investing in Buddy's publishing rights, a startled Pa
McCartney was presented with the cuff-links that had been fasteni
Buddy's shirt when his body was carried from the wreckage.

first double-side of non-originals, and the 45 before that – 'Heartbeat' – had merely bubbled under even loyal Britain's Top Twenty.

'The Big Bopper's Wedding', however, was steaming up *Billboard*'s Top Forty – but, though issued in the immediate wake of his passing, the Bopper's third single, 'Walking through My Dreams'/'Someone Watching over You', did not. On the other hand, the rise of Ritchie's 'La Bamba'* accelerated, climbing almost to No. 1 after the words 'the late' were inserted before his name in the publicity for his only performance on celluloid – miming 'Ooh My Head' (derived from Little Richard's 'Ooh My Soul') in the Jimmy Clanton vehicle, *Go Johnny Go*. Nevertheless, until the *La Bamba* bio-pic in 1987 and Los Lobos' million-selling version of its title song, Valens – and the Bopper – were remembered by John Citizen as the guys who died in the same air crash as Buddy Holly.

Other olde-tyme rock 'n' rollers went down too: Chuck Berry to prison, Little Richard to the Church, and the Everly Brothers to the marines – while babysnatching Jerry Lee Lewis was hounded from Albion's shores. Like Buddy Holly, Eddie Cochran was to be more permanently absent. Another similarity was that they were both better loved in Europe than at home.† In the same boat was Eddie's bosom chum Gene Vincent with whom he co-headlined a package tour of England's 'scream circuit' in spring 1960 with an indigenous supporting line-up that included Billy Fury and other charges signed

---

* With its fast three chord arrangement, this was to be categorised by some as nascent punk.
† Cochran's 'Three Steps to Heaven'/'Cherished Memories' was a posthumous UK No. 1 but a flop in the States. A further affinity with Holly was that Cochran was accompanied by the Crickets for his last recording session.

up by the celebrated pop svengali Larry Parnes. After the show at the Liverpool Empire, local agent Allan Williams arranged another Merseyside spectacular with Parnes on 3 May for the two Americans – but, in the end, Eddie couldn't make it, incapacitated as he was by his death in St Martin's hospital in Bath late on Sunday 17 April. En route from the Bristol Hippodrome to London airport, a tyre burst on the A4 through Chippenham, and the speeding driver rammed a lamp post. Sitting in the back between his fiancée and Vincent, Cochran was hurled against the roof and then out of the door.*

Despite fractured ribs and collar-bone plus injuries to his already calipered left leg, Gene, with characteristic obstinacy, honoured existing British dates, using the microphone stand as a surgical support and paying respects to his friend with a heavy-hearted 'Over the Rainbow'. Years later, he would be surprised in backstage alcoves addressing an unseen Cochran. When called to go on stage, he would reply sadly, 'Tell Eddie I'll be right out'.

Two months after 'Three Steps to Heaven' fell from its perch, Johnny Kidd and the Pirates were up there with the unforgettable 'Shakin' All Over'. One of the few home-grown rockers who never went 'Bobby'-smooth, Kidd could generate a sweaty intensity rarely experienced in UK pop before 1962. As a result, he always had more bookings than he could possibly keep,

* Dave Dee, who was then a police cadet, was on station duty that fateful night and was responsible for Cochran's possessions, including his guitar, until their removal back to the States. As the Man Who Killed Eddie Cochran, the chauffeur – on top of being fined and banned for dangerous driving – is, reputedly, still beaten up regularly by West Country Teddy Boys.

with or without record success. For such a tireless tourer, by the law of averages, there was bound to be some major transport mishap sooner or later and for Johnny it came when the group's van was smitten head-on by a skidding lorry near Radcliffe, Lancashire on 7 October 1966. On the television news the next day, it was reported that twenty-seven-year-old Johnny had been among the fatalities.

Kidd had been thinking aloud about an album consisting entirely of Gene Vincent numbers. As the 1970s approached, Gene could have used the publicity and, more, any writer's royalties as he'd been threatened with court over maintenance for an English ex-wife. He could also foresee a time when his now steadfastly painful leg would have to be amputated. Backed by Alice Cooper, he was overweight and weeping drunk at the Toronto Rock Festival in 1969, an event that astonished those who thought he was already dead – and one that failed to bring him back from an outer darkness of back-of-beyond dance halls in northern Europe. While denying that his alcoholism was critical, he'd wake up thick-tongued after another bender, swearing not to touch another drop but sinking three fingers of hair-of-the-dog Martini within half an hour of dressing.

It might be seen as proper that his last booking was in England where a considerable hard core had never ceased to adore him. Back in Los Angeles, his missus had cleared off with the children, the car and half the house. Gene gave up. Boozing steadily but not eating, days slipped by until, on 12 October, he slumped to the floor of his mother's caravan, vomiting blood. He was buried beside the highway where he'd spent his life travelling to the next show.

On *their* last legs, the Sex Pistols had fallen back on

classic rock. A pronounced liking for Eddie Cochran was evidenced in rehashes of his 'Something Else' and 'C'mon Everybody' which both sliced to No. 3 in the British charts. These were sung by the unstable Sid Vicious who replaced bass guitarist Glen Matlock after his exit from the Pistols in March 1977. A stronger qualification than hit-or-miss musicianship had been the new recruit's hand in beating up a journalist during one of the combo's many recitals at London's 100 Club.

Few deserve the status of folk hero less than John Beverley Ritchie. As the bloodily exhibitionist 'Sid Vicious', he came up through the ranks to stage centre when a harrowing US tour ended with the sacking of the Pistols' front man, Johnny Rotten, who had refused to co-operate with manager Malcolm McLaren's plan for the outfit to record with Great Train Robber, Ronald Biggs. Vicious too was to be absent from the sessions, poleaxed as he was by heroin addiction. Moving to the States in September 1978, he had for all practical purposes left the group and would record a New York concert album (*Sid Sings*) with a scratch band. This was issued just after Sid's soul went to the Lord while awaiting trial for the murder of his 'constant companion' and fellow junkie, Nancy Spungeon, after one of their little games turned nasty in the midst of the crumpled bedclothes, food leftovers and overflowing ashtrays of a hotel room.

Out on bail, his sniffing round a girl in a night club with the subtle chat line, 'I ain't had it since Nancy', finished with a fracas during which someone got knifed. Up before the beak the next morning, Sid was remanded in Riker's Island jail to undergo detoxification. On 1 February 1979, he was deemed fit enough to go free, but he wasn't so weaned off heroin that he could prevent injecting himself almost immediately with a lethally injudicious dose.*

Stray paragraphs in the music press nudged forward the notion of a Sex Pistols renaissance with a reinstated Matlock who was to tell his side of it in a 1989 autobiography. This mentioned in passing that his parents had named him after the mild-mannered conductor Glenn Miller, whose aeroplane had disappeared over the Channel on 15 December 1944. The late Glenn's continued fame warranted a romanticised 1954 bio-pic, an Oscar-nominated soundtrack LP and a reissued 'Moonlight Serenade' in the UK hit parade. Though Ray McKinley, Buddy de Franco and their successors were its nominal leaders, Miller controlled the orchestra from Davy Jones' Locker in that his original scores were regarded as definitive by those multitudes who put repackagings of what RCA called 'The Real Glenn Miller and His Orchestra' high into the international charts as late as 1977.

While 1977 was a fat year for both Miller and the Sex Pistols, neither a 'Greatest Hits' collection, nor anything new from John Lennon showed its face in either the British or US album tabulations. Until his final weeks, not a melody or lyric was heard from him commercially after 'Cookin'', a self-satisfied donation to *Ringo's Rotogravure* in 1976. What right had anyone to expect more? He said as much in a reluctantly given press conference in Japan a year later.

Belying the growing myth of John as 'The Howard Hughes of Pop', a chance encounter with him on holiday in Bermuda caused one newshound to report that John's songwriting well was not as dry as folk imagined. This

* Provided, on her own admission, by his mother.

101

was confirmed in August 1980 when he and Ono taped material sufficient to fill two albums – the first of which, *Double Fantasy*, was released that autumn. There were even enough numbers left for Lennon to give four to Ringo when, that November, they met for the last time.

'John who?' Pete Best, Starr's percussive predecessor in the Beatles, had spluttered from his shaving mirror when Mrs Best shouted the news upstairs that creepy December morning on Merseyside. Through a travesty of legitimate fan worship, Lennon had been shot on a New York pavement by one – henceforth referred to by Ringo as 'the arsehole', and by George Harrison as 'the Devil's best friend' – who was mad about the Beatles in the most clinical sense. 'Are you John Lennon?' asked one of the cops in whose squad car the victim was raced to hospital. 'Yeah,' gasped John. Then he died.*

The tragedy bequeathed unto *Double Fantasy* an undeserved 'beautiful sadness'. The album was, after all, a smug, slight statement by a rich, refined couple long detached from the everyday. Be that as it may, morbid Beatlemania reversed the drop of *Double Fantasy* and its '(Just Like) Starting Over' 45 from the charts and, as a further tribute, Yoko engineered her Top Forty début without him – and, for the first time since 1968's *Two Virgins*, Lennon's bum made the cover of *Rolling Stone*. As quills were sharpened for numerous – and notorious – biographies, repromotions of his own and the Beatles'

---

* After the media had sensationalised Lennon's remark in 1966 that the Beatles were more popular than Christ, the possible in-concert slaughter of the artistes by divine wrath – or someone acting on the Almighty's behalf – improved attendances on the quartet's final US tour. A firework that exploded on stage in Memphis gave all four a horrified start. Recalling a similar incident in Melbourne in 1964, an eye-witness deduced that 'George has an incredible fear of being killed'. Who hasn't, sport?

records plus a rash of tribute discs invaded the charts within a month of the cremation.

'The leader of the band's arrived!' bawled an *NME* reader's letter, presuming that Lennon was being conducted to the top table in some pop Valhalla. A spiritualist *au fait* with John's afterlife adventures knew of his affair with a long-departed Hollywood actress – intelligence that might have enraged his volcanic widow whose *Season of Glass* album sleeve depicted a pair of blood-stained glasses while the follow-up, 1982's *It's Alright*, employed trick photography to show a spectral John standing next to her and Sean in what looks like a recreation ground.

There'd been other Beatle deaths too. The first and least sudden was that of the gifted Stuart Sutcliffe, the Beatles' first bass guitarist. In late 1961, he gave notice to the Beatles and recommenced his studies at Hamburg's State School of Art under Edouardo Paolozzi – but not for long. Splitting headaches worsened to faints and temporary blindness. Expecting the worst but ever the artist, he requested internment in a *white* coffin. He got his wish after suffering a cerebral haemorrhage on 12 April 1962. Lay supposition would trace its origin to two years earlier when he'd stumbled beneath the kicking winkle-pickers of a gang who'd ambushed the Beatles outside a Merseyside palais.

When Stuart was still a member of the group, Lennon had – as a best mate's privilege – poked ruthless fun at him. A new outlet was found in manager Brian Epstein, later butt of John's paraphrasing of a 1967 B-side title as 'Baby You're a Rich Fag Jew' – a dig at the public school anti-Semitism and homo-eroticism that helped make Brian what he was. The expiry date of Epstein's contract with the group that August would mean – as he himself anticipated – a reduction in both his cut and say in their affairs. However, there was no loss of mutual affection, and certain of the Beatles' entourage urged each other to warn Brian of the inherent dangers in the over-prescribed tablets he took compulsively to sleep, stay awake, calm his nerves and lift his depressions. Their concern was justified after his lonely life ended through, so the inquest decided, 'incautious self-overdoses' during the August bank holiday.

Not putting all his eggs in one basket, Epstein had taken on other acts too – such as the Fourmost for whom he secured an eight month season in a 1964 variety presentation at the London Palladium. According to *The Times* correspondent, 'for sheer charm, they stole the show' but, though their *raison d'être* was centred on comedy, there was a lake of off-stage tears. Just before the Palladium stint, guitarist Mike Millward had felt off-colour. The diagnosis was cancer. Sharing Gene Vincent's the-show-must-go-on stubbornness, he wouldn't let the lads down. If a huge, scalp-revealing tuft of his hair fell out the very moment the compère spoke their name, he'd get someone to stick it back on with sellotape. When he could no longer keep such a level-headed grip on himself, he asked bass guitarist Billy Hatton if he ought to throw in the towel. 'I said yes,' remembered Hatton, 'and it was the hardest yes I've ever had to say.' In a Cheshire hospital, nothing more could be done for Mike, and he died peacefully on 7 March 1966.

The following month, 'A Night for Mike' took place at the Grafton Rooms in Liverpool 6, scene of many a rough night at the dawn of Merseybeat. 'A Host of Top Show Business Stars' was promised but mostly these consisted of beat groups who were unable to take chart placings for granted anymore; plucky anachronisms battling through 'Twist and Shout' for those for whom Merseybeat had become a dim recollection.

Back at the Grafton twenty-two years on, old friendships and rivalries were renewed once again when some of the same outfits blew the dust off their instruments for a fundraising concert for the family of John Banks, the Merseybeats drummer who died in comparative poverty. From this occasion sprang the formation of 'Merseycats', a committee who facilitate reunions of 1960s outfits for a children's charity.

At such a function in May 1989, they played before a mock-up of the graffiti-covered Cavern wall – and, at stage left, a ghostly photo enlargement of Rory Storm. Though much-loved locally, he and his backing group, the Hurricanes,* missed the boat in 1963 when commercial expediency drove even the slowest-witted London talent scout up north to grab other peas from the same pod. By the early 1970s, he was commuting as a disc jockey between Benidorm, Amsterdam and the Silver Blades Ice Rink back home. In September 1972, denied the acclaim he might have merited as a pop star, he never woke from a slumber induced by a cocktail of pills prescribed for a respiratory complaint and an ill-judged quantity of whisky. The next morning, his mother found him lying across his bed, and, with her golden boy's demise so soon after that of her husband in May, she joined them in the hereafter within the hour. A couple of the national tabloids that ran the story tapped Ringo for a quote about his old boss – with whom he'd long lost touch. No, he would be at neither

---

* With whom Ringo Starr rattled the traps prior to becoming a Beatle.

the cemetery nor the wake because 'I wasn't there when he was born either'.*

Most saddening to the Beatle 'family' had been the loss of road manager Malcolm 'Big Mal' Evans. When the group split up, he'd so missed the activity and reflected glory that he deserted his wife and children for sunny California where, thinking they needed him, he plumped down on the bar stool next to John, Ringo and the Who's Keith Moon: hard drinkers all – enduring a premature male menopause, marital problems or both. Having gained no contentment from following his former masters, his later slaughter in a Los Angeles apartment by gun-toting police – after some mean-minded woman he'd picked up had alleged he'd threatened her with a revolver – was said by some to have been a form of suicide.

While Mal's extinction was unexpected, few were entirely caught unawares on 7 September 1978 by Keith Moon's body's final rebellion after a lifetime of violation. A known prankster, he could create mayhem from nothing, the most documented examples being his disruption of a party in Chertsey by steering a Rolls-Royce Silver Cloud into the host's swimming pool, and parading around London clubland in Nazi attire.

After accidentally running over his chauffeur in 1970, Keith began punishing up to four decanters of spirits on rising 'just to get things moving'. More likely to sling a bottle at a television screen than rise from the armchair to switch it off, his fee for his last UK tour with the Who was a paltry forty quid after they'd sub-

* Certain record industry executives would check what Starr tracks they'd be entitled to rush-release if he didn't survive emergency surgery on 13 April 1979 to remove five feet of blocked intestine.

tracted compensation for damage he'd inflicted along the way.*

Moon had thrown an extravagant soirée on completing a bit part in *That'll Be the Day*, a movie set in summer 1959. He'd been in character as a drummer in a holiday camp combo, Stormy Tempest and the Typhoons. In silver jacket and hair stiff with lacquer, Tempest was played by Billy Fury; a touching instance of type-casting for the ailing rock-a-balladeer, soon to undergo a second by-pass operation.

Fury dominated national news bulletins on 28 January 1983 when – as he knew it would – a heart attack finally finished him. In the small hours, he had returned to his London home after a lengthy studio session. Then he collapsed and was dead by noon. Public sorrow was either exorcised or exacerbated by a special edition of *Unforgettable*, a Channel Four nostalgia romp, on which he was seen running through 'Halfway to Paradise', 'Like I've Never Been Gone' and other of his best-loved hits for the people who loved them – and him – most of all.

This frail Liverpudlian died with a record ('Devil or Angel') in the charts – just. However, there hadn't been time for him either to commence a comeback tour of Britain (backed by Pepsi and the Colas) or complete *The Only One*, his farewell album. All the same, his was *the* showbiz funeral of the year.

On 30 May 1959, Fury had sung on the final edition of *Oh Boy!*, *Six-Five Special*'s less pious successor. Also in

* As he drifted away on the tide of twice the recognised lethal intake of a potion to combat his alcoholism, his last utterance was for a girlfriend to get lost. He was carried from the same London flat where portly Mama Cass died of a heart attack while munching a ham sandwich on 29 July 1974.

front of the cameras was Dickie Pride, another Parnes creature with the look of fated youth. 'The Sheik of Shake', his voice and trademark convulsions were still slaying audiences in 1960 when he recorded *Pride without Prejudice*, an album of Tin Pan Alley chestnuts with Ted Heath's orchestra. This ploy might have set him on the road of the 'all round entertainer' had not his dabbling with amphetamines alienated him from Parnes and precipitated a fall from grace that found him delivering coal and nursing debilities that brought him to an even earlier grave than Billy Fury.

Before *her* death in March 1966, Alma Cogan, larger-than-life perennial of peak-time television variety, had been attempting to escape from the lightweight, tulle-petticoated jauntiness that had made her – 'Banjo's Back in Town', 'Twenty Tiny Fingers' *et al* – by sifting through the sheet music, LPs and – if lucky – demo tapes of beat groups. The most obvious expression of this policy was her cover of 'Eight Days a Week' by the Beatles who liked her well enough to accept an open invitation to the liberty hall that was her Kensington flat. She had taped a few hitherto unissued titles under the direction of Andrew Loog Oldham when, like Matt Monro, a routine spell under the scalpel (to remove her appendix) disclosed cancer. She coped by burying herself in work but, during a trek round Scandinavia, the disease overtook her.

One of Alma's few concessions to C & W had been a concert reading of 'Your Cheatin' Heart' from the Hank Williams portfolio. Accompanied by the Drifting Cowboys and with a white fedora his only superfluous adornment, this gangling Alabaman's popularity guaranteed standing room only for virtually all his two hundred annual one-nighters.

His fame spread – and so did his notoriety as a drinker before he graduated from Southern Comfort to amphetamines and worse. The short-lived magic of narcotics eased the agony of a distorted spine but, giggling drunk or on another planet, it was a miracle he could even totter on stage some evenings. Becoming an erratic performer, he walked a self-destructive line between shambles and dazed inspiration. A booker's risk, many of his shows degenerated into slanging matches with onlookers miffed because he wouldn't do yodelling 'Lovesick Blues', a number he'd come to loathe. His nadir as a showman was the night that disgruntled paying customers tried to lynch him.

The latest single, the pessimistic 'I'll Never Get Out of this World Alive', was nearing the top of the country chart when twenty-nine-year-old Hank made a curious statement to his wife – 'I think I see God coming down the road' – just before a local teenager, Charles Carr arrived to motor him from his home in Montgomery to a New Year's Eve bash in Canton, Ohio. The aeroplane that was to take him to Charleston for the next day's engagement was forced down by foul weather over the Blue Ridge Mountains so Carr was retained for an overnight drive. The journey was not without incident. While a Tennessee highway patrolman was issuing Charles with a speeding ticket, he nodded towards the open-mouthed figure in the back, remarking 'that guy looks dead'. He was, too – as his chauffeur discovered after stopping to ask directions at a West Virginia petrol station.* If provoked by excessive ingestion of alcohol

* For reasons best known to themselves, Williams' investors put it about that he'd perished in 'a road accident' – which he had in a way. At the funeral, the plot was too small for the coffin so some airmen interred nearby were dug up to make room.

and drugs, the all-embracing 'natural causes' brought the curtain down on Hank Williams. To long-suffering Drifting Cowboy Jerry Rivers 'the news was shocking but not unbelievable'.

If Hank was 'hard', Jim Reeves was pure 'sweetcorn'. Treacly enough to switch smoothly to pop, his style embraced both the harmless bounce of his mid-1950s smash, 'Bimbo', and, riven with a C & W undertow of guilt, infidelity and loss, the prototypical 'He'll Have to Go' in which 'Gentleman' Jim dials his inamorata when she and a rival are entwined on the sofa.

He became the most renowned addressee of the Tennessee town of Hendersonville whose civic authority approved an annual public holiday in his honour. It was to here that the 'Bimbo Boy' – a nickname invented by a bored disc jockey – and manager Dean Manual were returning from a show in Carthage, Arkansas by private aircraft on 31 July 1964 in heavy rain. A few miles before the estimated descent, the aerodrome controllers saw it vanish from their radar screens. A full-scale search was mounted immediately but it took two days for a four-hundred-strong search party to find the crashed plane in surrounding woodland and to recover the bodies. Jim's remains were taken back to Carthage where hundreds filed past the casket before its flight to a necropolis in East Texas. Flags fluttered at half-mast in Hendersonville where a memorial service for Manual and Reeves was conducted the Sunday after, attended by most of nearby Nashville's country music in-crowd.

When introducing posthumous hits like the 1966 No. 1, 'Distant Drums', on *Top of the Pops*, Jimmy Saville dubbed Reeves 'Mr Forever' but an article in *Record Mirror* had proclaimed that 'The Late Jim Reeves Has Five Years to Live' – intimating that there were insufficient Reeves tracks 'in the can' to warrant, say, four or five singles a year beyond 1969. Actually, they carried on until 1977 via the superimposition of 'Nashville Sound' backing tracks to sketchy demos and even previously-released items.*

Despite criticism from the Official Fan Club of Great Britain that 'Jim's music should be left as he himself intended', his dedicated cult-following kept coming back for more – and none were more dedicated than a woman from Sunderland who believed that, by entering the loins of her (now estranged) husband, a spectral Bimbo Boy had impregnated her with the son she would later christen 'Jim Reeves'. Yearly, she embarks on a pilgrimage which culminates with the laying of a posy on the grave in Texas.

Bob Marley, too, attracted an unsolicited quota of nutcases. Their fanaticism reflected his major part in convincing post-Woodstock rock consumers to take their reggae medicine neater. Marley's pragmatic interventions in Jamaican politics brought him both a murder attempt and, in 1978, a Third World Peace Medal.

A later channelling of his music back to the black market for which it was always intended was curtailed by cancer of his brain, lungs and liver developing from a football injury. Treatment necessitated the planing of his dreadlocks – roughly as traumatic for a Rastafarian as inadvertently devouring pork would be to a Muslim. Yet sacrifice of religious tenets was in vain for Bob's health worsened and he died around midday on 10 May 1981 in the Cedars of Lebanon Hospital, Miami. There was now no sense in an uneasy press maintaining its

---

* The same questionable methodology had already been employed to spin out Buddy Holly's leftovers.

silence, and the news was flashed across a world wondering where he'd been hiding since the previous September. Back in Jamaica, the Rude Boy from dirt-poor Trenchtown shanty was given an official state funeral attended by both the island's Prime Minister and the Leader of the Opposition. The day after his passing, Marley's was the lead eulogy in *The Times* following several parched weeks of no Big Deaths.

If we're still grubbing round for strange patterns in God's purpose, we find that January is a cruel month for pop entertainers. Hank Williams faded away on the 1st; Larry Williams on the 2nd.* Elvis Presley's twin brother was still-born on the 8th. The 10th was when kidney complications took Howlin' Wolf. Soul fatman Billy Stewart and three of his band went in a car crash on the 17th while uraemia claimed Alan Freed on the 20th – and, on the same day eighteen years later, Ozzy Osbourne was hospitalised with rabies after biting off a bat's head on stage. Jackie Wilson's time came on the 21st.

April is unlucky for Greenwich Village folk singers – with 1966 a vintage year for psychedelic decease as Paul Clayton jumped out of a window after a three-day LSD trip, and Richard Farina, his psyche boggling likewise, had a fatal motorbike crash near Carmel, California on his wife Mimi's twenty-first birthday. Ordered out of Bob Dylan's limousine for daring to suggest that 'Can You Please Crawl Out of Your Window' wouldn't be as big a smash as 'Like a Rolling Stone'†, Phil Ochs took to heart Dylan's flinging after him an insulting comment

---

* Of gunshot wounds in his Los Angeles home in 1980. It was never established if it was murder or suicide.
† It wasn't.

about his mediocre ability as a songwriter. It didn't improve when Phil hit the bottle with a vengeance in the later 1960s, and then fell prey to a schizophrenic condition that caused him to demand to be addressed as 'John Train'. Incompletely cured, embarrassment at his former behaviour and fear of another such episode contributed to his decision to hang himself at his sister's house in 1976 on the 9th day of . . . April.

The 24th to the 26th of the following month was open season on blues singers as the respective mojos of Elmore James (in 1963) and Sonny Boy Williamson (1965) stopped working. On the 27th in 1968, Little Willie John – who notched up two million-sellers in the late 1950s – died of pneumonia in the Washington prison where he was doing bird for manslaughter.

Leaving the calendar for a while, shall we look again at presageful song titles? What about 'When the Day Is Done', last track side two of *Everybody's Welcome At* (the late) *Mrs Mills' Party*, eh? Look too at Gerry Monroe, a tenor who went in November 1989. His go at 'My Prayer' first entered the charts in *November* 1970. This had been the follow-up to Gerry's revival of Johnnie Ray's 'Cry' – and hadn't Johnnie, 'the Prince of Wails', stated categorically that 'you won't see (the moon) shine' 'A Hundred Years from Today' on his in-concert *At the London Palladium* in 1954?* Three years later, he was in the Top Ten with 'Look Homeward Angel' – and where do angels live, pray?

Jerry Lee Lewis called the place 'the by-and-by', adding 'Lord, it won't be long' during his inspired 1973 interpretation of Charlie Rich's 'No Headstone on My Grave' ('I want a monument!', hollered Jerry Lee). That

* Johnnie died of liver failure in Los Angeles on 26 February 1990.

November, the self-styled Killer's son, Jerry Lee Lewis Jnr – very much a chip off the old block – would overturn a jeep (a coming-of-age present from his sire) and break his neck when the tow rope to the car he was pulling snapped. Jerry Lee had the corpse put on an aeroplane bound for Junior's last resting place beneath a heart-shaped tombstone in Clayton, Louisiana. En route, a collision with a large falcon splintered the window of the cockpit.*

1955 was the year of Jerry Lee's successful audition for Sun Records as young North America tuned into rock 'n' roll's unhinged go-man-go sorcery. Britain struck back with the saturnine Dickie Valentine, direct from fronting a palais bandstand, who knocked Bill Haley and the Comets' 'Rock Around the Clock' off the top with 'Christmas Alphabet'. He used to wind up his act with 'Luck Be a Lady', Marlon Brando's party piece in *Guys And Dolls*, 1955's big movie. All this preamble is simply to tell you that though it was the last number in the set it did not prove a lady on the 1971 night when Dickie died in a car crash on the way to the next booking.

Claudette Orbison and her husband were thundering home from a drag race on 7 June 1966. As befitted the occasion, she straddled a BMW, and he a more powerful Harley-Davidson. Dusk found their greasy steeds slowing down to pass through Gallantin, a small town only miles from their opulent ranch-style spread in Jim

* Two of Jerry's three sons plus a wife were taken from him as a result of accidents. His turbulent years were also crowded with high-living, destitution, Niagaras of booze, stimulant abuse, more marriages than Henry VIII, last-minute tour cancellations and his shooting of a bass guitarist. Lengthy convalescence from a near-fatal stomach operation in 1981 brought a halt to his concert schedule and his refusal of a kind invitation to hammer the ivories on the Rolling Stones' *Undercover* album.

Reeves' Hendersonville. A thirty-year-old truck driver named Kenneth Herald zoomed out of a side-turning – and that was that for Claudette.

The week after his wife's burial at Nashville's Woodlawn cemetery, Roy's latest 45, 'Lana', jumped from thirty-six to eighteen in the British charts; his highest position for over a year. With all the publicity generated by Claudette, it couldn't miss. Hot on its heels, MGM nipped in with another single infinitely more tear-jerking and profitable, 'Too Soon to Know' ('if I can forget her').* Leading off with Chopin-esque piano *arpeggios*, this was a despondent *lied* but a heaven-sent means whereby Orbison could be catapulted back into the public eye after a perturbing run of comparative flops. The company had, after all, practically gone into hock to sign him.

More my meat was 'Memories', hidden away on a 1968 album. Claudette's spectre effuses from the speakers with Roy's elegant resignation as loaded as his sonorous howls had been amidst the high tide of 'It's Over'.

In 1968 too, MGM thought they'd got another Claudette-type commercial miracle to restore Orbison to the Top Forty. Since 'Too Soon to Know', tilting for hit records had become incidental to a livelihood centred increasingly on personal appearances on the chicken-in-a-basket trail where current chart status had no relevance. Thousands of latecomers had been turned away from such a venue in Ipswich. Of these, a few were unwholesomely inquisitive. Inside, they looked at Roy

* 'Too Soon to Know' was produced in Nashville by Jim Vienneau whose speciality had been death discs. Jody Reynolds' 'Endless Sleep', Mark Dinning's 'Teen Angel' and Ray Peterson's 'Tell Laura I Love Her' were all his.

and wondered what that solitary mister was thinking. Onstage was not a common-or-garden pop star but a man from hell.

At 5 a.m., on 16 September in Bournemouth's Royal Spa Hotel, Orbison's road manager, Bob Blackburn, had been roused by the telephone. When Bob panted into the foyer moments later, the night porter looked up from the day's first edition of the *Daily Sketch*. Blackburn asked for a doctor.

A little later, with the drowsy MD at his elbow, Bob shook Roy gently and came straight to the point: 'Your house has burnt down. Roy and Tony are gone.' These were two of his three children. In the middle of the American night, the wooden structure and air-conditioning of his home fed thirsty flames. The boys had been messing about with matches in the basement where petrol was stored for their father's collection of antique cars. Devoid of will, Orbison was transported to Heathrow through pouring rain.

Though it made headlines, the blaze didn't procure the hit his wife's motorbike crash had done. That would come during the final chapter of Orbison's tragic but triumphant life in 1988 when an intangible buzz in the air told the old trouper that 'You Got It' – applauded almost as ecstatically in concert as any of his 1960s smashes – would slam him into the Top Ten, possibly all the way up, for the first time in many a long year. In doing so, he found a new audience among those too young to have ever heard of him before. With George Harrison, Bob Dylan,* Jeff Lynne and Tom Petty, he was one of the

* In the same month that Claudette Orbison had her motorbike accident, Dylan had one too. He woke from a week's concussed oblivion with a busted neck, mild paralysis and amnesia. He wouldn't return to public life for at least a year. Through similar mishaps, the

116

casual Traveling Wilburys (*sic*). But sadly, in spite of what looked like the start of fresh successes for Orbison, on 6 December 1988, death chose to blight the Orbison family yet again.

A hectic afternoon out of doors with miniature aeroplanes had been too much fun for Roy who was troubled by a tightness and then shooting pains across his rib cage. In the bathroom near eleven o'clock, his exhausted heart came to a standstill after a seizure of shuddering gasps and cold sweat.

Certain denizens of the media speculated on who would be the new Traveler. In the running was another with a big voice, understated image and cautious business acumen. Del Shannon had also recorded with Petty, Lynne and Harrison. However, the possibility of his enlistment became academic when Del, having conquered alcoholism, was so overwhelmed by a fit of deep depression in February 1990 that only a shaking muzzle against his temple could lift it.

When her poet husband died after a mere year of blissful wedlock, singing Celtic harpist Mary O'Hara did not assuage her dejection by blowing *her* brains out. Instead, she joined a nunnery. After twelve years within its cloisters, however, she elected to face the world again. Picking up the threads of her musical career, Mary accrued a qualified fame whereby she could pack out the Royal Albert Hall where a highlight of the show there on Guy Fawkes' Night 1977 was 'Forty-Five Years', an opus about a long and happy marriage.

Allman Brothers Band lost two members when singing guitarist Duane Allman swerved to avoid a lorry on 29 October 1971, and, within a mile of the same spot, Berry Oakley, the bass player, also died in the saddle just over a year later.

A different kind of pastoral lyricism and acoustic emphasis pervaded the original line-up of Renaissance, a quintet that reunited two ex-Yardbirds, Jim McCarty and Keith Relf for just one album in 1969. Seven years later, a plan to regroup as 'Illusion' was quashed after Keith was electrocuted while tuning a guitar through an unearthed amplifier on 14 May 1976. Illusion carried on without him for two albums before sundering. Nevertheless, rooting through dusty spools in McCarty's attic, Richard McKay – a diehard Yardbirds fan for whom no information connected with them is too insignificant to be interesting – compiled enough remaindered Illusion tapes for a third collection, *Enchanted Caress*. Whilst not initially intended for Joe Public's ears, McKay's most alluring selection was 'All the Falling Angels', Relf's last demo.*

Anticipating Relf's mode of departure by three years, ex-Shadow John Rostill was found *rigor mortis* and clutching an electric guitar in his home studio in Hertfordshire. On the previous 3rd May, Stone the Crows' road crew assumed that some youths loafing about and grinning mischievously during the soundcheck in a Swansea palais were backstage staff. Stepping forward at showtime to make an introductory announcement, the outfit's guitarist Les Harvey† touched a microphone –

* It also utilised time on *Musical Spectrum*, a cassette tape compiled by McKay of Keith's 'private home unreleased recordings'. Mostly a fly-on-the-wall patchwork of sounds not usually thought of as musical, *Musical Spectrum* may have had Relf turning in his grave. The death disc aesthete's attention must also be drawn to Keith's solo 45 of 1966, 'Mr Zero', and his 'Farewell' ('to future days') composition for the enigmatically-titled *Yardbirds* LP that same year. On 1968's *Little Games*, he sings 'deep within me I die' in 'Only the Black Rose'.
† Younger brother of the leader of the Sensational Alex Harvey Band who suffered a fatal heart attack in Zeebrugen, Belgium on the last date of a European tour.

and, because persons unknown had been up to no good with the wiring of the PA system, promptly absorbed more than enough high voltage to kill him.

For any roving minstrel, every silver lining has a potentially lethal cloud – as demonstrated by Johnny Kidd who joined the angels straight after knocking a northern audience cold. Professional West Country yokel Adge Cutler was one who, stunning 'em too, followed in Kidd's tyre tracks in the mid-1970s – and didn't Marc Bolan go after his travelling companion Gloria Jones wrapped their Mini round a tree* on 16th December 1977, just before his thirtieth birthday?

Over in the States, the smart way to go was by air. The Reaper got four in one go in the early evening of 5 March 1963. Carrying C & W stars Cowboy Copas, Patsy Cline and Hawkshaw Hawkins back to Nashville after a charity concert in Kansas City, the man at the wheel of a twin-engine Comanche didn't see the side of a mountain coming.† Georgia soul shouter Otis Redding and all but one of his Stax record label's second-string house band, the Barkays plus his valet and the pilot found themselves chanting everlasting hallelujahs after their wind-buffeted plane dived into an icy lake near Madison, Wisconsin on 10 December 1967, three days after the taping of '(Sittin' on) the Dock of the Bay'.‡ Its lyrics were flavoured with a soupçon of

---

* Flowers are still left at the spot near Barnes Common.
† On hearing the radio reports, Roger Miller and Carl Perkins were two who joined the party searching the area near Camden, Tennessee. Of all the departed, the artiste most missed by country fans was Patsy Cline, queen of the heartbreak ballad who could 'cry on both sides of the microphone'. In 1981, Nashville producer Owen Bradley's skills with sampler, vari-speed and editing block brought together her and Jim Reeves on record with a duet of 'Have You Ever Been Lonely'.
‡ But one day short of three years since Redding's role-model Sam

premonition but its rise to No. 3 in Britain was not entirely on 'sympathy sales' as it was also Redding's most direct bid on vinyl to become the darling of more than just highbrow soul specialists.

Droopy moustachioed Jim Croce's popularity graph made a similarly sharp upward turn after a booking at Northwestern Louisiana State University on 20 December 1973. On its way to Jim's next show in Sherman, Texas, the private aircraft failed to gain altitude and crashed into a tree at Natchitoches, Louisiana, killing him, guitarist Maury Muelheisen and a road manager. As Otis Redding had been voted Best Male Vocalist in a British music weekly's reader's poll for 1968 so Croce – talented but no Bob Dylan – had a posthumous US No. 1 with 'Time in a Bottle', and became temporarily the greatest singer-songwriter who ever picked up a guitar.

Seated in a rocking fuselage, half of group Lynyrd Skynyrd beheld heaven's ladder when the aeroplane sliced into woodland near Gillsburg, Mississippi on 20 October 1977. A month later, their sixth album, *Street Survivors*,* began its ascension to a UK No. 13, a position unequalled by any Skynryd platter before or since.

I'm nothing if not vulgar. One of my wife's best friends went off me because I said I didn't like Nick Drake, an ex-public schoolboy whose trio of early 1970s albums were aimed at the self-doubting bedsit diarist

Cooke was mortally wounded with three bullets in a Los Angeles motel room whilst offering hospitality to two ladies neither of whom was his wife. Thrown together on an aeroplane in 1966, Otis and Roy Orbison had mulled over the feasibility of cutting an album together, even bestowing it with the provisional title *Big O: Black and White Soul*.
* With a cover portraying the outfit standing amidst a wall of flames.

rather than incorrigible old rockers with a bad attitude. Nick went in for what was coined 'self-rock' if you liked it, 'drip-rock' if you didn't. Its confessional fragility was, declared one reviewer half-admiringly, like 'intruding on someone else's phone conversation'. Drake had a nervous breakdown in 1972 and he wanted to tell everyone about it on his fourth album. Sessions were underway but, a chronic insomniac, he started swallowing slightly more than he should have done of a drug prescribed to send him to sleep. On the evening of 24 November 1974, it did the trick rather too well. His intimates were sceptical about the official 'death by suicide' verdict because he'd considered it 'too cowardly' but even today fans pore over his records, gaining deep and lasting pleasure from alighting on omens of death.

Though he too had been recovering from severe depression when he died, Graham Bond was both physically and artistically of more robust stamp than Nick Drake. His pop pedigree was also more cultivated. Quite at ease playing alto sax and organ simultaneously, he'd worked with Jack Bruce, Ginger Baker and saxophonist Dick Heckstall-Smith in a modern jazz octet before the four of them, preferring the earthier sounds of rhythm-and-blues, formed the first Graham Bond Organisation in 1962. Graham broke up the band in the late 1960s to try his luck in the USA before he and his singing wife, Diane Stewart, teamed up with Cream's lyricist, Pete Brown. Next came various unrewarding outfits whose overall ethos reflected Bond's fascination with occult practices. This got so out of hand that he started professing that his father was Aleister Crowley – although evidence shows that the much-misunderstood black magician would have had to have been in two places at once to have managed this. Prone to bouts of drug addiction, Bond was at a personal and professional low as 1974 loomed. On 8 May, he went for a stroll, hoping that the rhythm of walking would inspire lyrics for a forthcoming studio session. Dragging his feet a little, he bought a ticket at Finsbury Park underground station. Whether he slipped or was overcome by a sudden urge to end it all, he finished under the wheels of a tube train, and the police took two days to identify the body.

A closer parallel to the case of Nick Drake was the private anxiety of Ian Curtis, epileptic vocalist with Joy Division, post-punk Mancunians who believed that they required no self-abasing humour to make themselves palatable to pop consumers. To prove the point, their 'Love Will Tear Us Apart' filtered into the Top Twenty only weeks after Ian hanged himself on 18 May 1979, unable to face a pending US tour.

Another on whom the demands of showbusiness took a profound toll was former Byrd and Flying Burrito Brother Gram Parsons who, with Rolling Stone Keith Richards, had been discussing possible fusions of country and classic rock. With ex-Family and Blind Faith guitarist Rick Grech* behind the console, Parsons was on the path to achieving this when heart failure whisked him to the Pearly Gates on 19 September 1973. That wasn't all. A week later, his road manager hijacked the coffin and consigned it to the flames at the Joshua Tree National Monument in the San Bernadino desert. This, he explained, was how Gram would've wanted it. †

* In 1978, Grech severed all professional links with pop to become a furniture salesman in his native Leicester where he died in 1989.
† On Bastille Day that year, another ex-Byrd guitarist, Clarence White, had been unloading a station wagon outside his California home when another vehicle flattened him. Gene Clark – who flew the nest in 1966 – died of the proverbial 'natural causes' in May 1991.

In the event, the autopsy turned up traces of narcotic substances in Parsons' blood stream.

The same brand of naughtiness led to the cashiering of bass player Pete Farndon from the Pretenders in 1982. A case of the blind leading the blind, he and heroin-addicted punk drummer Topper Headon were trying to get something going when thirty-year-old Pete snuffed it on 14 April 1983.

While sharing the light of heaven with the saints, he might have been reintroduced to the Pretenders' guitarist, James Honeyman-Scott. Weakened by a detoxification course, his death on 16 June 1982 – the day after Farndon's sacking – occurred after snorting cocaine at some *demi-monde* function in London.

Moving from the rank-and-file to the central microphone – and back in time to 28 February 1968*, we enter a bathroom in New York's West 153rd Street precinct. A syringe rolls across the lino. Sprawled next to the tub is Frankie Lymon, his eyes like catherine wheels. You would not think to look at him that he had once been the Michael Jackson of the late 1950s. You couldn't switch on a wireless in North America without a blast of 'Why Do Fools Fall in Love', 'I'm Not a Juvenile Delinquent' and other smashes by pint-sized Frankie with or without his brothers, the Teenagers. At thirteen, he was ordering champagne, smoking nought but the finest Havana cigars and had masses to talk about with women three times his age. His hypodermic 'works' were an established if discreet part of dressing room paraphernalia. Inevitably, the bubble burst and, after

---

* Rolling Stone Brian Jones' penultimate birthday – his twenty-sixth – prior to drowning, woozy with spirits and tranquillisers, in his overheated Sussex swimming pool on 2 July 1969.

his try at 'Little Bitty Pretty One' stalled at No. 58 in 1960, he couldn't get another hit to save his life. By 1964, he was mainlining and enmeshed in the financial turmoils of no less than three broken marriages. A new 45, 'I'm Sorry', was cast adrift on the vinyl oceans in April 1968 but, caring only for junk, Frankie Lymon had had his last fix by then.

Allegedly, thanks to heroin, Janis Joplin gave to fish and the air that which she had refused to men – well, *some* men – when her ashes were shed on to the Pacific just over a week after her death on 14 October 1970.

Son of comedy-actor-with-a-dash-of-religion David Kossoff, Free guitarist Paul's habit brought on two heart attacks in 1975. The first rendered him 'technically dead' for half a minute; the second – while dozing in an aeroplane seat on 19 March – had him 'technically dead' to this day, when repackagings of his post-Free output* – rubbished the first time around – receive rave notices.

Tim Hardin's art suffered too through a heroin habit. Compared to less worthy contemporaries, he enjoyed little chart success but, nevertheless, became renowned for other artists' interpretations of 'If I Were a Carpenter', 'Misty Roses' and further of his compositions. However, standards dropped so much that 1971 saw a Hardin album, *Bird on a Wire*, consisting entirely of non-originals. *Homecoming*, a concert set from an Oregon auditorium, indicated a belated return to form – but it was also Tim's epitaph preceding as it did an overdose in Hollywood on 29 December 1980 – a passing over-shadowed by that of John Lennon who had still not recovered from being dead after three weeks.

In a Wiltshire hospital on 4 January 1986 – January

---

* Including a track entitled 'Rock 'n' Roll Junkie'.

again, note – Thin Lizzy's Phil Lynott, unconscious for nearly a week, would cease hovering between life and death after drug abuse dragged him down.

A few months prior to his demise, Lynott had made the UK Top Ten with 'Out in the Fields', a duet with Gary Moore whose 1987 Album, *Wild Frontiers*, would contain a Thin Lizzy-fashioned requiem to his old colleague.

A chance to play the title role in a planned Jimi Hendrix bio-pic had landed in Lynott's lap during his final months. The twentieth anniversary of the genuine article's death was celebrated in 1990 with myriad retrospectives on record, the printed page and even a jeans commercial. As with Paul Kossoff, Jimi's latter-day efforts when in the land of the living had been dismissed by pundits as regurgitations of old ideas, even if his snow-blinded fans applauded his strings of bum notes as enthusiastically as his most revelational solos during his tired performance at the 1970 Isle of Wight Festival. On 17 September, Jimi 'sat in' with Eric Burdon's new combo at London's Ronnie Scott's club, having such a good time that he promised to show up the following evening. When he didn't, Burdon 'knew that something heavy had happened'. He wasn't wrong because some sort of medication on top of a tuna fish sandwich had led poor Jimi to suffocate in his sleep after inhaling his own vomit. From his 1968 double album*, *Electric Ladyland*, Voodoo Chile (Slight Return)' was lifted as an obvious 45, which soared to No. 1 by November.†

* Only five Hendrix LPs (including a compilation) were issued while he was alive but, an incurable 'blower', he'd jammed with all and sundry, frequently when tape machines were on. As a result, over three hundred albums with Jimi as their selling point have been released since 1970.

† Eric Burdon reckoned that Hendrix wrote a suicide note but no one else has ever seen it.

It hadn't furthered the Beach Boys' quest for hip credibility when Jimi had mumbled something about 'you'll never hear surf music again' on the Experience's psychedelic quasi-instrumental, 'Third Stone From the Sun'. The Beach Boys' most publicised encounter with death was with Charles Manson, a grubby acquaintance of drummer Dennis Wilson, who, no longer the 'harmless freak' he'd never been, masterminded the Sharon Tate bloodbath in 1971. Dennis himself became increasingly the worse for booze over the years that followed and, despite all kinds of incentives, was not strong-minded enough to let the blue devils be sweated from him. Finally, he was suspended briefly from the group for overall unreliability. On 28 December 1983, he drowned in a Californian marina; his judgement of the water's temperature and his own fatigue impaired by too much vodka.*

This Russian beverage had also seen off Led Zeppelin's John Bonham in 1970, who, to show what a hell of a fellow he was, held down sixteen large ones during a pub luncheon on 24 September 1980. At a rehearsal-cum-social gathering round Jimmy Page's Windsor gaff that afternoon, he carried on imbibing until he was poured on to a bed to snore it off. By the next morning, he'd turned blue.

When the ex-members of Led Zeppelin were coaxed into regrouping for *Live Aid*, John's absence was regrettable but by no means disastrous. Much the same opinion, albeit mistaken, had been reached by Canned Heat after their myopic counter tenor and general factotum, Al 'Blind Owl' Wilson, out-of-sorts after enduring

---

* 'Farewell My Friend' from his only solo album was played at the memorial service held shortly before his burial at sea, a custom usually reserved for sailors.

concussion in a car accident, passed away in a sleeping bag in singer Bob 'The Bear' Hite's Topanga Canyon back-garden on 3 September 1970. Some tablets had spilled from a bottle in his grip. Waiting for his arrival in Berlin, the others decided that Al would have wished the European tour to go ahead without him. They were able to continue in a recognisable form but, though Wilson's guitar was propped up ritually on every stage they played, Canned Heat sorely missed his creative input. Depending more and more on earnings on the road, Hite especially had a rough time financially, and was forced to sell part of a record collection that had made him the very Lord Beaulieu of blues. On 4 April 1981 after a booking at the Palomino on Sunset Strip, a combination punch of liquor and drugs plus his uncompromising obesity knocked thirty-six-year-old Bob into eternity.*

Clyde McPhatter's craving for firewater eventually swallowed up his house. In 1954, national service had compelled him to quit the Drifters† but, as a demobbed solo vocalist, he'd registered over twenty singles in *Billboard*'s pop chart before the bubble burst in the mid-1960s. Drifting from pillar to post professionally, soon hardly a day would go by without a

---

* The life-and-soul of impromptu blues sessions, Hite's personality had already been celebrated in song in 'The Bear' on John Mayall's *Blues from Laurel Canyon* in 1968. Portent freaks might be intrigued too by the 1968 Canned Heat's B-side, the traditional 'One Kind Favour', with its 'see that my grave is swept clean', two white horses 'to take me to my burying ground' *et al* – not to mention Al Wilson's self-penned 'My Time Ain't Long' from 1970.

† Previously, he had been one of Billy Ward and the Dominoes. Later, Jackie Wilson auditioned for a post in this vocal group but was not taken on until McPhatter had left because pianist and singing coach Ward was not prepared to employ two homosexuals at the same time.

drinking binge. What had once signified a week's work became a month's, and his last recording sessions yielded nothing worth releasing. A year before liver, heart and kidney problems killed him on 13 June 1972, he was interviewed by a journalist who claimed to be a fan. Clyde blinked sadly at his feet, muttering, 'I have no fans.'

Let's have a random round-up of some other pop stars who were too fond of old John Barleycorn. Scorning his doctor's advice that backstage frolics during a 1972 tour would probably kill him, Ron 'Pigpen' McKernan of the Grateful Dead succumbed to alcoholic poisoning the following March. After swigging more than his fill, AC/DC's Bon Scott joined the legion of the lost from the back of a car in south London on 19 February 1980. Former Traffic woodwind player Chris Wood also overdrew on a misspent youth. Studio time he'd booked for autumn 1983 to finish a solo project had to be reallocated after milk-floats braving the dawn of a July Tuesday in 1983 pulled over on hearing the agitated clang of the ambulance speeding Chris, clutching his abdomen, to Birmingham's Queen Elizabeth Hospital. His ill-treated liver had finally collapsed and, when the city woke, he was on a more sedate ride to the morgue.

There's nothing new under the sun. Of stimulant-related pop casualties, the daddy of them all was Stephen Foster, nineteenth-century composer of such as 'Beautiful Dreamer', 'Old Folks at Home', 'Old Dog Tray', 'Old Uncle Ned', 'Old Black Joe' and 'Massa's in de Cold Cold Ground'. A gifted but improvident chap, his wife left him for the second time in 1861. Almost penniless three years later, he billeted himself in a hotel in the Bowery, New York's seediest corner. There, he scraped together enough cash to promote an alcoholic black-out of such depth that he never came round.

Tobacco was the undoing of Nat 'King' Cole who had complained intermittently of chest pains for several years – and, in September 1964, it was confirmed that he had lung cancer and that his days were numbered. With this intelligence, he cancelled outstanding concerts but gamely put in one more recording session before slipping away on 15 February 1965. Wiping her eyes, his widow tried to sue the manufacturers of Nat's favourite brand of cigarettes but her energies were better spent on the founding of the Nat 'King' Cole Cancer Foundation.*

Their second daughter, Natalie, inherited her beauty and his vocal projection, and was encouraged from the cradle to think of pop as a viable living. Her surname ensured her records a fair hearing but Joe Public so distanced her from Nat – something that could not be done with, say, Julian Lennon or Ziggy Marley – that she racked up quite a respectable tally of hits by the late 1980s. She was even able to get away with a tour billed as 'An Unforgettable Evening: Natalie Cole Sings Nat "King" Cole' in the wake of a 1991 Top Ten entry with 'Unforgettable', a technological cobbling-together of her and Dad's voices over a state-of-the-art facsimile of his original 1951 recording's backing track. Natalie also worked him into the accompanying video.

The late Sir Laurence Olivier was seen as a hologram in drummer-turned-entrepreneur Dave Clark's *Time*, a West End musical praised largely for its spectacular audio-visual effects. On the album, the knighted

---

* Cole died at the age of forty-five – and they hadn't been quiet years. In April 1956, British bandleader Ted Heath had witnessed him being half-killed by white racists midway through his act before a mixed audience in a theatre in Birmingham, Alabama. Having heard Cole on the radio, they assumed he was Caucasian because his vocal mannerisms were so similar to those of Bing Crosby and Perry Como.

thespian's recitation of 'The Theme from *Time*' came out as a single in 1986. When the show ran and ran, Cliff Richard gave up his leading role owing to previous commitments. His place was taken by Queen's Freddie Mercury beside whose bed Clark was sitting when Mercury 'just fell asleep' when the most menacing ailment of the eighties took him on 25 November 1991. Predictably, a single featuring the deceased – Queen's 'Bohemian Rhapsody' – sliced to No. 1 as easily as a wire through cheese within a fortnight. The following April, an all-star Wembley memorial concert to Freddie – with profits going to AIDS charities – was satellite-linked to even more millions across the globe than *Live Aid* had been, thus reasserting the extent to which a star can elicit adoration from the grave.

Chapter Six

Fabulous Nobodies

Dead pop musicians are two-a-penny. Holly, Elvis, Lennon . . . there are plenty more where they came from – or, rather, where they went. But now is the time to spare a thought for the nonentities who pegged out in the name of pop. Top of the heap are fabulous nobodies like Miss Christine of the GTOs – Girls Together Outrageously – fans centred in Los Angeles who became notorious for their skills in evading the most stringent security barricades to impose themselves on their idols. The GTOs aspired to orgasms at the thrust of the famous so well that some were rewarded with relationships more enduring than a swift knee-trembler in the romantic seclusion of a backstage broom cupboard. Some – including Miss Christine – were taken on as domestic staff by Frank Zappa who, intrigued, invited them to record an album, *Permanent Damage*, for his Straight record label.

It would be gratifying to report that the GTOs became stars – for they had everything it took except the talent. Documentary rather than recreational, *Permanent Damage* winged its way into the bargain bin and, sadly, the only trappings of pop stardom that the girls acquired were vices instanced at their most extreme by Miss Christine's fatal heroin overdose on 5 November 1972.

Petty crook and would-be titan of teen, Charles Manson was similarly patronised by the Beach Boys

who, urged on by his main champion Dennis Wilson –
'Charles is the most tuned-in dude I've ever met' –
recorded his song, 'Cease to Exist' (retitled 'Never Learn
Not to Love') as a 1968 B-side. Although it was Dennis
whose property he and his 'Family' fleeced, the Beach
Boys were not Manson's favourite group. The Family had
1968's *The Beatles* on instant replay as they prepared for
the Tate murders on 8 August 1969, having heard revolutionary messages in Paul McCartney's 'Helter-Skelter'
and George Harrison's 'Piggies' – an attack on clichéd targets 'in their starched white shirts'. Translated by Manson
as a call to arms was the throwaway line, 'What they
need's a damn good whacking', suggested by George's
Mum to rhyme with 'there's something lacking'.*

The Word made vinyl in the comfort of your own
home, many – especially in the States – listened as
reverently as Manson to the Beatles' gramophone records
backwards and at the wrong speeds and even normally.
Every millimetre of their covers and labels were scrutin-
ised for veiled but oracular *communiques*. By 1969, clues
from as far back as *Sgt Pepper's Lonely Hearts Club Band*
supported a widespread rumour that Paul McCartney
had been beheaded in an auto accident three years
earlier, and replaced by a *doppelgänger*. Surely you can
hear John say 'I buried Paul' in a daft voice in the last
seconds of 'Strawberry Fields Forever' – and somewhere
else he goes 'Paul is dead. Bless him, bless him, bless
him . . . ' The front cover of *Abbey Road*; hasn't it got a
car number plate '28 IF' on it? Like, Paul would've been

* From gaol, Manson arranged for the release of 1970's *Lie*, an album
containing 'Cease to Exist', 'Old Ego Is a Too Much Thing' and other
ditties taped under the Beach Boys' aegis. If it's printed salaciousness
you're after, there's *The Family: The Whole Charles Manson Horrorshow*
by ex-Fug Ed Sanders (Panther, 1972).

twenty-eight *if* he hadn't died in 1966. In the foreground, there's a funeral march across the zebra crossing with John leading the way as The Priest, then barefoot 'Paul' the Deceased, scruffy George as the Gravedigger and Ringo the Sexton. It's obvious, isn't it?

As you'd expect, most of these theories came from the USA, where a Detroit disc jockey had set the ball rolling after an anonymous phone-in caller explained the *Abbey Road* symbolism. None of them were hits but there was an impressive array of 'Paul Is Dead' discs behind shop counters by the end of 1969. Penetrating the ether most were 'Brother Paul' by Billy Shears and the All-Americans, 'Saint Paul' from Terry Knight* and Zacharias and his Tree People's 'We're All Paul Bearers (Parts 1 and 2)'. Later, Lennon's snigger was almost audible when, not content with airing grievances against McCartney in the press, he sniped at him on record with 'How Do You Sleep' from 1971's *Imagine*, confirming that Billy, Terry, Zacharias *et al* 'were right when they said that you were dead'.

A less publicised case of pop insanity occurred in 1987 when twenty-five-year-old Richard Dickinson trampled his poor old mother to death to the accompaniment of Bob Dylan's 'One More Cup of Coffee', after she moaned about him playing it at four o'clock in the morning. Investigating what were not ordinary weekend screams, a neighbour discovered Richard sprinkling coffee granules on the bleeding corpse. In the police station, he

---

* One of these 'pop singers who can really sing'. Within weeks of the record's release, he withdrew from the main spotlight to manage Grand Funk Railroad. In a vocational slow moment after his million-selling version of 'Light My Fire' in 1968, José Feliciano (under an alias) issued a 'Paul' 45 too.

133

elucidated that he'd thought he was the evil 'Isis' on the same Dylan LP. Found guilty but insane, Dickinson was banged up in an asylum.* After five years as a model inmate, he was allowed a day out – to go to a Dylan concert. The institution medics were worried intitially about what might happen if Bob sang 'One More Cup of Coffee' or 'Isis' but concluded that there'd now be little risk if he did.

The supposed subliminal commands in the grooves of certain Heavy Metal albums persuaded at least four US record buyers to do themselves in. The artistes concerned, Ozzy Osbourne (ex-Black Sabbath) and Judas Priest, were both from England's Black Country where enthusiasm for Heavy Metal was such that some of its patrons would insert their heads into yawning speaker bins to receive the full mega-decibel churn of bass guitar. In this teenage wasteland – 'Sabbath territory' – the brain-damaging practice of 'headbanging' was born. The annual festival at Castle Donington, thirty miles north-east of Birmingham, became the most important date in the Heavy Metal year.

As is their wont, our colonial cousins exhibited a fanaticism that left UK Heavy Metallurgists gulping dust. In 1990, Judas Priest were in dead trouble when taken to task over the 1978 track 'Better By You Better Than Me' which was linked to the suicide of two youths who, according to the letter they left, had stumbled on the words 'do it' whilst running a tape of the number

---

* Drummer Jim Gordon was similarly incarcerated for matricide – a crime attributable to the chemicals that were common currency when, with Delaney and Bonnie and Friends, he'd muscled in on a 'superstar' élite that included the likes of Eric Clapton and Leon Russell. Jim's story was the basis of 'The Ballad of James Gordon' by up-and-coming British country star Terry Clarke.

backwards. During the much-protracted litigation by the children's guardians, the entire album was heard like this but the most coherent statement that could be understood from the gibberish seemed to be 'it's so fishy, personally, I'll own it'.

Osbourne had also been sued – unsuccessfully – for multi-million-dollar damages in 1986 by the parents of eighteen-year-old John McCollum, a Californian youth who took his own life after much hard listening to the vocalist's 'Suicide Solution' – actually about alcoholism. Although all the free publicity was a bonus, Ozzy left the Los Angeles Supreme Court not wholly reassured by the judge's comment that 'the whole thing sounds like the plot of a cheap horror movie'.

There were elements of this in Osbourne's concerts. As a visual aid, a dwarf – named Ronnie after Ozzy's replacement in Black Sabbath – was hired to be 'hanged' during one number. It was not an original idea as mock-executions of Alice Cooper – via gallows, guillotine and electric chair – had been going on since the early 1970s. Outlines between stage and 'real' life had dissolved in 1974 when a thirteen-year-old Canadian boy's party trick of dolling himself up like Cooper and mimicking the hanging bit went dreadfully wrong when he wasn't taken down after the usual few seconds.

A more cheerful ending to this chapter might be the saga of French twin brothers who were fans of Hersal Thomas, a Texan boogie-woogie pianist. Admiration turned into obsession, and soon they were neck-and-neck in a race to acquire a complete set of his records. When one was only a disc short of the finishing flag, the loser was found composing a suicide note but was dissuaded from going through with it when his sibling, after much soul-searching, proposed combining collections.

Chapter Seven

The Greatest Star of All

We never see the man. We only see his art. I mean this most sincerely, friends. Was Queen's spot on *Live Aid* motivated by a simple wish to help the starving or, as one of its organisers reckoned, 'Freddie's chance to prance about in front of the world?' Even if Mercury was still around, how could we ever know? The same would apply to anyone sufficiently thick-skinned to have recorded a tribute to him in time for the Christmas sell-in that immediately followed his death. Anyone who knew the ropes could have got started on something at the very moment of the official announcement that he had AIDS. It could have been in the shops and on the Radio One playlist in time for the funeral.

Within hours of Roy Orbison's passing, while estate agents were still debating who would be doing the probate assessment, and publishers liaised with biographers, the *Sun* had compiled a dial-a-tune megamix of six of his hits at thirty-eight-pence a minute, and a Major Bill Smith was hard at work in a Fort Worth studio, taping a monologue entitled 'Big O' – with an impersonator in the background yawling an ancient Orbison smash like a lovesick coyote.

Roy himself had been among the many who had eulogised Elvis Presley on vinyl. He was also one of the few with, he reckoned, 'the credentials to sing it', having known Presley from 1955 when 'it was Elvis who made me a motorcycling fan'.* From an idea of his second wife Barbara in 1974, 'Hound Dog Man', with a no-frills arrangement and unvarnished narrative about 'my old friend', concluded an Orbison album five years later – which was, explained Roy, 'long enough after all the exploitation. It wouldn't bother me if no one heard the song. I really did it from me to him' – and it was true enough that the Big O had no need of the second-hand celebrity† accrued by Danny Mirror, a blond Dutchman who enjoyed the approbation of Presley's UK fan club for his 'I Remember Elvis Presley (The King Is Gone)' – spiced with a vignette from 'Are You Lonesome Tonight' – which, six weeks after that fateful August Tuesday, had progressed at a more-than-funereal pace to No. 4.

Though a one-hit-wonder, Danny had more luck than the red-eyed unshaven fellow who accosted Jonathan King the very morning after Elvis turned up his toes. He'd got on the job as soon as he'd heard, he told King, and was still adding the finishing touches to it over breakfast. Nevertheless, he'd set aside a few seconds to decide which company should have the privilege of releasing this first tribute to Elvis – and had chosen the man who'd given 'Johnny Reggae' and Sakkarin to the world. It must have been a pretty ropey number, for even King, apparently, 'sent him packing'.

It might have been 'The Greatest Star of All' by Skip

---

* After Roy had taught her to ride and bought for her birthday her own machine, his wife Claudette's passion for the sport would last for as long as she lived.
† Nor did J. D. Sumner, the *basso profundo* on Presley's 'Way Down' – but he went ahead all the same with 'Elvis Has Left the Building'. Its picture sleeve had the two of them together at one of a podgy Presley's Las Vegas pageants.

Jackson in which steel guitars weep behind a sort of Illinois Cockney who declares in a flat tone that Mr E. A. Presley's early singles 'seemed to make me get on up' and regretting that one more 'great record to make it all complete' hadn't been forthcoming. All the same, 'I know we've all had a ball' is his unconvincing conclusion. After a spell on the deletion rack, Skip's 45 had a second lease of life as a much-requested spin on a section of disc jockey Kenny Everett's BBC radio programme devoted to his pick of the worst records ever made. I don't think 'The Greatest Star of All' was *the* worst but it was a strong contender.

So were the likes of 'Elvis Goodbye' by Bobby Freeman, 'The World Loves You Elvis' by Wesley Gillespie, 'The Legend of Elvis Presley' by Dub Crouch, 'Elvis Is Gone But His Spirit Lives On' by Bob 'Lil Elvis' Harrison, 'The Legend of a King' by Warren Jacks, 'Farewell To the King' by Jimmy Jenkins, 'Goodbye Elvis' by Jim Whittington, 'Elvis Presley: El Rey Del Rock 'n' Roll' by Mexico's Juan Ramos y Los Principes, 'I Remember Elvis' by Roy Williams plus 'The Legend's Still Alive or It's Great To Be an Idol' by Ray Hebel – who had another go with just plain 'Elvis'. Despite the suspect taste of the record-buying proletariat *en masse* none of these items were hits and all the artistes involved were consigned hastily to the haphazard oblivion from which they'd barely emerged.

Not putting all his eggs in one marketing move, Paul White mourned Elvis while celebrating the festive season as best he could with 'Elvis, Christmas Won't Be Christmas' – and still-born Jesse Garon is there to welcome his twin brother in Paul Marshon's 'God Called Elvis Home'. If it *was* a tribute, then Lonesome Tone's – issued after a decent interval of three years – was the best of the bunch, extending a farewell not only to Presley but to the 1950s era from whence he sprang. A pin-up of him smouldered no doubt in the twilight of the bedroom where Tone lay, with the words 'Mum, Dad, Love, Hate and Elvis' – the title of the single – tattooed about his person.

How many are the forearms similarly emblazoned with the names and images of the giants of classic rock – or pairs of family pets called, say, 'Gene' and 'Vincent', 'Duane' and 'Eddy' or 'Don' and 'Phil'? What Teddy Boy doesn't know – and respect – the true believer who plans his life and bank balance around every Jerry Lee Lewis tour of Britain?*

In the States, while 'It Doesn't Matter Anymore' petered out at No. 13, a tribute to Buddy Holly – and the other two – hovered two positions *above* it; gesture mattering more, seemingly, than substance. 'Three Stars' by Tommy Dee† had him whimpering about the Big Bopper's ascension to 'new fame and fortune' in heaven with Ritchie Valens as a celestial social worker helping any 'boy or girl who might have gone astray' – and Buddy 'singing for God now'. Commensurate with death as the great leveller, all three get exactly one verse each between 'gee, we're gonna miss you' choruses by the Teen-Aires and Carol Kaye. It was covered (and improved upon) in Britain by Ruby Wright (with narration by Dick Pike) but untainted by opportunism was

---

* A chief contender amongst the London Teds must be Sunglasses Ron. A fearsome hybrid of Edwardian rake and Mississippi riverboat gambler, Ron – so it is fabled – has worn his trademark shades day and night since Buddy Holly died.
† Apparently, an advised pseudonym of a noted Nashville-based songwriter.

Eddie Cochran's version in which the lyrics were altered to make them more of a direct address rather than sounding like he was reading the roll of the fallen on a cenotaph – and, because Cochran was a buddy of Holly, his emotion-charged voice on the 'Buddy, I can still see you . . .' section wasn't just hammy exhibitionism – well, not enough to make you laugh out loud. It was issued posthumously after a dispute with his record company over Eddie's wish to donate royalties to the bereaved families.

As sincere in its way was 1961's 'Tribute to Buddy Holly' by Mike Berry and the Outlaws. According to its composer, Geoff Goddard, it 'just sort of "came out"', having resulted 'from my interest in spiritualism'. It was produced by Joe Meek whose suicide* would take place on the eighth anniversary of Holly's plane crash. As he – and to a lesser degree, Goddard and Berry – were so avidly engrossed with the Texan singer, the approval of the Buddy Holly Appreciation Society – and Buddy too – was essential before release – when the record was promptly banned by the BBC for 'morbid concern over the death of a teen idol'.

It was the Remembrance Day march tempo of 'Tribute to Buddy Holly' as much as the words that spurred this censure – which was why Goddard's 'Just Like Eddie' for a disinclined Heinz slipped the net. A combination of two half-finished songs, it featured an uplifting guitar riff† and a light-hearted call to anyone feeling

---

* On top of financial difficulties and poor mental health, a row with his landlady was the last straw for lonely, insular Joe who turned a twelve-bore on her and then himself.

† In 1964, Meek wrote and Heinz recorded the more obvious 'Tribute to Eddie' as the title track of an LP consisting principally of revivals of Cochran favourites.

blue to take the vocalist's advice and find some isolated haven to 'play your guitar just like Eddie' – Cochran that is, a surname unmentioned but tacitly implied to stir up almost-but-not-quite enough controversy to provoke another BBC banishment. Coupled with Heinz's Viking good looks, 'Just Like Eddie' was guided with near-mathematical precision into the Top Ten.*

Returning briefly to Buddy Holly, I ought to bring to your notice 'Gold Records in the Snow' by Barry Barnes – and, especially, 1979's 'The Real Buddy Holly Story' by ex-Cricket Sonny Curtis. This was less an overdue tribute than an articulation of Sonny's disenchantment with a dramatised film biography of his late colleague in which 'Buddy' – amenable and everybody's best pal in real life – punches out a Nashville big-wig during a 1956 session. Moreover, not a solitary frame is allocated to the Crickets' catalytic mentor Norman Petty.

Using Holly's passing – on 'the day the music died' – as a starting point, Don McLean had got a lot off his chest about pop in general via the imagery of 'American Pie' in 1972.† If one more bedsit bard of the early 1970s, Don was nowhere near as precious as high-pitched, quavering Neil Young, a drip-rock colossus who carried what others merely implied to absurd lengths of morosity. He was still at it in 1979 with 'Rust Never Sleeps' in which lines like 'it's better to burn out than to fade away . . .' blurted the inane live-fast-die-young philosophy involuntarily played out by Holly, Hendrix,

* It was revived by the Silicon Teens, and adapted as a soccer chant – 'Just Like Kenny' (after Kenny Dalgleish) – and for an ITV commercial (as 'Just Like Shreddies').
† Holly also inspired Philip Norman's 1989 television screenplay *Words of Love*. 'Vincent', McLean's follow-up to 'American Pie', was his detailed appreciation of the painter Van Gogh.

Morrison, Joplin, Vicious and like unfortunates. 'For what?' enquired John Lennon during one of his last interviews. 'So that we might rock? If Neil Young admires that sentiment so much, why doesn't he do it?'

Updated whenever necessary for stage performances, the Righteous Brothers' recorded arrangement of 'Rock 'n' Roll Heaven' (where 'they got one hell of a band') was glutinous with both gratuitous orchestration and dropping with buoyant pride the names of 'Janis', 'Jimi', 'Jim' and suchlike. Neither of the unrelated siblings admit that it was the sex-and-drugs-and-rock-'n'-roll lifestyle that contributed to many of the heroes' wretched ends. And they don't mention those who were chewed up and spat out by the pop industry – such as Johnny Banks of the Merseybeats or Florence Ballard, an ex-Supreme who, aged thirty-two, died a pauper on 21 February 1976, having received but cursory payment for her hand in the trio's run of hits.*

Closer – but not close enough – to the realism behind the 'wonderful-to-be-here' glitz of pop entertainment were records like 1967's 'The Madman Running Through the Fields' – fame-induced psychosis – by Dantalion's Chariot, and Bad Company's 'Shooting Star' – concerning the rise and deadly fall of Top Ten idol Johnny. In 1974's 'Stardust' by David Essex, he's called Jim Maclaine, the character played by Essex in *Stardust*, a film about another pop dream that goes fatally sour. A hybrid of all these aspects – fame, madness, death (possibly metaphorical) – David Bowie's *Rise and Fall of Ziggy Stardust and the Spiders from Mars* was hinged loosely

---

* At the burial, Diana Ross – fresh from her Oscar-winning role in *Lady Sings the Blues* – was photographed cuddling one of Florence's twin daughters. 'I love you, Blondie' was the message on the wreath she'd ordered.

on Vince Taylor's apotheosis to a career-extinguishing sermon at the Paris Olympia – a veritable 'Rock 'n' Roll Suicide'.*

On Bowie's next album, *Aladdin Sane*, 'Time' logs a 'Billy Dolls' – drummer Billy Murcia of the New York Dolls. After a visit on 6 November 1972 to London's fashionable Speakeasy his life was terminated in a young lady's flat where he fell asleep (assisted, presumably, by 'quaaludes and red wine') only to expire through 'accidental suffocation', said the coroner, when, for whatever purpose, his host poured black coffee down his throat to revive him. The other Dolls – including the late Johnny Thunders – were no saints either, what with instances of alcoholism, heroin addiction and matters that a natural prudity forbids me from specifying.

Many unsavoury habits are passed on from one generation of musicians to the next. An unusually high percentage of the older bluesmen – Robert Pete Williams, Bukka White, Leadbelly, Son House and Muddy Waters' guitarist Pat Hare – were jailed for murder, and plenty more went to Abraham's bosom by violent means. Possibly through poisoning, Robert Johnson – one of the few to deserve the epithet 'legendary' – 'died like a dog with a bark' in El Seven's 'Robert Johnson's Photograph' – a purely symbolic title until a snap of Johnson surfaced in a recent biography.

Considering his lifelong dedication to the form, it is scarcely surprising to find pieces honouring blues grandees in John Mayall's canon. He dedicated two items – 'The Death of J. B. Lenoir'† and 'I'm Gonna Fight For

* The hook-line of this piece quotes Jacques Brel's 'You're Not Alone (Jef)'.
† In a 1967 car crash in Chicago.

You J. B.' to this obscure post-war artist he much admired, and 'Sonny Boy Blow' to the blues musician who was also the subject of the Paul Jones' 1967 B-side, 'Sonny Boy Williamson'.

Before God summoned him in the early 1960s, Forest City Joe Pugh pre-empted both Mayall and Jones with 'Memory of Sonny Boy', one of many such memorials to blues artists made by their friends – and relatives. 'Dedicated to Otis' by Lucille Spann, for example, was for her husband the barrelhouse pianist Otis Spann who died of cancer at the age of forty on 25 April 1970.

The Otis you might have been thinking of was in William Bell's 'A Tribute to a King' three years earlier. Its chart placing in Britain is symptomatic of the esteem in which Otis Redding is held here. Echoing both Redding's breakthrough into the white market and the age – twenty-six – at which he met his end, Johnny Ace had been the posthumous recipient of 1955's 'Salute to Johnny Ace' by the Ravens, and the Five Wings' premise that 'Johnny's Still Singing'.

If we agree that Ace and Redding's music was derived from blues, and accept, with skiffle scribe Brian Bird, that 'blues is the main content of jazz', then now's the moment to throw in Dory Previn's 'A Stone for Bessie Smith', a therapeutic commendation of this 'classic blues' hollerer's extrapolatory influence.* Blind New York composer Louis 'Moondog' Hardin (obit) – who flitted briefly across the pop forum during its fleeting 'classical'

---

* Bessie Smith was also taken in a road accident – in the grey of morning on 26 September 1937 when she struck a stationary lorry while driving through Coahoma, Mississippi on her way to an engagement. The title song of Previn's *Mary C. Brown And The Hollywood Sign* concerned an actress who, when global fame proved elusive, hurled herself to her death from the said sign.

144

Some of the Grim Reaper's greatest hits: a random compilation. *(Mary L. St Clair)*

Moments after take-off on 3 February 1959, this Beechcraft Bonanza crashed, killing the pilot and his three passengers – Buddy Holly, the Big Bopper and Ritchie Valens. *(Pictorial Press)*

'Three Steps to Heaven': Marty Wilde poses with Gene Vincent and Eddie Cochran during the 1960 tour of Britain which ended with Cochran's death. *(Pictorial Press)*

After Roy Orbison *(below)* taught his wife Claudette to ride, her passion for motor-cycling would last for as long as she lived. *(SI)*

'Feast of the Mau-Mau': Screamin' Jay Hawkins used to be quite a shy fellow with a warm baritone not unlike that of Nat 'King' Cole. *(Pictorial Press)*

Right Lord David Sutch: god-father of British horror-rock.

Below This highly collectable 1965 concept EP by The Downliners Sect contains a self-referential version of Jimmy Cross's 'I Want My Baby Back' – in which two lovers reunite inside a coffin.

Left 'Love me now, for now is all the time there may be.' On 31 July 1964, aerodrome controllers saw the craft bearing Jim Reeves vanish suddenly from their radar screens. *(Pictorial Press)*

Below left Johnny Ace's pastime of playing Russian roulette backfired during a backstage round on Christmas Eve, 1954. *(Pictorial Press)*

Below As well as John Leyton's 'Johnny Remember Me', Geoff Goddard also composed tributes to Buddy Holly and Jim Reeves. *(Geoff Goddard Collection)*

Funeral Services

of the late

MR. JOHN M. ALEXANDER, JR.

(Johnny Ace)

CLAYBORN TEMPLE A. M. E. CHURCH

SUNDAY, JANUARY 2, 1955—2:30 P. M.

Right Though her 'Terry'
was without doubt a rocker,
Twinkle was actually more
of a London dolly-bird.
(Pictorial Press)

Below The Shangri-Las'
'Leader of the Pack'
apotheosised what might
have been Terry's North
American blood brother.
(Pictorial Press)

John Lennon, seen here with actor Jack McGowran on the set of *How I Won the War*, once asked the *New York Times* 'who'd want to be an eighty-year-old Beatle?' *(Michael Towers)*

Left Many listeners found John Entwistle's macabre compositions, such as 'Boris the Spider', the most attractive aspect of The Who. *(Pictorial Press)*

Below Ex-Yardbird Keith Relf was cut off in his prime by faulty electrical wiring. *(Pictorial Press)*

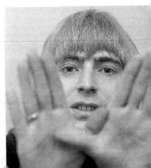

'I Don't Live Today': Jimi Hendrix on 'Ready, Steady, Go!', 1966. *(Alan Clayson Archives)*

'My Time Ain't Long' – but it wasn't a smoker's cough that carried off Canned Heat's Al Wilson *(top centre)* and Bob Hite *(bottom centre)*. *(Bob Baker/Redferns)*

'Hellhound On My Trail': if his songs were anything to go by, Robert Johnson was tormented by an entire inferno of devils, phantoms and ectoplasmic monsters. *(Pictorial Press)*

Above left Alice Cooper: glam rock from the charnel house. *(Pictorial Press)*

Above right Napalm Death: these entertainers' 'Divine Death' comprised twenty seconds of headache-inducing electronic distortion and guttural utterances. *(Earache Records)*

Below Former gravedigger Dave Vanian fronts The Damned, who by 1986 were smooth enough to score their biggest hit with 'Eloise', lovingly copied from Barry Ryan's string-soaked 1968 original. *(Erica Echenberg/Redferns)*

period in the late 1960s – paid his respects to groundbreaking alto saxophonist Charlie Parker* in 'Lament 1 (Bird's Lament)' after 'we even talked about doing a record together. One night, I met him in Times Square and shook a shaking hand, not realising that would be the last time we would meet'.

Seen by some as more in the tradition of an improvisational musician like Parker, Jimi Hendrix had spoken to Miles Davis and Gil Evans about recording together after the 1970 Isle of Wight Festival. We'll never know what the outcome might have been but it was, none the less, fitting for Jimi Hendrix's life to be commemorated on disc by acts that weren't like Danny Mirror or Zacharias and the Tree People. Thus we have 'Song For a Dreamer' from Procul Harum, Rod Stewart's Top Ten revival of Hendrix's 'Angel' in 1972, and less a tribute than a cautionary tale, John Mayall's 'Accidental Suicide'. Though Steve Stills' début solo LP was dedicated to Jimi alone, it was extended to Al Wilson and Duane Allman on a 1973 Stills track, 'Blues Man'.

Rockabilly balladeer Jack Scott from Ontario had acknowledged an artistic debt in 1960 with *I Remember Hank Williams* on which he sang 'the tunes as though he'd inhaled the Nashville air for months'. As a Nashville resident for years, not months, and a Southerner to boot, Roy Orbison with his advisers felt entitled, eleven years later, to take more liberties with the original arrangements on *Hank Williams the Roy Orbison Way* – such as grafting the undulating *ostinato* of Johnnie Ray's 'Such a

---

* 'Bird' was toppled from his perch by a heart attack attributable to pneumonia on 12 March 1955.

Night' on to 'Jambalaya', and jarring accent shifts on to 'Cold Cold Heart' and 'I'm So Lonesome I Could Cry'.

During Roy's final months, musicians decades his junior had been buzzing round him. Backtracking from their punk genesis, U2 had tumbled upon Orbison through 1985's *Blue Velvet* soundtrack, and had composed an opus for what came out as his valedictory album. The most staggering conversion was that of guitarist Steve Jones, formerly of the Sex Pistols, who as both a person and would-be songwriting partner was, to Roy, 'just a sweetheart; real open and honest'.

As Major Bill Smith would do with 'Big O', so the Cash Pussies cashed in on Steve's confrère, Sid Vicious' exit with the delicate '99% Is Shit' – featuring the dear departed's tape-looped voice repeating this phrase. Described with vague accuracy in a tabloid as 'a sort of dirty old man of punk', Ian Dury had emitted his feelings about *his* hero in 'Sweet Gene Vincent', 'young and old and gone' – and also icon of the rockabilly craze that followed punk.

The late 1970s was the wellspring of many eulogies to the dead as a device whereby many acts hoped to buttress their standing with credible influences. Keith Moon's demise at the beginning of the puny 'Mod revival' was an excuse for the Jam to crank out 'So Sad About Us' with slightly more guts than the Who original. The same could not be said of Siouxie and the Banshees' go at T. Rex's 'Twentieth Century Boy' soon after Marc Bolan met his Maker. Rather than rehashing a Rolling Stones number, Psychic TV came up with their own 'Godstar' to Brian Jones on the twentieth anniversary of his 'chlorine dream'. That was what Jim Morrison called Brian's drowning in 'Ode to L. A. While Thinking of Brian Jones, Deceased', printed the week after in *Disc*. Do you notice how both of them died in water on the same day of the year (3rd July)?

This may seem a tenuous connection but, overdosing on morphine, Lenny Bruce expired on a bathroom floor on *3* August 1966. Under the auspices of their Apple Corps, the Beatles had considered marketing a *twenty-four album* retrospective of him talking dirty in hip restricted code. Action speaking louder than words, Frank Zappa organised the release of a Bruce double-LP, edited from one of his shows. Both Tim Hardin and Bob Dylan thought enough of the man to lionise him in song. The former's 'Eulogy to Lenny Bruce' ('never again will we get together to die') was covered by the late Nico* – romantically linked with both Brian Jones *and* Jim Morrison, believe it or not – who'd found Bruce side-splitting 'for that thing . . . that nothing is wrong to do or to say or to take . . . he really destroyed himself in the end'.

In 1966, she had a role in *Chelsea Girls*, Andy Warhol's most famous movie, and was an adjunct to the Velvet Underground in which she was sometimes given star billing to the chagrin of the outfit's chief protagonist, Lou Reed, whose perspectives on seedy-flash New York low life were taking tangible form as literary-musical wit. Nico had joined as 'featured singer' at the behest of late Pop artist Warhol who let the combo rehearse in his Greenwich Village studio, The Factory, and incorporated them into his mixed-media 'Exploding Plastic Inevitable' troupe.

When Warhol was within an ace of death after being

* This doom-laden Teutonic entertainer suffered a cerebral haemorrhage in July 1988 after a bicycle ride on a hot day while holidaying in Ibiza.

shot by Factory acolyte Valerie Solanas, Reed sat down with his guitar to compose 'Andy's Chest' which expressed bottled-up affection for his father figure with a few side swipes at the girl who'd put him in hospital. For years afterwards, Andy's wounds continued to play him up, often reopening if he over-exerted himself. Come 1987, he was back in the operating theatre for the removal of a potentially gangrenous gall-bladder but failed to come round from the anaesthetic.

If Warhol finished up as a bland media 'personality' with an intriguing past, maybe that was almost the point. Married and commuting to the Big Apple from rural contentment on a New Jersey farm, Lou Reed had gone the same way – though he had not invited his old guru to the wedding. Hurt, Andy had confided to his diary – published after his death – that 'I hate Lou Reed more and more, I really do'. Shrugging it off as waspishness, Lou collaborated with the Velvet Underground's multi-instrumentalist John Cale on *Songs for Drella*.* A fourteen-part 'look at the life of Andy Warhol' ran the programme notes when the suite was performed in a Brooklyn church in January 1989 with the deceased's portrait hanging over the stage. Described as 'a fiction' on the subsequent album, *Songs for Drella* dealt less with Warhol's life than with Reed's interpretation of it. And so it was, for some of the time, the Lou Reed story too.

One of Warhol's 'multiple paintings' of 1962 was of Norma Jean Mortenson who had, that year, found her adult life as film actress and comedienne Marilyn Monroe more than she could bear. To the tune of 'Who Killed Cock Robin', Pete Seeger blamed her suicide on every-

* A combination of 'Dracula' and 'Cinderella', 'Drella' was Cale and Reed's nickname for Warhol.

148

one from top Hollywood moguls to the humble fan (i.e., 'Who'll catch her blood?/"I", said the fan, "in my little pan"' – you get the drift) in his 'Who Killed Norma Jean'. Elton John weighed in with 1974's 'Candle in the Wind', his wordsmith Bernie Taupin's tribute to Marilyn – which I was vexed at hearing myself humming whilst typing this.

It was the manner of James Dean's death in a car smash rather than his meagre output on celluloid that ensured his immortality. It hardly needed the Beach Boys to reword the traditional 'Their Hearts Were Full of Spring' to remind us that, 'known forever more as the Rebel Without a Cause', 'A Young Man Is Gone'.

A well-meant genuflexion towards another icon of youth culture was 'Alan Freed' (who 'recognised our need') by Shakin' Stevens and the Sunsets. This lauded the Ohio disc jockey who played a considerable part in bringing rock 'n' roll – an expression Freed was alleged to have invented – to the general public. The group left him spinning his records still, electing not to spoil things with verses about Freed becoming a scapegoat as the payola storm clouds gathered in 1960. His irreversible vocational decline was punctuated by an ill-judged migration to Los Angeles, heavy drinking and, in 1964, accusations of tax evasion. Freed was incapable, however, of standing trial as he was bedridden with the uraemia that would extinguish him a year later.

Most US disc jockeys like Freed had been unmindful of whatever was gripping a backwater like Britain in 1963. However, the Beatles' subjugation of North America had the Englishmen swamping the Top Twenties of the United States and Canada, five or six singles at a time, by autumn 1964. The first US Beatle-related 45, 'My Boyfriend Got a Beatle Haircut' by Donna Lynn, was not to be the last.

A Johnny Guarnier's 'To Kill a Beatle' was taken to heart by the fan who gunned down John Lennon sixteen years later – and reactivated the Beatle tribute industry. Head and shoulders commercially above efforts like 'Elegy for the Walrus' and 'It Was Nice to Know You, John', George Harrison's 'All Those Years Ago' was the promotional 45 from his *Somewhere in England* album, and the reason why George by association was to end 1981 seven places behind Lennon as tenth Top Male Vocalist in *Billboard*'s awards. Regardless of its singalong mediocrity, another incentive for buyers was the superimposed presence of Ringo and Paul who had taken a break from another project in George Martin's Monserrat complex to add their contributions when the unmixed version arrived from Harrison's studio in England.

Lennon was an artist with whom Bryan Ferry, via a *Melody Maker* article, articulated a wish to collaborate. Bryan may have told the man himself when, in 1974, he dined with John, George and Ringo in New York. Touring the Fatherland with Roxy Music the week after the slaying, Ferry suggested closing the show with uxorious 'Jealous Guy' from John's *Imagine* album. A German record company executive ventured that it would be a sound choice for the next single but Ferry felt it might appear tasteless. Nevertheless, after further deliberation, Roxy Music tried an arrangement during an exploratory session in a Chertsey studio. With the oblique 'A Tribute' on the picture sleeve the sole reference to the motivation behind it, 'Jealous Guy' scudded all the way up the UK charts, the only Roxy Music 45 to so do.

Sean Lennon's godfather, Elton John got no further than No. 51 with his 'Empty Garden' tribute in 1982. Though he procrastinated for even longer, Mike Oldfield – with sister Sally on lead vocals – slummed it on *Top of the Pops* with 'Moonlight Shadow' in 1983 which addressed itself to the horror outside the Dakota on the night it happened.

The central figure of Oldfield's ditty was not John but Yoko who'd sanction and partly compere 1990's televised and international tribute to her husband at Liverpool's Pier Head. George Harrison had nothing to do with her Merseyside extravaganza but, while they declined to show up in person, Paul and Ringo each sent a filmed piece; Starr's 'Hi, Liverpool!' and supergroup rendering of 'I Call Your Name', a minor Beatles track from 1964, bridging a gap between Hall and Oates and Dave Edmunds' John Lennon Tribute Band. Conspicuously uninvited to appear were any Merseybeat groups from when the world was young.

Back in 1963, the British pop papers had announced the Beatles' forthcoming US trip on the same November day that John F. Kennedy was assassinated. Some would predicate that the four's American walkover was an antidote to the depressing months that followed the tragedy in Dallas, 'a place not known for war'. So ran 'Lincoln Limousine' by Jerry Lee Lewis, a breezy, Macgonagall-esque album filler that remains my all-time fave rave of requiems to any dead celebrity – especially with its inane 'Oh Lord, it would have been better if he had stayed at home' line and a piano riff reminiscent of the Searchers' 'Needles and Pins'. 'He might just be sincere', whined *Record Mirror*, 'but it doesn't sound in good taste'. The sleeve notes called it a 'touching eulogy' but it's actually more like an advertisement for the vehicle in the sights of the 'twenty dollar rifle' that 'took the life of this great man' as the Killer leads up to the truism that 'you never know who's your enemy or your friend'.

The Joseph Kennedy Jnr, Foundation for Mental Retardation was the beneficiary of profits from budget-priced *John Fitzgerald Kennedy: a Memorial Album* (which included his inaugural speech in its entirety). Produced and broadcast by a New York radio station within half a day of the shooting, it shifted four million copies in less than a week. After its spin-off 45, 'The Voice of the President', nestled uneasily between Bobby-ballads and surf instrumentals on juke boxes, JFK waded in with a second hit LP, *The Presidential Years*.

By bilious coincidence, on 21 November – the night before the murder – the folksy Brothers Four had taped 'Long Ago Far Away', a scrubbed-clean diatribe about us being no better than Rome's bloodthirsty crowds or Attila's hordes what with all these atomic bombs, Ku Klux Klan lynchings *et al*.* Over the following months, the Brothers found they could whip up unresponsive audiences with a swift burst of 'Long Ago Far Away', now topical with its 'things like that don't happen no more nowadays' pay-off.

With a certain mental athleticism, 'The Warmth of the Sun' by the Beach Boys could be seen as a reaction to Kennedy's passing but the Byrds struck harder with 'He Was a Friend of Mine'. The seasons came and went and he came to be described in song as either as significant a loss to post-war youth as James Dean – e.g.,

* It was also something else: a composition by Bob Dylan, then a protest singer who few visualised as the quasi-messianic enigma he was to become.

'Kennedy Say's (*sic*) by Terry and Gerry – or, nihilistically, as just another bourgeois liberal with inert reactionary tendencies. In Adam and the Ants' delightful 'Catholic Day', there'd be no more 'messing about with Monroe, soft drugs or playing the space race' for JFK now that his wife was cradling 'his brain on her knee'.

When Robert Kennedy died at the trigger-jerk of another lunatic in Los Angeles in June 1968, Ireland's singing actor Richard Harris put immediate pen to paper, and saved the resulting poem, 'The Morning of the Mourning of Another Kennedy', replete with lines like 'the worms and decay of his brother quivered at the thought of their food', for an off-beat 1970 B-side. The news reached the Rolling Stones in the midst of a session for 'Sympathy for the Devil'* – lyrically, nearly a diabolical inversion of reproachful 'Long Ago Far Away'. Infallibly pragmatic, the Stones made the line 'I shouted out, "Who killed John Kennedy!"' plural ('the Kennedys').

Along with riots in over twenty US city ghettos, the gunning down of another political leader, Martin Luther King, from a balcony in Memphis, Tennessee two months before Kennedy Minor, had the Rascals at No. 1 for a month in the States with their tribute, 'People Got to Be Free' – though no one thought to smack out a King spoken-word platter *à la* 'Voice of the President'. Nevertheless, composer Dick Holler was quick off the mark with 'Abraham, Martin and John'. Killing three birds with one stone, this litany was the medium of Dion's chart comeback and, in 1971, disc jockey Tom

* Which was taking place before director Jean-Luc Goddard's cameras for inclusion in a movie of the same name.

Clay's maiden US Top Ten placing. On the same label (Tamla Motown) as Clay, Marvin Gaye's was the only version of this rare – and rather cloying – tribute 'standard' to crack the charts in Britain – and it was forever warbled by Andy Williams on his globally networked television series.

The matrons of middle America might have lapped up Williams and other Mister Wonderfuls but their left-wing blue-stocking daughters went equally cow-eyed over the late Cuban guerillero, Ernesto 'Che' Guevara whose mug adorned their hostel-room walls. Whereas President Kennedy's utterances had been pressed on to two albums and a single in the USA, the less affluent Cuba made do in 1966 with an EP of Guevara's verbal reinforcement of his khaki-jacketed chief Fidel Castro's policies. A few dozen copies of *Carta del Che Leida por Fidel* may have filtered overseas strictly for use as display – a hipper-than-thou university student could pull it artlessly from his record collection as a handy working surface for rolling a joint. It might be slotted on to the stereo once or twice for the same reason as a British holiday-maker on the Côte d'Azur might purchase *Le Monde* and pretend to read it with understanding on the beach.

Making more sense in English-language areas was the United States of America's 'Love Song for the Dead Che' which, minus its title, could be mistaken – with its 'wine and candlelight' scenario – for something as lovey-dovey (albeit more attractively so) as Andy Williams' 'Can't Take My Eyes Off You'.*

Other counter-culture worthies were exalted with less

---

* 'Che Guevara' by Birmingham's Ravenshead was issued in 1980 – the fifteenth anniversary of the Cuban revolutionary's death.

soppy devotion. Peter Gabriel incorporated a field recording of South African anti-apartheid activist Steve Biko's funeral in 1980's 'Biko'. Before it was taken up by protesters during the Springboks tour of New Zealand, it had been sneaked into many a Transvaal seat of learning to irritate the police when they arrived to arrest subversives. It was also sung *en masse* by cast and onlookers during the finale of a London spectacular held in order that those who so desired could make a fuss over Biko's luckier colleague, Nelson Mandela.

Also a gaol-bird, US black militant George Jackson had managed to get his views published in book form – *Soledad Brother* – before becoming one of the fatalities in a prison riot in 1971. Harking back to his protest roots, Bob Dylan sympathised after a self-conscious, pop-starrish fashion with the lad's ignominious passing via a single containing two takes of 'George Jackson' and a rude word – probably included to confuse readers who observed that Dylan hadn't sworn once in a recent and lengthy *Rolling Stone* interview. Bob was to cry out for justice too in 'Hurricane' (1976) for ex-boxing champion Ruben Carter, imprisoned for homicide.

Who the famous person was in Ultravox's 'I Remember (Death in the Afternoon)' is anyone's guess. The only clues – and they're remote ones – are its release date (1981) and the line 'we tuned the dial; we heard the news'.

The Stranglers* recorded an unsentimental requiem for a non-fictional fan, 'Dagenham Dave', one of an army of stalwarts who enacted bloody reprisals against anyone

---

* The Stranglers' 'No More Heroes' lists Che Guevara – and Leon Trotsky whose skull was fractured with an assassin's ice-pick in 1940.

who slighted their favourite group – and the Beatles alluded in 'A Day in the Life' to one of their moneyed hangers-on, Guinness heir Tara Browne who 'blew his mind out in a car'*. Furthermore, when Fairport Convention's van skidded off the motorway on the way back from a Birmingham engagement, of the two passengers killed, it was not drummer Martin Lamble but a mere associate of the outfit, clothes designer Jeannie Franklyn,† to whom Jack Bruce dedicated 1969's *Songs for a Tailor*.

Chief among homages to deceased relatives are 1992's 'Tears in Heaven' by Eric Clapton to his son Conor, and, twenty years earlier, Elvis Presley's 'Mama Liked the Roses'. Immediately after Mrs Presley's funeral in August 1958‡, her son in his khaki regimentals was encircled by the press corps, thrusting stick mikes at a gaunt face whose mechanically moving mouth spewed forth unblinking copy for tomorrow's newspaper. No autographs please. One or two sick jokes were cracked that morning during Dave McEnery's recording session for 'New Angel Tonight', his tribute to 'the mother of our rock 'n' roll king'. Whoever Dave was, 'New Angel Tonight' became his epitaph too as, following this bid for the big time, he vanished from the pages of history.

* The reason offered for this in Eric Burdon and War's eleven minute revival of 'A Day in the Life' in 1976 was that Tara 'didn't notice that the lights were stoned'.
† A cousin of Phil Ochs. Death stalked Fairport Convention again on 21 April 1977 when former member Sandy Denny fell down a flight of stairs.
‡ Gladys Presley's fatal heart attack came on the same day (14 August 1958) as that of rural bluesman Big Bill Broonzy.

Chapter Eight

Empty Saddles

They came from beyond the pale of mainstream pop – from badlands of cacti, stony hills and seas of dry *mesquite* grass. The hissing hi-hats and finger snaps were almost audible as they rode imperiously down the trail, shadowy human shapes with only a glint of spurs, their white stetsons and six-shooter barrels peeping from holsters reflecting the early morning sunshine. Pistoleros, bronco-busters, rustlers, card-sharps – they'd come to stake their claims in the hit parade in which the handful of forts and settlements gained so far only emphasised its emptiness, its trackless wastes.

Their leader was Frankie Laine whose career on celluloid would focus largely on his disembodied voice carrying main narrative themes concerning gun law in the Old West. He could be heard as the credits rolled for the likes of *Man with a Star*, the *Rawhide* television series – and, of course, *High Noon*; its satisfactory upshot reiterated in Laine's 'Gunfight at the OK Corral' with the killers (killed by Wyatt Earp, Doc Holliday *et al*) pushing up daisies on 'Boot Hill, so cold, so still'.

Frankie's sidekick was Marty Robbins from Glendale, Arizona, an embodiment of C & W's right wing 'redneck' posturing – but it was only when the contents of country and black music merged that he was able to transcend regional popularity. And yet, it was the lengthy, waltz-time 'El Paso' from 1960's *Gunfighter Ballads* that marked

157

his international breakthrough. As in 'The Deal', the ghost tells the story – of a ménage à trois, the rivals' shoot-out and the victor's run from justice which culminates in a return to the scene of the crime because 'my love is stronger than my fear of death'. Unhappily, the lady serves him as he had served the other fellow and, presumably, collects the reward.*

'El Paso' was backed with 'Running Gun' (composed by Robbins' protégés, the Glaser Brothers), a tale of a bounty hunter with 'twenty notches on my six-gun'. As homespun a saga was Johnny Cash's self-penned 'Don't Take Your Guns to Town', a mother's unheeded warning to Billy Joe who is mortally wounded in a bar room fracas after his first slug of liquor. His final words? You guessed them.

'Don't Take Your Guns to Town' – or anywhere else – was a maxim that the 'poor cowboy, wrapped in white linen' in 'Streets of Laredo'† – also recorded by Cash – might have done well to have adopted. So might the feuding Terills and Hannerys in the 1958 movie *The Big Country*. Then they might have been spared the loss of their respective paterfamilias when – as expressed most evocatively in 'The Death of Buck Hannery' in Jerome Moross' soundtrack – a dispute over water rights came to a head.

Conclusions were also reached with firearms in 'Ringo'

* In Britain, 'El Paso' was covered by Vince Eager who sounded rather too mundanely Home Counties to stand a chance of checkmating the original. The traditional 'Lily of the West' (recorded by Joan O'Bryan, Joan Baez and Bob Dylan amongst others) painted much the same picture of jealousy and treachery.

† This traditional C & W stand-by is a cousin of 'The Unfortunate Rake' and, also Irish, the happier 'Bard of Armagh'. A send-up 'Streets of Fontana', was taped by Frank Zappa in 1962 but remains unissued.

by Lorne Greene – 'Pa Cartwright' in the cowboy television series *Bonanza* – in which a fictitious desperado turns out to be too decent – fatally so – to take advantage in a duel against the lawman who had once saved his life. 'We're even, friend,' yelled Ringo, but he was pumped with more lead than the other bloke had dug out of him when they first met, when Ringo was sprawled 'face down on the desert sand'. Taken expediently from the 1964 LP *Welcome to the Ponderosa* during the Beatles' invasion of the USA, just the title* of Greene's otherwise unconnected talkover was enough to get it on radio playlists and *all* the way up *Billboard*'s *Hot 100*.

On the surface, the force of order also seems to lose in 1974's 'I Shot the Sheriff' from Bob Marley and the Wailers – but, as Bob elucidated, it was self-defence because 'sheriff' is a metaphor for 'wickedness'. Well, what else would you call someone who gunned down his own deputy?†

Your time could be more gainfully spent listening to the late Eamonn Andrews' workmanlike cover of Rusty Draper's 'The Shifting Whispering Sands Parts One and Two' in a brogue that rides roughshod over schmaltzy strings, cursory eldritch yelps and the Mike Sammes Singers. Peaking two places higher in the 1956 charts than a US version by Billy Vaughn‡, the Irish chatshow interlocutor's gold prospecting monologue dwelt on the passing of an 'aged miner' – 'I could not but

---

* In unconscious reciprocation, many early Merseybeat groups functioned under fierce Wild West nomenclatures: Clay Ellis and the Raiders, the James Boys – after Jesse – Johnny Ringo and the Colts, the Raving Texans and so forth.
† Eric Clapton's cover of 'I Shot the Sheriff' is better known than the original. In 1981, it was a minor UK hit for Light of the World.
‡ Whose orchestra would be another act who recorded 'Mack the Knife' (as 'Theme from the Threepenny Opera') in 1956.

wonder if he died by human hands' in a deserted chapparal with bleached bones and desolate panorama.

A younger television personality but of similar vintage to Andrews, Robert Horton – 'Flint McCullough', scout of *Wagon Train* – turned his back on city bricks to dig in a desert which even Eamonn's coyotes would shun. Robert didn't find any gold but he made a most evocative song-and-dance about it in 1960's 'Sail Ho!'. After his mule flakes out, he staggers the scorching, dust-dry plain. Unless he finds water, he's a dead man. He meets an old man in the same plight. Though a human rag with an empty canteen, the latter is buoyed up by the mirage of a rescue ship surging through the rocks and cacti. He dies within earshot of Horton's sneering mockery. Nevertheless, as the swirling orchestral arrangement sinks to violin pizzicatos and mournful mouth-organ, the singer himself is doomed as he falls prey to the same vision.

Concealed without even a composing credit on a B-side, 'Sail Ho!' was deprived of the 'standard' status that was granted to the much-covered but similarly hallucinatory 'Cool Water'. Frankie Laine's was the only version to pace, with his pard, Dan, into the UK hit parade in a quest for 'cool, clear warder' (*sic*) and was distinguished by a backing vocalist chanting 'water' as insidiously as a dripping tap. Vaughn Monroe – with an incongruous big band jazz passage – and the Sons of the Pioneers (whose Bob Nolan wrote the song) roamed the same barren wastes without a trace of the desired liquid.

Tom Jones would crave it as well. On the same 1966 album – *Green, Green Grass of Home* – he'd also try Monroe's 'Riders in the Sky'. This did not outshine the original any more than a version in 1960 by Shadows copyists, the Ramrods* or Pinky and Perky's vari-speeded rendition on the 1962 EP, *Out West*. A year later, both the surfin' Chantays and yodelling Frank Ifield had a go too but there'd be a two-decade wait for a more-than-mediocre rendering by King Kurt who dismantled and stuck it back together again so imaginatively that you could almost picture the dung-spattered clouds over which the Devil's herd were chased.

On solid ground, Michael Holliday's jog-trotting but tart 'Phantom Rider (on the Hopi Trail)' – a deceased paleface scalped for illicit gold-mining in Injun territory – underlined the string-pulled action in ITV's *Four Feather Falls* which, with its marionette thespians and talking animals, was aimed squarely at the kindergarten set. Meanwhile, back on the ranch, there was 'something strange in the old corral' in the threnody for the Old West that was the Sons of the Pioneers' 'Empty Saddles'.† You might come across the same rusty guns, death-watch beetles, broken wagons and cobwebs in a stable in Lonesome Tone's descriptive 'Ghost Town' with its silent nickelodeon, listlessly swinging saloon half-doors and graffiti tallying gunfight results.‡

In 1980, Kenny Rogers' 'Coward of the County' (i.e., Tommy, a convict's son) takes the law into his own hands when, to deadly effect, his patience with the Gatlin boys runs out after they have performed unspeakable atrocities upon his wife.

Over in South Africa, another bandit family 'died in

---

* Though, to be fair, the Shadows' 1980s policy of raiding the catalogues of long-gone rivals embraced a Top Twenty lift of the Ramrods' scoring of 'Riders in the Sky'.
† Beware of the group's inferior remake of 'Empty Saddles' on the 1960 album *Cool Water*.
‡ Where are you, Lonesome Tone?

the Transvaal dust' in the title song – co-written by mouth-organist Larry Adler – of 1961's *The Hellions* in which its singer, Marty Wilde, had a bit part. Other British attempts to stage gunfights in song included Houston Wells and the Marksmen's 'Only the Heart-aches',* an account of a saloon bouncer's infatuation with the landlady. His dedication to the job was epitomised by the observation that 'the notches on my gun are twenty and three'. An earlier Wells 45, 'North Wind' was also produced by Joe Meek whose doom-soaked lyrics have a chap who murdered his girl and her illicit lover begging the angels to 'tell me I'm forgiven now, don't send my soul to hell'.

Guilty of a similar *crime passionel*, the cuckold attempts to flee the 'sordid scene' in 1985's tart 'Three Sheets to the Wind' by the Lost Weekend but is too dazed with beer to 'hotwire the car', and is still trying to sober up as wailing sirens and 'lights a-flashing' – not to mention 'the sound of furies and hellhounds on my trail' – close in.

More crassly amusing was Benny Hill's chart-topping saga of fifty-two-year-old 'Ernie (The Fastest Milkman in the West)', who bites the dust when struck by 'a stale pie' thrown by Ted the baker, a rival for the hand of Sue, a merry widow whose subsequent splicing to the survivor is marred by the hauntings of the slain Ernie from 'that milk round in the sky'.

Similarly, I have to confess to being 'into' Charlie Drake's 1960 cover of Larry Verne's US smash 'Mr Custer'. Most of its appeal lies in the incongruity ('what am I doin' 'ere?') of the diminutive English funnyman's Bow Belled ad libs from the depths of the blue uniform of a Seventh Cavalry trooper en route, presumably, to

---

* A Val Doonican version would appear on a 1964 B-side.

he battle of Little Big Horn where Custer and two hundred soldiers would be slain in the famous 'Last Stand' by Crazy Horse's Sioux and Cheyenne command. Having dreamed the previous night that 'there I was standing with an arrow in my back', Charlie joins his file despite increasing trepidation after the introductory redskin whooping subsides to a steady chant over a stock throbbing tom-tom rhythm and ominous organ flurries. Pathetically, he cries 'I don't wanna wind up dead all bald', asking his yellow-haired Colonel, 'May I be excused for the rest of the afternoon? I want to change my library book.' He's then distracted by the first of many whistling arrows: 'Oi Wyatt, duck yer 'ead! Ugh! Bit late on that one, son. I bet that don't 'arf 'urt.'

Drake's unfortunate comrade is not the same Wyatt whose frequently deadly law-enforcing feats were serialised in the late 1950s ITV series *The Legend of Wyatt Earp* starring Hugh O'Brien who also sang the title theme with a chorus that was corrupted to 'Wyatt Earp! What a twerp!' by British schoolchildren.

The fame of Earp was, however, more calculable than that of buckskinned Davy Crockett – especially in 1950s Britain. North America was over its Crockett craze when we were bombarded with its attendant coonskin caps, quiz games, checked shirts – and Bill Hayes crackingpaced 1955 hit single from Walt Disney's *Davy Crockett*. Let me hear you now – 'Daveeeeee! Davy Crockett! King of the wild frontieeeeeer!'

In the last shot of the film, Davy (played by Fess Parker) is shown flailing his rifle like a club at the snarling bayonets about him at the Alamo* – a conclusion sufficiently open-ended not to upset younger

Where the historical Crockett was killed in 1836.

viewers who might also have been interested in th
planned 1956 sequel, *Davy Crockett and the River Pirate.*
The song too stopped short of the unmentionable – ba
the passing of Mrs Crockett and its effect on her husban
(whose 'grief was gall') in some among the multitude o
covers of 'The Ballad of Davy Crockett'.* On the F
side of Fess Parker's version, the lady pops up again i
'Farewell' as Davy, its apparent co-writer, leaves for 'th
land of the stranger'. Make of that what you will.

John Wayne's grizzled and charismatic Crockett get
what's coming to him in the seven minute climax of tota
massacre in 1960's *The Alamo*, expressed with graphic
unhummable gusto – all trumpet flourishes and berser
xylophones – in 'Charge of Santa Anna/Death of Davi
Crockett/Final Assault' from the ubiquitous Dimitr
Tiomkin's soundtrack LP. This collection was beefed u
with a Marty Robbins adaptation of 'The Ballad of th
Alamo' which, after a token reference to the presen
ruined fort-cum-shrine's ghostly defenders, scratches th
surface of the background to 'the thirteen days of glory
when Texas didn't even belong to the USA but was par
of Mexico. The essence of the matter was that growin
immigrant infiltration of the northern marches of it
empire worried the Mexican government. Worry becam
alarm when the newcomers revolted against the militar
dictatorship of President Santa Anna who had seize
power in 1823. Hence the arrival of Crockett, Jim Bowi
Colonel Travis and his cannon plus their men at th
Alamo to buy time for General Houston to marsha

* Among them those of 'Tennessee' Ernie Ford, Max Bygrave
future Beatles music publisher Dick James, Gary Miller (with aberra
new words about 'the buckskin buccaneer'), Pinky and Perky and, a
late as 1977, English painter and performance artist, Humphre
Ocean.

the forces that would eventually rout Santa Anna at San Jacinto.

Watching the movie, you find yourself willing the lads on the ramparts to hold out until the army gets there – even though you know they won't. Virtually the only survivor was a youth sent on horseback by Travis to deliver a progress report to Houston. This was the first straight acting role for Bobbyish pop starlet Frankie Avalon who, none the less, managed not to make a fool of himself. He was not, however, permitted to sing – not even to fill needle time on the soundtrack release. Instead, the job went to Robbins – and Washington's Brothers Four whose bland 'Green Leaves of Summer'* (similar lyrically to the Pete Seeger's 'Turn! Turn! Turn!') pales beside that heard on tear-jerking celluloid by an anonymous *a capella* choir. When isolated from the movie, this simple air still knots the stomach in its yearning for times past when you were 'close to the Earth'. Whatever your understanding of the situation at the Alamo or any sympathies you may or may not have with John Wayne's political stance,† it still gets you right there too when Wayne-as-Crockett displays more sensitivity on-screen than he did off with speeches – included on Tiomkin's album – that bind his motley Tennesseans to the task in hand after Travis offered them the opportunity of surrender or escape. '"Repub-lic"', he tells them in his pedantic but irresistible drawl,

* Also recorded by Mantovani and, in 1962, by Kenny Ball and his Jazzmen.
† Director as well as star of *The Alamo*, Wayne had endorsed the McCarthyite witch hunts in the 1950s, and was to participate in a 1968 movie, *The Green Berets*, which, like Staff Sergeant Barry Sadler's obscene ballad, lent uncompromising support to the US presence in Vietnam.

'is one of those words that makes me tight in the throat', and, after his boys had spilt their blood, the Lone Star State – until officially annexed to the Union in 1846 – enjoyed the best of both worlds as a unified, quasi-imperial republic that could still claim affinity to the wider world in the north.

Back in the UK, Dave Dee, Dozy, Beaky, Mick and Tich went in for a measure of epic westernising with 1968's 'Legend of Xanadu'. Though set in a 'black, barren land' in some Latinate region, Dee sticks to his Wiltshire accent for the spectral spoken verse as yet another besotted chump lays down his life for some heartless woman. When presented to the Queen Mother years later, Dave was remembered by her as 'the one with the whip' – because he wielded one during the costumed promotion* of 'Legend of Xanadu' on *Top of the Pops*. Its crack was emulated in the studio by slapping two plywood scraps together as an empty lager bottle zipped down the fretboard of an electric guitar.

The much covered 'Frankie and Johnny' told a similarly tragic tale and is certainly as worthy of an album devoted to its many different scorings as the one actually issued in the 1980s devoted to 'Louie Louie'. When a Mississippi work song of the nineteenth century, the couple were Frankie and *Albert* – and the scarlet lady Nellie Bligh, became Alice Fry in some later versions. The outcome of Frankie's enraged shooting of her perfidious boyfriend varies too. Lonnie Donegan invokes her mother's understanding that 'there's no damn good

---

* So effective was the group's stage enactment of the number that there were serious discussions with a film company about a full length movie (to co-star Esther and Abi Ofarim) based on the plot outlined in 'Legend of Xanadu'.

in men' while Brook Benton in 1961 – who begins in the middle and changes the locale to Broadway – makes a sympathetic chief-of-police say 'you should have shot him forty times' and offer to be a witness for the defence. Looking the camera straight in the eye in 1962's *It's Trad Dad*, Acker Bilk concocts the most unusual consequence of all with Frankie and the judge tying the knot and living happily ever after in a mansion with jazz-loving children.* With Donna Douglas and Elvis Presley in the title roles, *Frankie and Johnny The Movie* in 1966 had gambling rather than fornication as the source of Frankie's displeasure – but it would have been an odd Presley potboiler if it hadn't ended in a romantic clinch.

The prize for the most adventurous 'Frankie and Johnny' must go to Lena Horne, veteran of Harlem's Cotton Club. Starting from the point of arrest, a tolling bell heralds a conversation in which the policeman accedes to the bartender's 'Aw, let's have one more before you take her, officer.' Then follows a flashback which, via quasi-symphonic dynamics, shows Frankie buying a .44 from a pawn shop on espying Johnny and Nellie Bligh in Ma Rainey's brothel. The deed done, she recalls dying Johnny's private sweetness and implores that he be rolled 'over real easy because bullets are hurting him so', bringing her face to his ear to whisper, 'I'll be with you 'fore very long'.

There are only so many renderings of 'Frankie and Johnny', however fantastic, that you can take in one go so I'll leave off on a sour note with the worst. 1960's 'The New Frankie and Johnny' by Kenneth Earle was none the less, wholly in context in the film *Meet Me in*

---

* 'Frankie and Johnny' was also recorded by Gene Vincent who had a cameo in *It's Trad Dad*.

Las Vegas ('a large scale musical of almost stupefying banality' decided one critic). Nauseating with jive talk, Earle's version wasn't even original as Bobby Darin's similarly syncopated 'Clementine' had been on the air several months earlier.*

As open to interpretations as various as those for 'Frankie and Johnny' is 'Pistol Packin' Mama' who 'shot out the light' and pursued her errant man for having too much fun 'drinking beer in a cabaret'. If this evokes visions of either a pleasure-seeker with money to burn in 1930s Berlin or high-stepping, gartered choreography in a Dodge City saloon, the fount of its creation was not so exotic. Roadside cafe proprietor Mollie Jackson's husband and brother operated an illegal whiskey still in the Kentucky mountains. Armed with a pistol for protection, she'd drive the family car out to transport them home at weekends. It became customary for her to call them from the road, and Mr Jackson to reply, 'Lay that pistol down, Ma, or we ain't coming' – an exchange noted by Texan songwriter Al Dexter who frequented Mollie's place where, during lean periods, she'd feed him without charge on the understanding that he'd think of her when he was famous.

Accompanied by his Troopers, Dexter's 'Pistol Packin' Mama' was executed in 'western swing' style – 'hillbilly jazz' – in 1943 to sell a million and imprint Al in his outsized white stetson in the public eye. Before the year was out, Bing Crosby and the Andrews Sisters did as well with a call-and-response adaptation. It was overhauled radically seventeen years on by Gene Vincent

* Starting from scratch, George Jones and Bouleaux Bryant came up with 'Who Shot Sam', a variation on the 'Frankie and Johnny' theme. It was revived in 1963 by Merseybeat-cum-C & W outfit Sonny Webb and the Cascades.

and the Beat Boys,* his English backing combo, with an arrangement by Eddie Cochran, to become Gene's last Top Twenty strike.

A female whose blood was up also figures in the traditional 'Banks of the Ohio' by which she stabs 'the only man I loved' because he's not prepared to commit himself to a long-term relationship. Just like the killer of Delilah, she instantly regrets her rashness. Olivia Newton-John's 1971 hit with this jogalong item† became, retrospectively, all the more poignant in the light of her broken engagement with its co-producer, Bruce Welch of the Shadows. Sensitive at the best of times, he was prostrated, allegedly, by frightening paroxysms of grief.

It's the 'double-timing gal' that gets what's coming to her in Georgie Fame's 'The Telegram'. Rubbing salt into her boyfriend's wound regarding his poverty and unemployment she sends him a telegram, as now she has a new man she can afford it. Something snaps inside Georgie and he takes an axe to her. He recounts his folly during the subsequent trial 'to end my life of misery'. Didn't Tom Jones remind us in 1968‡ of how mocking 'Delilah' disturbed the balance of her man's mind too? 'I felt the knife in my hand and she laughed no more', he bellowed before pleading with the corpse for forgiveness just as the squad car arrived. In Waylon Jennings' 'Delia's Gone', the magistrate exercises leniency with

---

* With Georgie Fame on keyboards, guitarist Colin Green, Brian Locking (bass) and drummer Brian Bennett. The latter two were to join the Shadows in 1962. Slade recorded an in-concert version in 1980.
† Recorded in 1964 by Joan Baez.
‡ Seven years later, the Sensational Alex Harvey Band's 'Delilah' also entered the UK Top Ten.

only a custodial sentence for a man who ends a quarrel with some flighty piece by plugging her full of daylight. To the melody of 'The House of the Rising Sun', he makes an immediate pilgrimage to her graveside on release.

'Hey Joe' was a ballad from time immemorial that managed even more of a comeback than 'Banks of the Ohio'. On a par with 'Louie Louie' and Them's 'Gloria', it was a fixture in the repertoires of the Byrds, the Shadows of Knight, Marmalade and countless mid-1960s 'garage bands' throughout the world. Though the intention was to make it *not* sound like any other act's version, Tim Rose's arrangement was the blueprint for the Jimi Hendrix Experience's 'Hey Joe', the 1966 smash that set Hendrix on the path to international success.

With no pause to consider whether he might have been mistaken in shooting down his woman after he 'caught her messing around with another man', Joe hightails it 'way down south' to the Mexican border. Hounded to the same destination was another who'd likewise gone a little barmy with the 'guns made of metal forged by the Devil's hand' in 'Ride Ride Ride' by the Journeymen.

Once captured, this horseman and Joe might both have succumbed to Johnny Cash's 'Folsom Prison Blues' when sharing a cell with the 'frontier lad who lost his love when he turned bad' in the Everly Brothers' 'Take a Message to Mary'. He requires an unnamed friend to inform Mary that their betrothal is off for any reason other than the truth – that he's been sent down for the jolly old 'shot from a careless gun' routine during a stagecoach robbery.

Further along the corridor is one with but an hour left to him before execution. Knowing that his lover is only too cognisant with the situation, the Bee Gees, sentimental to the last, put the sentence 'I've Gotta Get a Message to You' into his mouth as the seconds tick by.

Conditions in the nick might have sparked off the insurrection rammed home by the Robins in 'Riot in Cell Block Number Nine* – which, like 'Framed' by the same 1950s vocal group, borrowed the tension-building riff from Muddy Waters' 'Hoochie Coochie Man'. An ill-advised dance 'at the local county gaol' led, in 1973, to another uprising so beyond control that National Guardsman Sergeant Baker was instructed by the governor to send reinforcements with rifles loaded with 10cc's 'Rubber Bullets'. Sadistically, Baker is disappointed that 'those slugs ain't real'. With his 'fool' grumblings and a neo-'baby' lead vocal, 'Rubber Bullets' was ostensibly a comedy record – even with lines like 'blood will flow to set you free' – but both it and 'Riot in Cell Block Number Nine' carried sociological implications (e.g., 'Uncle Sam is the one who belongs in the exercise yard').

In 1962's 'Don't Go Near the Indians', Rex Allen – a sort of Arizona 'answer' to Roy Rogers – took the scalping of his infant son by Yellow Sun, a Red Indian brave philosophically. Rather than bottling up his mingled sorrow and hatred, he gets even by abducting a child of near enough the same age from the tribe to rear as his own. The question of incest arises when the boy reaches puberty and declares his wish to wed Nola Lee, a redskin maid. Both are unaware that they are actually brother and sister. Gently, the foster father sits the lad

---

* Covers of this song by Dr Feelgood, Shakin' Stevens and the Sunsets and, in 1991, Mike Smith (ex-Dave Clark Five) were but the thin end of the wedge.

down and reveals their irregular kinship, consoling him with 'though you're a full-blooded Indian, son, I love you as much as my own little fellow that's dead'.*

The matter-of-fact 'Old Tige'-esque tenor of Rex's rootin'-tootin' monologue is such that you imagine that the youth accepted the impossibility of his marriage to Nola Lee as part of life's small change, and that matters between him and his doting guardian would be exactly the same as they'd always been.

It was flattery of a kind and a witness to longevity that 1961's 'Big Bad John' by Jimmy Dean was adapted (to 'big bad Dom') thirty years later to extol the virtues of Domestos. In form, it was a recited progenitor of 'Ringo' but John was not a man who defied the law – though hearsay had it that, during a punch-up over a 'Cajun Queen', he'd 'sent a Louisiana man to the Promised Land'. Perhaps because he was still starting at shadows, John preferred his own company but he was respected as a steady if reserved wielder of the shovel down the mine round which the community had grown. One day, the timber props of one particular tunnel gave way, shutting off John's gang from the surface. His mighty shoulders checked further collapse until rescue came from 'this man-made hell' – rescue, that is, for everyone except John who made the ultimate sacrifice, proving that he was 'big' of heart as well as physique – as the 'marble stand' erected in front of the closed shaft testified.

Coal from the late John's place of work might have powered the train driven by 'O'Brian the Brave Engineer', a 1962 rewrite by Karl Denver of 'Wreck of the Old

* The British cover version was by Lorne Gibson. It also prompted a spoof in Sheb Wooley's 'Don't Go Near the Eskimos'.

172

'97'. At their most rugged, the Four Pennies gave Leadbelly his due two years later in their Top Twenty update of his railway crash-insanity crossover, 'Black Girl'. Miming it on television, vocalist and rhythm guitarist Lionel Morton got so carried away that he abandoned his six-string altogether during the instrumental interlude, a display repeated during the Pennies' British tour with Freddie and the Dreamers, which followed a vexing attempt to shoot a promotional film for 'Black Girl' in Paris.

The industrial accident was similarly 'mined' in Robin Hall's *au naturel* 'Blantyre Explosion' and Alan Price's 'Trimdon Grange Explosion', written in 1882 as a 'whip round' song after a Durham mining catastrophe. A mordant 'Oranges and Lemons', Idris Davies and Pete Seeger's 'The Bells of Rhymney' served as a moritorium for a Welsh colliery disaster and the subsequent tribunal report about which 'even God is uneasy'. 'Put the vandals in Court' and 'all would be well if, if, if . . . ' are two other phrases that provoke further doubt.

The sepulchral echo of a recording complex's dark, twisting staircase after a late session, and news of the schoolchildren buried alive by a shifting slag heap in Aberfan in 1966 combined to inspire the Bee Gees' imaginary 'New York Mining Disaster 1941', the contemplations of a pitman trapped by a subterranean landslide.

When in 1968 *The Good the Bad and the Ugly* hoisted Clint Eastwood* to international acclaim – and Hugh

---

* Who'd played *Rawhide*'s 'Rowdy Yates', second-in-command to cattle herder 'Gil Favor' – actor Eric Fleming who was to drown in a river whilst on location for a movie set in South America.

Montenegro and his Orchestra to the top of the British hit parade with its title tune – all ocarina, electronic mouth-organ and wordless, grunted vocals, it started a vogue for spaghetti westerns with sound tracks that matched the action shot for shot. Thus Hugo was well-placed to secure the commission for the follow-up, *Hang 'Em High*. Its theme, however, had some of its thunder stolen by a version from Booker T and the MGs. Nevertheless, Montenegro was hired again for 'Man with No Name' Eastwood's *Dollars* films for which he conducted pieces such as 'The Vice of Killing', 'Sixty Seconds To What?' and 'Almost Dead'.

It is a common misconception that Georgie Fame's 'The Ballad of Bonnie and Clyde' was in the film – when its actual theme music was a bluegrass breakdown by banjo-pickin' Lester Flatt and Earl Scruggs. His income depending on the day-to-day mundanities of record sales, Georgie's opportunism (complete with machine-gun sound effects) paid off with the biggest smash of his career – but another London-based act, the Artwoods, missed the boat. Vocalist Arthur Wood realised that, hitless and poor, the group 'badly needed a gimmick'. Therefore, sniffing the wind, they re-christened themselves St Valentine's Day Massacre and rush-released an unrevised revival of the Depression anthem, 'Brother, Can You Spare a Dime'. This was gilded with a suitable wardrobe and stage presentation, a publicity stunt involving Faye Dunaway (who'd been 'Bonnie' in the flick) – and an abysmal distribution network which made the chances of making the Top Fifty slender.

The record was B-sided by the self-composed, 'Al's Party' – after Capone, the brains behind the historical Massacre on 14 February 1929 in Chicago. Mental pictures of similar carnage by wide-lapelled hitmen riding on the tail-boards of Buicks had already been evoked by 1948's 'Slaughter on Tenth Avenue'. Composed by Richard Rodgers for his own bio-pic (*Words and Music*), although its interweaving melodies weren't instantly hummable, it snowballed into a murderous mood whether by Sidney Torch and his Orchestra in the 1950s, as the title track to a 1974 album by Mick Ronson or by latter-day Yardbird John Knightsbridge, as adept a Jeff Beck stylist as Ronson.

A recipient of irrelevant notoriety because John Dillinger was watching it when he was chased and shot dead, 1934's *Manhattan Melodrama* movie also provided a title for a cordite-smelling saga by Shakin' Stevens and the Sunsets, and there were elements of this in Eno's 'Dead Finks Don't Talk' on 1974's *Here Come the Warm Jets*. Dipping into the same deadly pot-pourri, we might also pull out Marc Hoffman's French language 'Machine Gun Kelly' or David Machin's godawful 'Shoot Shoot Johnny' which, vocally, betrays an absorption of the worst aspects of David Bowie. Though it moved the clock forward from the Roaring Twenties, organised crime pervaded the 1964 James Bond thriller that put Shirley Bassey into the Top Thirties of both Britain and the States with 'Goldfinger', a vilification of 007's Latvian adversary with his 'kiss of death'.

Of greatest antiquity in the concrete-booted genre is Berthold Brecht and Kurt Weill's 'Moritat von Mackie Messer' from 1928's *Die Dreigroschenoper* or, if you prefer, 'Mack the Knife' from *The Threepenny Opera*. This prologue from the bi-centennial updating of John Gay's *Beggar's Opera** is sung by a Soho busker who

---

* A 1948 arrangement of *The Beggar's Opera* by Benjamin Britten is recommended.

summarises the eye-stretching exploits of Macheath (alias Messer), a wide boy lurking in the shadows to avoid recognition. Translated from Berlin street slang into English by Mark Blitzstein, its comparison of Messer to a shark, and mention of cement bags, a jack-knife and bodies bleeding in gutters indicate that Mac isn't small-time. There is also more than a suggestion that he's a devil with women too.

1956 was a boom year for 'Mack the Knife' in one form or another with four versions appearing in the US Top Forty in the same month via Louis Armstrong, Ella Fitzgerald, and, confusingly, of the twenty-odd other renderings, one by Dick Hyman (with a swing instrumental as 'Moritat') and another by Richard Hayman.

If that wasn't enough, Bobby Darin selected a jazzed-up 'Mack the Knife' for *That's All*, a 'sophisticated' 1959 album designed to turn him from the rock 'n' roll shouter of 'Splish Splash' and 'Queen of the Hop' into a coltish Sinatra. Booked for Dick Clark's *American Bandstand*, when Darin, with the confidence of the newly famous, remarked that he intended to début it on the show, its clean-cut host supposedly retorted, 'If you want to turn your career to chopped liver, so be it'. Clark was to eat his words when Bobby's polished 'Mack the Knife' lingered at the top of *Billboard*'s pop list for nearly two months.*

Bobby, however, never quite metamorphosed into a

---

* But the hits fizzled out in 1963 – bar 'If I Were a Carpenter' three years later. The artist also attempted a rebirth as a singer-songwriter *à la* Dylan, even calling himself Bob Darin for a spell – as disturbing in its way as, say, Mick Mouse, Tone Hancock or Frank Laine. On 20 December 1973, Darin died after an artificial heart-valve inserted two years earlier ceased functioning. In 1979, a reissue of 'Mack the Knife' rippled the UK chart – as did a 1984 version by King Kurt.

second Sinatra – but one who could have done so had he chosen was Scott Walker. It is less his perfect control of a golden-brown baritone that merits a paragraph here than his co-writing of the Walker Brothers' 'Deadlier Than the Male' – lethal beguilement by a wanton – for a distasteful 1966 movie of the same name in which a Goldfinger-like personality directed nubile henchpersons to captivate and then bump off an oil millionaire.

While their involvement in *Deadlier Than the Male* exacerbated the schism that would sunder the Brothers, a 1954 movie, *New Faces* – the old backstage plot – had been the making of Eartha Kitt whose first chart penetration was but a year away. However, it would not be with the film's novelty number, 'You Can't Chop Your Poppa Up in Massachusetts, Lizzie Borden'.* Hardly Hilaire Belloc, this nonsense was centred on a 'problem kid' whose naughtiness drove her Ma and Pa to bawl '"Lizzie, cut it out!", and that's exactly what she did'. On butchering her father, she exclaims a hope that he'll go to heaven 'because he wasn't wearing shoes'. I cannot go on . . .

* Other artistes who recorded this 1952 composition by Michael Brown include the Coronets, Billy Cotton and his Band and Penny Nicholls and the Canadians. US mental hospital inmate-turned-cult-celebrity Roky Ericson came up with a belated 'answer' disc in 'Chop Chop Away Lizzie Borden'. A charming Ericson ditty of the same vintage is 'I Love The Sound Of A Severed Head Bouncing Down The Staircase'.

Chapter Nine

Danse Macabre

If you can't be Elvis, be macabre. There's plenty you can do with red lipstick and liberal dollops of tomato ketchup – while twenty messy minutes with cold scrambled eggs, cherry food-dye and some old tights will result in glisteningly convincing intestines. Then you can pick up some musty, Bible-black funeral gear from a jumble sale, a coffin from a mortician's bankrupt stock and – to gild the image and transport the group and equipment – a cheap ambulance or hearse from a car auction.

It was Screamin' Jay Hawkins' inspired notion to have his road crew drop handfuls of rubber bands from the gallery and stage-whisper 'worms' during an act which began with his slow and sulphurous emergence from a coffin, bathed in eerie fluorescence. Garbed in, perhaps, a turban, zebra-striped formal attire and pink cloak, he would produce props like a cigarette-puffing skull mounted on a stick and an array of powdery potions, while his singing flitted fitfully through warbling mock-operatics, half-spoken recitative, insane falsetto shrieks, low grumbles – 'wurrrrrr' – and the raucous, blood-chilling dementia of someone in the throes of a fit. Some watching might remember a shy chap from Cleveland, Ohio, with a warm baritone not unlike that of Nat 'King' Cole's. Hawkins had also served a showbusiness apprenticeship honking tenor saxophone in various black dance bands before seizing command of his fate in 1953.

Sparkling among otherwise unastonishing early singles, 1954's 'She Put the Whammy on Me', provided the most blatant clue of what was to come.

After a further two years' thankless slog of one-nighters and flop records, Hawkins struck gold with 'I Put a Spell on You'. With the best of intentions, he'd bustled into the studio with a light, romantic ballad. The session wasn't going particularly well, and some liquor was purchased to loosen the tension. Several takes later, the song had mutated into the manic, goggle-eyed exorcism of a man so drunk that he was recording flat on his back.

The rest, as they say, is history. Refining his cartoon scariness, Hawkins became a treasure of classic rock, guaranteed well-paid work for as long as he could stand up. On the disc front, 'I Put a Spell on You', was virtually his only major hit – but royalties poured in from 1960s covers by the Animals, the Alan Price Set – the only version to breach Britain's Top Ten – Them, Nina Simone, the Crazy World of Arthur Brown and Creedence Clearwater Revival among others.* Reworkings of the formula included 'I Hear Voices', 'Feast of the Mau-Mau', 'Little Demon' and an inopportune 1980 remake of 'I Put a Spell on You' which, through Keith Richards' advocacy, landed Hawkins a support spot on a Rolling Stones US barnstormer. Better suited for the intimacy of theatre or club than stadiums designed for championship sport, Jay's subtleties were wasted on a mob impatient for the Stones, who chattered restlessly among themselves or headed for the toilets to partake of

* The Hawkins original was exhumed for the soundtrack of 1984's monochrome *Stranger in Paradise*. However, most of Jay's performance of the song in American *Hot Wax*, the 1978 film biography of Alan Freed, glided on to the cutting room floor.

whatever soft drugs were on offer. Most professionally, he flogged his time-honoured act for all it was worth until the usual smoke-filled exit and weak applause from an audience hardened by years of grosser excesses by Black Sabbath, Alice Cooper and others for whom Screamin' Jay's pioneering accomplishments had been received wisdom.

In the 1950s, Hawkins was the master of *pop macabre* – and possibly its only serious practitioner.* Nevertheless, among 45s keeping up with the adolescent craze for escapist horror movies were 'Screamin' Ball at Dracula Hall' by Brooklyn's Duponts, 1958's 'Frankenstein's Den' from the Hollywood Flames, the Frantics' 'Werewolf', 'Haunted House' by Johnny Fuller and 'The Creature (from a Science Fiction Movie)' by Buchanan† and Ancell. Among better-known artistes who dabbled were the Coasters with 'The Shadow Knows' – flop follow-up to 'Yakety Yak' – and a pseudonymous Frankie Ford who, as one of 'Morgus and the Ghouls', recorded 'Morgus the Magnificent', a novelty tribute to a Louisiana television personality of Vincent Price bent.

In Britain, we had 'Cool Gool' (*sic*), 'the ghost with the most', by Sharky Todd and his Monsters – session musicians earning their tea break – which was spun a lot on ITV's *Cool for Cats* by host Kent Walton who was later to drop this 'teenage rubbish' to become a wrestling commentator. A former grappler, Doctor Death ran the 2 I's, the Soho coffee bar that was the shrine of UK pop. Skifflers Harry Webb, Reg Smith and Terry Nelhams used to entertain there before changing their respective

---

* Although a Mr Undertaker recorded a one-off 45 on the Music City label entitled 'Here Lies Love'.

† Bill Buchanan also teamed up with Richard Goodman for 'Frankenstein of '59'.

names to Cliff Richard, Marty Wilde and Adam Faith. Receiving less immediate chart acclaim were such hit-makers of later eras as Spencer Davis, Gary Glitter and, all the way from Glasgow, Alex Harvey.

There was also a certain David Edward Sutch who one 1959 night had screwed himself up to climb on a pub stage to entertain drinkers with a parody of a pop star. With amused cheers still ringing in his ears, David decided to become the antithesis of the Presley lookalikes competing for Doctor Death's attention, after persuading a Sudbury instrumental outfit that, although he had originally intended to manage them, he could better serve as front man. Screaming Lord Sutch and the Horde of Savages' first paid booking at a Harrow working-men's club brought instant parochial notoriety. Following appearances at the 2 I's, some Sunday news-papers and a BBC documentary team homed in on Sutch, remarking mostly on his pre-Rolling Stones long hair – briefly dyed green – before mentioning the leopard skin loin cloth, the woad, a bath (for 'Splish Splash'), bull horns, monster feet, a collapsible cage, a caveman's club, the inevitable coffin and whatever else he'd laid his hands on in an endless effort to elicit career-sustaining publicity. On one occasion he performed with an alligator and on another with a Himalayan bear.

Sutch's routines on the boards verged on music-hall slapstick, embracing an 'operation' on a colleague with the wrenching out of heart and liver (bought from the butcher's that afternoon), and the simulated murder and mutilation of a 'prostitute', i.e., a Savage in wig and padded bra. In 1966, he underwent a temporary name change when, as 'Lord Caesar Sutch and the Roman Empire', he rode on stage in a chariot, resplendent in toga and laurel wreath, at a benefit for Johnny Kidd's widow.

Many nights were spent in police cells for sundry breaches of the peace, and he was barred from the Granada cinema circuit after plummeting through an organ during a rash jump from the footlights to the orchestra pit. And at Brand's Hatch, a dim view was taken of his Lordship pretending to black out at the steering wheel in the middle of a celebrity race (the old wooden overcoat was then sent out to collect the 'corpse').

The music, of course, came second. In 1960, he'd been discovered by Joe Meek who organised the début 45, 'Big Black Coffin' which had to be retitled ''Til the Following Night' to humour the record company. This set the pattern for future singles which were divided evenly between horror spoofs and rock 'n' roll ravers. 1963's 'Jack the Ripper' – 'nauseating trash' sneered *Melody Maker* – brought him closest to a hit. With David in full regalia and long-bladed dagger stalking Victorian tearsheets – extremely outrageous at the time – a promotional film found its way on to the short-lived 'Scorpitone', a video juke box prevalent in the early 1960s. I was present in Macari's cafe in Aldershot when two bus conductors spent their entire lunch hour and half a satchel of silver watching 'Jack the Ripper' repeatedly, their faces alight with the vacant ecstasy once reserved for public hangings.

While their point was frequently lost without accompanying visuals, the commercial progress of most Sutch A-sides was also hindered by restricted airplay, outright bans and many venues limiting entrance to his shows to the over-twenties. Yet, even cumulatively, the likes of 1963's 'Monster in Black Tights' – with its 'wrinkled-up chin where the worms have been' – 'She's Fallen in Love with the Monster Man', 'Dracula's Daughter', the self-composed 'All Black and Hairy', 'Wailing Sounds', the nine-minute 'Hands of Jack the Ripper', 'Monster Ball' and 1992's 'Murder in the Graveyard' were no more harmful than a ride on a fairground ghost train, even if isolated cases of fainting and hysteria were not unknown.*

Both in the studio and criss-crossing Europe in draughty, overloaded vans, Sutch was accompanied by many nascent stars, among them guitar icons Jeff Beck, Jimmy Page and Ritchie Blackmore. A host of renowned ex-Savages were the 'Heavy Friends' who turned out for their old boss after his part in a jam session at the Los Angeles Club, Thee Experience, led to a profitable two-album deal with Atlantic Records in 1970.

A lighter heavy friend, pianist and 'prostitute',† Paul Nicholas – future film and television actor – admitted that 'with David Sutch being more theatrical, I was learning another aspect of the business'. Before Sutch first visited the States during the fag-end of 1964's 'British Invasion', Alice Cooper were soberly attired, mop-topped Vince and the Spiders. Back home, acts in his artistic debt spanned decades from the Ghouls and the Mersey Monsters in the 1960s to the Damned who, even with a record in the Top Thirty, felt honoured one evening to bear Sutch's coffin onstage. In 1989 he assembled an eleven-piece band that included the late

---

* Composed by Joe Meek and Geoff Goddard, 'Monster in Black Tights' was a revision of 'Venus in Blue Jeans' (Mark Wynter's cover of Jimmy Clanton's US million-seller). 'All Black and Hairy' and 'She's Fallen in Love with the Monster Man' were revived, respectively, by North America's Gravediggers and Scotland's Revillos.
† His own words.

trombonist Don Lang and assorted ex-members of Deep Purple, Cliff Bennett's Rebel Rousers and – by a stretch of the imagination – the Rolling Stones* for a Hallowe'en engagement in the London Dungeons that was broadcast by BBC Radio One. Frowned upon by the Corporation in a more innocent age, the antics and music of the most renowned English pop singer who never had a hit could hardly have been witnessed in surroundings more blood-curdlingly appropriate.

'The Bloody' (a dance) coupled with 'Let There Be Fright' (some nonsense about psychedelic graveyards) might have been an attempt by a Doctor Shock to put himself forward as Sutch's colonial rival but, however funny their names, whatever their activities in concert, most US titans of trash ploughing the same furrow in the 1960s played it safe on vinyl with bandwagon-jumping covers and trite material in the style of the day. Naz Nomad and the Nightmares, for instance, gouged their deepest wound with a xerox of the Electric Prunes' 'I Had Too Much to Dream Last Night', and Cannibal and the Headhunters – all Latinate pompadours and olive complexions – went in mostly for discotheque fodder such as 'Land of 1,000 Dances' and the self-penned, non-horrifying 'Headhunters' Dance Party'; though, to give them credit, they whoop with glee at the gunfire effects and the 'shoot the boy running now' line in a retread of Junior Walker's 'Shotgun'.

Britain was also blessed with acts whose names were at odds with their output whether the remarkable Zombies, Ghost – a 'nice little band' of 'progressive' persua-

---

* Namely, drummer Carlo Little who stuck it out with Jagger and Co. for a fortnight before deciding that prospects with Sutch were more attractive.

sion – or Dickie Hart and the Palpitations with 1975's 'That's a No No', a sexual pilgrim's frustrated discourse. More agreeable than either of the latter two were the Undertakers, a pre-eminent Merseybeat combo whose recorded legacy was derived largely from the throat-tearing R & B motherlode resounding round local clubs and Hamburg 4. In 1964, their arrangement of Rosco Gordon's 'Just a Little Bit' had shown at No. 49 in the charts – not brilliant but enough to hold on hoping. Nevertheless, if their fans couldn't have cared less, middle-aged promoters and media executives were more than slightly aghast when, true to its name, the quintet rolled up in a hearse to walk on stage in frock coats and top hats with black crape to their 'Death March' signature tune. When subsequent discs fell short of the 'Just a Little Bit' precedent, the group mothballed some of its funerary trappings and abbreviated to the 'Takers. However, these concessions and a plug on ITV's *Thank Your Lucky Stars* in September 1964 for their version of the Drifters' 'If You Don't Come Back' – a tale of lovesick insanity, rarely heard over on BBC – won not even just a little bit more hit-parade action.

Although worlds away from the Undertakers, even the Beatles had been accused of theatrical morbidity. In 1966, Brian Epstein had had to calm friction over a US album, *Yesterday and Today*, with a jacket depicting the Moptop Mersey Marvels as white-smocked butchers jubilantly going about their grisly business. That heads and limbs of dolls were among the gory wares hadn't mattered when the picture was plastered across *Disc*'s front page to advertise 'Paperback Writer'. Such a scene was comic opera in a land that housed Madame Tussaud's Chamber of Horrors and Lord David Sutch – but, with boy soldiers already being blown to bits in

Indo-China, the 'butcher sleeve' was hurriedly withdrawn from circulation in the sensitive USA.

Should you bring out an overlooked copy at a vintage record fair, dealers will buzz round like wasps to a jam jar. At one such event recently, a friend of mine assisted a customer who was after a 45 in which 'this geezer keeps going on and on about fire'. The Crazy World of Arthur Brown had come into being in the watershed year of 1967 when philosophy graduate and cosmic ham Arthur teamed up with organist Vincent Crane and a drummer with the technicolour name of Drachen Theaker. The toast of London's psychedelic dungeons, the act was as good as it would ever get when the Crazy World 'went public' on gaining a recording contract. Robed and sporting a helmet spouting flames (originally a candlestick attached to a sieve), Brown had the vocal arsenal of a Screamin' Jay Hawkins as he cavorted and stared psychotically while Crane bucked and lunged at the keyboards, and Theaker toiled busily over his kit. Twice, things went dangerously awry and both Arthur's drapery and, indeed, a howling Arthur were set ablaze to ovations from cross-legged hippies who thought it was part of the act.*

The group nodded to prevailing trends on their first single with the droll 'Give Him a Flower' but its A-side, 'Devil's Grip', was a truer reflection of the Brown dialectic with its lyrical update of 'She Put the Whammy on Me'. After this created a stir, the Crazy World of Arthur Brown went for the jugular with 'Fire' – Arthur as 'god of hell-fire' will 'destroy all you've done' – a *tour de force* that was their only hit – a No. 1, mind – before a

---

* At the second and most critical fire mishap – in Windsor at a Bank Holiday festival – Brown was saved by some quick-thinking onlookers who doused him with ale.

troubled US tour finished with the resignations of Theaker and Crane.

The God of Hellfire fulfilled outstanding commitments with replacements while an album track, 'Nightmare', was pressed as a stopgap 45; its subsequent failure indicated how quickly crazy Arthur had become *passé*. Brown then travelled down many avenues – new bands, image transformation, an unrealised plan for a presentation with water where there had been fire, a part as the Priest in Ken Russell's *Tommy*, onstage nudity, meditation, entertaining Israeli troops with just a guitar and a musical reunion with Vince Crane.* Each led the same way – to a painting-and-decorating business in Texas and letting off steam with a casual weekend combo. En route, he recorded a revival of 'Endless Sleep' and, with Kingdom Come, *Galactic Zoo Dossier*, a 1971 LP reviewed in *Record Mirror* as 'a nightmare cacophony of horror', exemplified by 'Creation' with Arthur as the very monarch of hell.

If Arthur was its *de jure* ruler, the fiery furnace's *de facto* overlords by then were Black Sabbath whose climb to fame was possibly more interesting than what occurred afterwards. They were connected genealogically to a smart-suited Erdington beat group called the Rest. However, the individuals who would become Black Sabbath first found each other in Mythology, a 'progressive' unit who switched policy and name with the advent of the late 1960s blues boom.

The passing of this wave of British blues obliged the band to seek a new direction. Manager Jim Simpson sent them to win their spurs at Hamburg's Star-Club where the need to '*mak schau*' for hours on end toughened the

---

* A manic-depressive, Crane swallowed a fatal overdose of sleeping tablets on 15 February 1989. Arthur Brown attended the funeral.

unit – now renamed Black Sabbath – for less demanding but more reputable tasks back home. It was, reasoned Jim, 'rather like training a thousand metre runner by sending him on five thousand metre courses'.

When they returned from the Reeperbahn, Black Sabbath's blues had fermented into an apocalyptic brutality which, layered by Osbourne's straining attack, affected a bleak but atmospheric intensity. Sporting inverted crucifixes and similar Satanic fetishist gear, they were smashing out self-penned pieces like 'Hand of Doom', 'Behind the Walls of Sleep', 'Children of the Grave', 'Paranoid', 'Electric Funeral', 'Rat Salad', 'Into the Void' and so on – that exhibited bass player Terry Butler's fascination with the novels of Dennis Wheatley. As to the tunes, 'most of the numbers are based on a certain riff', explained Butler with quiet pride. 'We don't use a melody, just a raw type of riff.' Simpson described his clients' recitals as 'basic, dirty and bad. It is an honest interpretation of their environment' – meaning that it was a product of England's industrial hub where, fouling the air and waterways, the thick black fumes and chemical waste percolating from the conurbation's furnaces caked employees' poky dwellings with soot and grime as indelibly as Lady Macbeth's damned spot.

The début album, *Black Sabbath* 'shipped enough units' – mainly by word of mouth – to gain a toehold on the charts within a month of release before slinking to a gratifying No. 8. Suddenly, the band were plunged into an exhausting but exhilarating round of zig-zagging European tours, radio sessions and television spots. A single, 'Paranoid', shot into Top Fives throughout the continent while at the top of many listings was the second album. From the latter stemmed Black Sabbath's global success – particularly in the States.

However, the scum of internal dissent was allowed to surface. It boiled down to a clash between guitarist Tony Iommi and Ozzy. First of all, Osbourne did not subscribe to the maxim that if a thing's worth doing, it's worth doing pedantically, and the painstaking Iommi's constant retakes and overdubbing of minor guitar fills were starting to pall. Bored silly, Ozzy occupied himself with an increasing intake of hard drugs, booze, sexual adventure and other transient kicks such as drawing random beads on his farmyard chickens with a rifle until there were none left squawking. Soon he was as nutty as the character he assumed onstage during 'Paranoid' and 1976's 'Am I Going Insane'.

With Osbourne's departure in 1978, the group started catering more and more for the kind of consumer for whom the information that a favoured group's latest album is just like the one before is praise indeed. Sometimes, they'd hear sick-making stories about their old front man's incarceration in asylums and detoxification clinics as a result of his wallow in crapulous debauchery. Allegedly, he relieved himself wherever he felt like it – on the site of the Alamo (for which he was punished with lifelong exile from that district of Texas), and in a motel lift. While emptying his bowels loudly and abundantly, his cheery 'It's OK I'm staying here' did not assure other occupants who got out at the next floor. Somebody else swore that he'd brought a press conference to a standstill by biting off the head of a white dove and swallowing it. True or false, the multiplying legends boosted sales of Osbourne collections like *Diary of a Madman*, *The Ultimate Sin* and 1988's *No Peace for the Wicked* plus their retinue of 45s like 'Mr Crowley', 'Suicide Solution', and 'Bark at the Moon' with its video of Osbourne as a werewolf.

Formed in the light of Black Sabbath's initial flush of success, Black Widow's luck ran out much sooner. Leicester local lads Zoot Taylor (keyboards), Clive Jones (woodwinds), Robert Bond (bass), James Gannon (guitar), and Clive Box (drums), teamed up with Oxford vocalist Christopher Trevor to create a 'progressive' musical style. This featured an onstage Black Magic ceremony (involving a naked girl) and pieces like the audience-participation number 'Come to the Sabbat' – the 1970 single lifted from their début album. Through a sniffy *Rolling Stone* article, a public warning from noted white witch Alex Saunders and similar publicity, attendances at the group's engagements were healthy but gave false impressions of their market standing as diminishing returns for later products demonstrated.

By the time of Black Widow's disintegration, Lou Reed was well into his post-Velvet Underground career – though he himself admitted that the yardstick by which his subsequent work would always be measured was his music with that group* – especially the earlier stuff. From this canon came 'Femme Fatale', 'Venus in Furs', 'Heroin', 'The Black Angel's Death Song', 'The Gift'† and all the other *demi-monde* perspectives on 1966's sensational *Velvet Underground and Nico* and its follow-up *White Light White Heat*. Its emotive vocabulary slopped over on to Reed solo albums like 1973's depressing *Berlin*, a kind of junkie *Cathy Come Home* in which its

* Who re-formed briefly in 1990.
† In this opus, a hapless suitor mails himself to a heedless girlfriend, who inadvertently decapitates him while opening the parcel with a buzz-saw. It's not impossible that 'The Gift', more a short story than a song, was inspired by Woody Guthrie's harmless 'Mail Myself to You'.

squalid heroine kills herself after her children are taken into care. His next studio effort was *Sally Can't Dance* – because drugs were killing her.

By the mid-1970s, old Lou seemed to be living his lowlife songs as Ozzy Osbourne was living 'Paranoid'. Emaciated and a bit gaga in conversation, he became the focus of an unofficial pop press sweepstake with odds on that his would be the next Big Death. Onstage, he'd get out a syringe to simulate the process of mainlining during 'Heroin' – a substance he would later say he'd never touched. The observations of others repudiated this claim. His bristling thatch was patterned with dyed Iron Crosses, and his travelling companion was a person of indeterminate gender named Rachel.

Stoned bohemian one moment, arch conservative the next, the old monster appeared to have settled down in the 1980s to fidgety chamber recitals*, marriage and commuting to the Big Apple from rural contentment on a New Jersey farm, entering middle life as a fully integrated mainstay of the 'contemporary rock' mainstream, a nodding acquaintance of such as Bruce Springsteen, Phil Collins, Dire Straits – all the usual shower.

The same could almost be said of Dr John Creaux the Night Tripper, announced as 'the only doctor in the house' when collared by Ringo Starr for a 1991 nostalgia tour of North America with an All-Starr Band that also embraced ex-personnel from Springsteen's backing unit, the Band and the soporific Eagles†. Time was when Creaux's voodoo circus would traverse the continent and

---

* In 1991, Reed released *Magic and Loss*, an album much concerned with death through cancer.
† Not the 1960s British instrumental group of the same name.

191

beyond with reverberant zombie wails, sibilant lead vocals, throbbing murk and choreographed Creole psychedelia, jittery with timbales and wordless choral passages. Then Doctor John vanished back to the Louisiana swamps – and his alter-ego Mac Rebennack to studio employment in Los Angeles. That his image was not entirely contrived became evident when, on meeting New Orleans-born Rebennack socially, many would be charmed by his linguistic gymnastics. This mixture of English, Cajun and rhyming mumbo-jumbo had also bled on to 1970s albums like *Gris-Gris*, *Remedies*, *The Sun, the Moon and the Herbs* and 1972's *Gumbo*.

By 1980, he'd been beckoned towards more generalised pop and had even notched up an entry in the *Hot 100* as early as 1973 with 'Right Place Wrong Time' playing down his Night Tripper image. Nevertheless, he lugged his feathers, beaded head-dress, amulets to ward off evil spirits and the rest of the Dr John paraphernalia from the attic, and reminded himself of the words to 'Right Place Wrong Time' and, the most up-tempo excerpt from the newest album, Johnnie Ray's 'Such a Night'. He wouldn't let the All-Starrs down – and, in thirty cities, he pounded his Yamaha grand, thumped drums as necessary and, for his ordained minutes in the limelight, belted out the old *Gris-Gris* magic – even if nobody was getting any younger.*

* Some years before *Gris-Gris*, the undead were woven into the rich tapestry of popular song through the Del-Aires' 'Zombie Stomp', one of their contributions to 1964's *The Horror of Party Beach*, 'the worst movie of the last twelve months', according to *Newsweek*. A merging of radioactivity and drowned mariners' skeletons produce ocean demons who harry a shoreline shindig just as tanned adolescents in swimwear cut a rug to the bossa nova-ish doggerel of 'Zombie Stomp'. As harmless as 'Headhunters' Dance Party', it informs us that zombies leave holes in the ground when they jitterbug.

In his mid-forties, Alice Cooper had long been a wanted guest – ideally with trademark vaudeville ghoul makeup – on US television games shows and at pro-celebrity golf tournaments with the likes of Bob Hope. Incredible that he'd been a pariah once upon a time when he and his group had flared up at the zenith of the Arab Woodstock Generation drip-rock. No one then combined theatre, androgyny, cheapness and thrills more effectively than Alice Cooper: glam-rock from the charnel house. In its fullest flowering, the crux of a stage show as slickly contrived as any Broadway musical was that, like Mr Punch, Alice got sentenced to death – via gallows, guillotine or electric chair – for all manner of felonies committed from the opening bars of the set. There were a lot of funny activities involving whips, dolls, chickens and a boa constrictor. The repellant fascination induced tended to distract attention from the quality of the music.

Much of it was borrowed – a Black Sabbath riff here, a muttered Lou Reed mannerism there – but, welded together, it amounted to a melodic, controlled strand of heavy metal underpinning a witty if gruesome lyricism summed up in titles such as 'Black Juju', 'Under My Wheels', 'Halo of Flies', 'Dead Babies' and, violating the ultimate sex taboo, 'I Love the Dead'. From 1971's *Love it to Death*, 'The Ballad of Dwight Fry' plunged into the lethal insanity of a real-life Hollywood actor whose speciality was ill-favoured underlings, sinister butlers and creepy bit-parts in general. Finally, he turned into a composite of them all.

Less madcap elder brother than batty uncle these days, Alice can still spice up a riveting presentation of good-old-good-ones with newer material such as

'Poison', a single that was a breath away from a Britis
No. 1 in 1989.

The bulk of orders for 'Poison' and suchlike were o
compact disc, a format of such clarity that, strainin
your ears just a little, you could almost make out th
impact of dandruff grains falling from a guitarist's spl
ends. Those of the old school liked a smudge of grac
saving dirt on their records – and they didn't come muc
dirtier than the archaic Cramps who went in for 'psych
billy' or 'Gothic punk', a collision of rockabilly an
psychedelia.

Because they dispensed with the previously obligator
bass guitar, many believed there was something missin
from the music – and that the Cramps themselves we
a brick short of a load on the strength of the lurid *non
de guerre* they gave themselves. With singer Lux Interio
guitarist Poison Ivy and drummer Nick Knox there f
the duration, Kid Congo, Fur, Touch Hazard an
Griensnatch were among a movable feast of secon
guitarists. The first of these, however, kept his ordinar
name but made up for it with a vengeance. As much th
public face of the Cramps as Interior, Bryan Gregor
radiated alarm with a penetrating stare, a half-whi
shock of hair and sunken, pock-marked cheeks. As othe
would collect stamps or old coins, publicity had it th
Bryan would scoop and bag dirt from the graveyard
every town the quartet worked. When he quit in 198
it was put about that he'd become a wizard.

The Cramps had enough going for them for Gregory
exit to be but a minor set-back. Unfettered by slicknes
the instrumentalists revelled in rudimentary chord-slash
ing, indifference towards tonality, kitsch visuals and th
impression that everything could fall to bits at an
second. Meanwhile, Interior lurched about the stag

oug-eyed with veins jutting on his neck, embroidering his fluttering *wellawellawella* vibrato with yelps, hiccups, high-pitched whines and foghorn bass as an initially gawping crowd tuned into his awareness of his own absurdity.

If based in New York, the group's deepest musical roots lay in the good-bad rawness of white-trash Southern rockabilly – the blues with acne – but, as composers, they chose not to get all that 'gone' on simplistic hep-cat couplets about clothes, lust, violence and doin' the Ooby Dooby with all o' your might. Instead, they delved into darkness with the ilk of 'I Was a Teenage Werewolf', 'The Surfin' Dead'*, 'Zombie Dance', 'I Ain't Nothin' but a Gorehound', 'Strychnine', 'Voodoo Idol', 'Aloha from Hell', and, on the other side of the coin, beatific 'Kizmiaz ('where everyone lays around in the clouds in a happy daze'). The Cramps were tasteful in their choice of covers too: Link Wray's 'Rumble', the Trashmen's 'Surfin' Bird', 'The Crusher' from the Novas and the Count Five's 'Psychotic Reaction'.

The packaging of 1986's *A Date with Elvis* – their first on compact disc – somehow encapsulated the Cramps' stance. Dedicated to the memory of Ricky Nelson, it was dominated by a diabolical Bunny girl on silken sheets littered with transparent plates of club sandwich, and publications of a mystical and religious nature. They were probably the last rock 'n' roll group. Unlike Reed, Cooper, Dr John *et al*, the group did not go soft or crave the attention of showbiz proper. Continually pressing on the nerve of how far they could take it, their shows

Recorded for the soundtrack of 1986's *The Return of the Living Dead*.

would climax with Lux stripped naked amid urine-hue
lights and clangorous, stomach-churning discords. Wel
I mean, he had a penis, hadn't he?

Bass player Captain Sensible of the Damned had on
too. It was there for all the world to see on the fron
page of *Sounds* after he had strolled on starkers at
London venue in 1977 when punk rock was fresh out o
shock tactics.

The Damned were in at the beginning, getting
record out weeks before the Pistols did. Though the ga
was swiftly closed and numbers such as 'Stretcher Cas
Baby' and 'Problem Child' fought shy of the charts, th
Damned outlasted most rivals by reconstructing them
selves along more commercial lines. By 1986, they wer
smooth enough to chalk up their biggest hit with 'Eloise
lovingly copied from Barry Ryan's string-laden 196
original. In its way, such a volte-face was as much th
apotheosis of punk nihilism as the self-immolation of Si
Vicious. Virtually all that remained intact from the day
of 'Stretcher Case Baby' were artifices like the talcur
powder that drummer Rat Scabies sprinkled on his skin
to shroud him in musky clouds before the end of th
opening number. The vocalist, Dave Vanian was sti
conducting interviews from his dimly lit flat with sound
tracks to horror films wafting in the background. Resen
bling a youthful Grandad Munster, this forme
gravedigger cut a vesperal figure in undertaker's attire
black-rimmed eyes, bat necklace and a skeleton trinke
dangling from one ear.

He was hardly the first Man in Black. Building on th
precedence of Johnny Cash, Roy Orbison and Dav
Berry, later monochrome misters such as Lou Reed (wh
pioneered black lipstick for men), Alvin Stardust, th
Stranglers and Vanian affected a sullen introspectio

196

offstage as well. The Who's John Entwistle went through this phase for a while. In the midst of the group's 'Anyway Anyhow Anywhere' finale of smashed amplifiers, smoke bombs, flares and feedback lament, he'd be stock-still with a countenance like a Tyneside winter, quietly ministering to overall effect with extrapolations of the song's principal riff.

A superb bass guitarist, John was also the outfit's second-string composer – and if you can't be first, be peculiar. A minority of listeners found his macabre, cynical creations the most attractive aspect of the Who. Indeed, the discerning Jimi Hendrix's favourite Who track was Entwistle's 'Boris the Spider', squashed against the wall while climbing in *A Quick One* – in which the hallucinating alcoholic of John's 'Whiskey Man' was condemned to a padded cell. You cannot easily dismiss a man who wrote pop ditties about miserliness ('Silas Stingy'), voyeurism ('The Window Shopper'), a deserted husband threatening suicide from a skyscraper ledge ('Thinkin' It Over'), and an insurance swindle via a faked death ('I Found Out'). That the boy had talent was emphasised further by his invention of a challenge to the Twist in 'Do the Dangle' – from the neck after you've kicked away the chair 'and you're dancing on air'. This was a highlight of the first LP by John's splinter group, Rigor Mortis – with a gatefold sleeve monopolised by a grave on the inside (with a headstone 'in loving memory of rock 'n' roll) and a coffin lid without.

The cover of Captain Beefheart and his Magic Band's *Trout Mask Replica* portrayed the combo's leader wearing one. On this double-album, Beefheart presents us with 'The Blimp' – a portentous shape roaming the countryside for human prey – 'Pachuco Cadaver' and 'Bill's

197

Corpse' – featuring his bloated 'goldfish in the bowl' and 'plains . . . bleached with white skeletons'.

Just as mordantly surreal as Beefheart, Scott Walker sank his teeth into the regrouped Walker Brothers' *Nite Flights** with the same relish as he had Jacques Brel's sordid 'Jackie' or 'Next'. As tortuous as the Brothers' 'The Electrician', which described the goings-on in a torture chamber – 'where lights are low' – Scott's title track is riven with pain – 'broken necks', 'raw meat fists', 'stitches torn and broke', 'blood light' – but worse was to come in a 1984 solo album. One critic cited *Climate of Hunter* as the wellspring of 'the most terminal songs ever written' – and you can understand why. Like cattle marked for the abattoir – or the soldiers queueing in 'Next' – most of Scott's compositions have numbers rather than names. It's just as well with some of them – especially 'Track Seven'. Otherwise, would you request a disc jockey to spin something called 'Stump of a Drowner'? Yet, because it's Scott Walker and not Bobby 'Boris' Pickett singing, it's not the musical equivalent of a video nasty. It might even be Art.

When Walker was at large in Hollywood in the early 1960s as bass guitarist with the Routers (a Ventures-style instrumental unit), Pickett had been a comedy actor while moonlighting in the Cordials vocal group. He was also making a go of it as a composer. All Bobby's professional skills coalesced on the 1962 narrative, 'Monster Mash', co-produced by the Hollywood Argyles†

---

* Needle time was divided in three so that each Brother wrote four songs each. Gary and John Walker chipped in with such as 'Death of Romance' and John Walker's 'Disciples of Death', 'Fury and the Fire' and 'Child of Flames', but, if similar in style, these did not acquire scratches and surface hiss as quickly as Scott's contributions.
† Their biggest smash was with 'Alley-Oop'. Its hook-line, 'look a

vocalist Gary Paxton whose latest 45 was 'Spooky Movies'. Couched in the inveterate I-VI minor- IV-V chord sequence with a standard 'middle eight' or bridge passage, it was as clichéd lyrically as, with responses from a skittish girlie chorus (the Crypt-Kickers), Pickett in a venerable Boris Karloff 'mad scientist' mode name-checks Wolfman, Igor, Dracula and other stock horror movie characters who are revellers at a dance party in Frankenstein's laboratory.

The timeless 'Monster Mash' was a US No. 1 in 1962 and, preceded by a plethora of minor chart re-entries over the years, sold a million all over again in 1973 after a radio presenter on a Milwaukee station started airing it seemingly non-stop. Other stations picked up on 'Monster Mash'* and, like a ghost from the recent past, Pickett and his dispersed touring revue reappeared on television as the monster rose once more from its slab into international Top Tens.

In the interim, Bobby had squeezed every drop of blood from 'Monster Mash' with an itinerant show of diluted Screamin' Jay Hawkins bent, and all manner of soundalike follow-ups: 'Monster's Holiday' (a Yuletide crossover), 'Sinister Stomp', quasi-instrumental

---

that caveman go', was adapted by David Bowie for his 1973 hit, 'Life on Mars'. An ancestor of Captain Beefheart's 'The Blimp', this humorous semi-spoken lope was covered by Dante and the Evergreens and the Dinosaurs among others. In Britain, it was done by Brian Poole and the Tremeloes – with an extrapolated reference to cartoon characters Pixie and Dixie – and in camper fashion by the Bonzo Dog Doo-Dah Band. Among less successful Argyles discs was 'You Been Torturing Me'.
* Notable revivals in the meantime had been those of the Beach Boys - recited in concert by their resident buffoon Mike Love in a green spotlight – and the Bonzo Dog Doo-Dah Band. Dare I suggest that the latter's version was an improvement on Pickett's?

'Transylvanian Twist' and the 1964 double-header 'The Monster Swim'/'The Werewolf Watusi'. He even brought to life 'Rabian – The Fiendage Idol' (werewolf protégé of Count Dracula who Frankenstein hopes will make him 'the Dick Clark of all the undead'). Overloading his artistic canvas, Pickett kept plugging away with Igor's machinations to work nights in 'Graveyard Shift', a thirsty Dracula in 'Bloodbank Blues', and a paean to a decomposing Egyptian lover with 1968's 'Me and My Mummy'.

1958's 'The Purple People Eater' incited a comparable quantity of rehashes – but these weren't by its originator Sheb Wooley who had played Pete Nolan – the steady older man in *Rawhide*. Not as uncertain of acceptance by humankind as the Blimp, the Purple People Eater – 'the thing a-coming out of the sky' – is willing to suspend its anti-social dietary requirements to achieve membership of a rock 'n' roll band, demonstrating its qualifications for the post with topical musical vignettes from 'Tutti Frutti', 'Tequila' and the Hollywood Argyles' 'Short Shorts'.

For whatever reason, Wooley's effort caught on to the extent that it was certified as the fastest-selling novelty disc of the previous five years. A mania took hold. Merchandisers moved in, and high-street stores were rampant with Purple People Eater hats, Purple People Eater badges, Purple People Eater T-shirts, dolls, pillows, nail-clippers, ironing-board covers, powder compacts, you name it. The Big Bopper tried to catch the lightning with 'The Purple People Eater Meets the Witch Doctor'.* Then there was 'The Cuban Purple People

* 'Witch Doctor' had been a US No. 1 for Chipmunk führer David Seville a few months earlier. It was overtaken in the British charts by a cover by Don Lang and his 'Frantic' Five.

Eater' (in cha-cha-cha rhythm) and the Yiddish 'Purple Herring Fresser'. As late as 1966, Screaming Lord Sutch placed the wretched creature in Swingin' London, and it was still going strong in the 1980s with television comedian Russ Abbott's 'The Purple People Eater Meets the Space Invaders'.

In the same season as Wooley's hit, the climb of John Zacherle's 'Dinner with Drac' up the *Hot 100* was grudgingly tabulated by a *Billboard*, blitzed by actively hostile disgust within the industry at Zacherle's tastelessness. Today, his clumsy limericks to a rock 'n' roll beat are no worse than any that might draw an embarrassed titter but no walk-outs in an after-dinner speech at Chequers but, in the late-1950s, they got the record banned in a Britain so prudish it would oblige Billy Fury to moderate his sub-Elvis gyrations.

Slipping such a net with ease, Geoff Goddard's tame rock 'n' roll party in 'Dracula's Castle' was sung in an odd London-Greek accent by Mike Sarne. In any case, it was buried on a 1962 album which failed to live up to market expectations. Therefore, ears corruptible or easily offended by the wireless were unlikely to learn of how the Count's guests 'drained the blood from their glasses' until dawn when a sexton's bells tolled 'The Death March', and 'back to their tombs they ran'.

Don't expect too much either of 1957's bland 'Zombie Jamboree (Back to Back)' by Nassau's Vincent Martin and the Bahamians. With a title also promising more than is actually delivered, 'Frankenstein', a mildly unsettling synthesiser instrumental by the Edgar Winter Group, owed its name to the copious editing it needed. Originally a B-side from 1972's *They Only Come Out at Night*, it captured the US public's imagination for probably the same inexplicable reasons in microcosm as 'The Purple People Eater'.

Me? From the very year of Wooley's triumph, I would recommend 'Lord Rockingham Meets the Monster' by Lord Rockingham's XI, the *Oh Boy!* house band, as possibly the greatest horror instrumental of all time, man. Part of the melody line is carried by voices and some electronically doctored caterwauling. Against dubbed audience hysteria from *Oh Boy!*, there are also rhythmically interpolated end-of-the-world screams and ogres' laughter ('hoo-hoo-hah-hah-hoo') leading up to what sounds like the Monster itself on the rampage amongst the girls in the front rows. 'Goodnight, children everywhere!', it croaks gratingly like a bestial Uncle Mac in a sudden lull before wreaking further havoc in the gallery.

While dishing out praise, I ought to note 1966's 'The Eggplant That Ate Chicago' by Dr West's Medicine Show and Junk Band*, David Bowie-as-Bill Sykes in 1981's 'Scary Monsters (and Super Creeps)' (with the line 'I love that little girl and I'll love her till the day she dies'), the bump-and-grind of 'I Eat Cannibals' by the all-female Toto Coelo (and their 'Dracula's Tango' the follow-up that didn't make it) – and, also from 1982, Visage's† 'Damned Don't Cry' in which train carriages

* Through whose ranks passed Norman Greenbaum who, in 1970, recorded the million-selling neo-spiritual 'Spirit in the Sky' and its follow-up – unpopular with pigs – 'Canned Ham'. Eighteen years later, 'Spirit in the Sky' bounced back to No. 1 in Britain when revived by Doctor and the Medics.
† With Chrissie Hynde and drummer Vince Ely (respectively, future members of the Pretenders and the Psychedelic Furs), Visage's Steve Strange was one of the Moors Murderers, a combo whose very name provoked controversial tabloid coverage – though its recording career progressed no further than demo tapes.

hurtle to oblivion through blackened landscapes. Not as freighted with symbolism is 'My Guitar Wants to Kill Your Mama' from *Weasels Ripped My Flesh* by Frank Zappa's Mothers of Invention who'd closed their début album, *Freak Out*, with twelve minutes of 'The Return of the Son of Monster Magnet', an 'unfinished ballet in two tableaux'. The first of these was 'Ritual Dance of the Child Killer' but it was hard to tell where it ended and the next one began because, commensurate with the record's blanket title, the whole track was simply the group and its hangers-on babbling and shrieking inanities while bashing around any old how on a couple of hundred dollars' worth of rented percussion equipment – an aural action painting.

Zappa acolyte and Los Angeles street busker Wild Man Fischer's unaccompanied repertoire included 'Who Did it Johnny', a third degree in a police interrogation room with him singing the parts of the inspector, the panicking prime suspect and a third party who, implicated for the homicide of Mary Ann by the frantic accused, placidly ripostes, 'Well, if he says I did it, I did it'. In another role on the same double-album, Fischer – a bona fide screwball by all accounts – is the one responsible for 'Miss Jennifer Jones . . . lying dead on my porch'.

Concluding our chronologically illogical round-up of creditable one-shot stabs at horror, we arrive at the title track of Michael Jackson's *Thriller* for which Vincent Price was hired for a cameo as the piece's undead, blood-lusting lurker-in-the-night with a rap – about 'grizzly ghouls', 'hounds of hell' and so forth – that dissolves into maniacal chuckling. 'Hanky Panky' bubblegum practitioners Tommy James and the Shondells crossed the same divide as Jackson from teenyboppers to adult stars when they 'went progressive' in the late 1960s. On 1969's *Cellophane Symphony*, they came up with an explicitly unbubblegum stanza (in 'I Know Who I Am') about a fellow suffering with 'chapped lips from eating too many potato chips'. The vocalist then cracks up with unkind merriment 'when he smiled at me and almost bled to death'.

Chapter Ten

Spirits Drifting

After Mick Jagger's oration for Brian Jones at Hyde Park and the freeing of the butterflies, the Rolling Stones dived into a two hour set which ended with 'Sympathy for the Devil' augmented by Ginger Johnston's African Drummers. During the play-out, Mick was already motoring across the Serpentine, bound for Ned Kelly's Australia and more lurid headlines concerning a girl and drugs. The girl was Marianne Faithfull and the drugs she took were Tuinals for sleeping off the jet-lag in Sydney's Chevron hotel. Lying next to an already sleeping Jagger, her thoughts were racing as she watched herself tip the tablets into her hand and send them down her neck with gulps of drinking chocolate. Soon, she was chatting to the late Brian until he slipped away forever. From a velvet-blue oblivion, Marianne came round in hospital in the thick of inserted tubes and drips, with the feeling that she had stood on a bridge crossing a limbo between the here and the hereafter.

She didn't speak about the experience in public let alone sing about it but there had been and would be myriad other artists probing the afterlife in popular song. Steve Winwood, a creative helpmate on Marianne's *Broken English* of 1979, had done so on Traffic's 'Dream Gerrard' (*sic*). This had been galvanised by a quatrain written by his house guest, Vivian Stanshall, after reading a biography of French surrealist poet, Gérard de

Nerval whose investigations into the symbolism of his own dreams were interrupted periodically by his committal to mental institutions until 1855 when he was found hanged from a Parisian lamppost. Reacting to both the aesthetic spirit of Stanshall's lines and de Nerval's vulnerability, 'Dream Gerrard' was opaque with cinematic mellotron which, juxtaposed with dissonant piano and immovable eight-note insertions on saxophone, conveyed all the other-worldly deliberation of a dream's slow motion.

Also a semi-instrumental grown from an abstract poem, Procol Harum's 'Glimpses of Nirvana' captured a similar mood – as did the group's fiercer and wordless 'Repent Walpurgis'. Even more incorporeal was Eno's 'Spirits Drifting' which, in its sparse arrangement, evoked vaporous souls in gossamer robes roving aimlessly beneath the chamber of the moon before fading at cock crow. More stylised willies were on offer in 'The Supernatural', an instrumental from John Mayall's Bluesbreakers, showcasing the sustained, resonant shivers of guitarist Peter Green. A counter-tenor vibrato had served the same purpose on 'Esquerita and the Voola' by Esquerita, once a pretender to Little Richard's throne.

An also-ran British outfit of the early 1960s, the Raiders, cast a less self-centred spell in 1960 following an audition for Joe Meek in a Muswell Hill church hall. They were quite amenable to the Great Man's insistence that they get rid of their vocalist – sixteen-year-old Rod Stewart – as Meek was specifically after an instrumental unit to record an opus entitled 'Night of the Vampire'. Remoulded as the Moontrekkers, the four-piece's acquiescence yielded one week at No. 50 in the charts, and a BBC ban because of the single's disconcerting sound effects (creaking coffin lid, howling wind and a scream from Mr Meek himself*). When a second 45, 'There's Something at the Bottom of the Well' did not improve on this achievement, half the group left, and the others muddled on with replacements to go out in a blaze of glory when a 1963 single rocketed into Sweden's Top Ten.

Other instrumentals with post-existence appellatives were usually much of a muchness as demonstrated by 1967's 'Spooky' by Classics IV or the Phantom Chords' throwaway 'Ghost Train' (which sounded more appealing when I accidentally spun it at 33 r.p.m.). Renowned Los Angeles session musician Plas Johnson's soundtrack LP to *The Addams Family* suited this television series' status as a poor man's *Munsters* in spite of titles like 'Morticia's Theme', 'One Little, Two Little, Three Little Tombstones' and 'Hide and Go Shriek'. Just as middle-of-the-road was George Martin's production of 'Hell's Bells' by Alyn Ainsworth and his Rock-A-Fellas. As expected, tubular bells turn up too in, well, *Tubular Bells* by Mike Oldfield from which the eeriest section was used as incidental music in 1973's *The Exorcist*, as over-valued in celluloid circles as Oldfield's 'work' was in pop. Yet *Tubular Bells* was the single biggest influence on Clifford White, Jon Land and other leviathans of today's New Age music – often derided unfairly as aural wall-paper and purchased with the same discrimination as you would three pounds of spuds.

'Under Your Thumb' (1981) by Godley and Creme has a female suicide's spectral form, perfume and voice

* Thriftily, Joe had grafted exactly the same collage on to Screaming Lord Sutch's 'Til the Following Night' a few weeks earlier. Why waste good noise?

bothering a gentleman sheltering from the rain in the derelict and stationary train that had been in service when the lady had flung herself from it.* The Devil himself had been, in 1956, the engineer of the Ken Colyer Skiffle Group's 'Down Bound Train' with a brimstone lamp, sulphur fumes and further scarifying details filling a passenger's tipsy imaginings during a journey under a sky as leaden and slashed by lightning as that in 'Under Your Thumb'.

That September, Old Nick had been up against Gene Vincent's dragster in 'Race with the Devil' with lyrics as appropriately incomprehensible and breathless as a thrill-packed hot-rod rally commentary.

The Prince of Darkness – or someone who told you he was – stood unchallenged by co-stars on such records as 1982's 'The Number of the Beast' – 666 – by Iron Maiden, who understood as much about decadent Edwardian sorcerer Aleister Crowley as Ozzy Osbourne did in his contemporaneous 'Mr Crowley'. Neo-paganism had become a turn-of-the-decade craze in teenage Britain like the Twist had been in a wider world. It was kinda groovy to be a Goth, wearing all the Dave Vanian gear and having strategically dog-eared Crowley publications strewn artlessly around your bedroom. Dropping buzz-words from *Moonchild*, *Diary of a Drug Fiend* or something else you'd got stuck halfway through was all very well but how much more fun to hold giggly seances and hang about in graveyards and ancient monuments the way Teddy Boys used to hang around in Expresso bars.

* As you might imagine from an in-demand audio-visual production team like Godley and Creme, this single was attended by a remarkable video.

The Rolling Stones had been there long ago when 'the blitzkrieg raged and the bodies stank' in 1969's 'Sympathy for the Devil'* – though diabolism had been present in the title and cover of the previous year's *Their Satanic Majesties Request*, and the group had acquired a rather over-attentive fan in movie-making Crowley disciple Kenneth Anger who wished to cast them in his screen adaptation of Dennis Wheatley's *Lucifer Rising*.

French director Jean-Luc Godard was more successful at securing the Stones' agreement for him to film the studio sessions for the fateful 'Sympathy for the Devil' as part of a drama-documentary he was compiling. As the number developed, so wordsmith Jagger's Lucifer surfaced as an elegant figure ostensibly on the fringe of events but sufficiently well-placed to stir kettles of fish for private amusement whether, say, as a face in the crowd at Golgotha for the Crucifixion, as a footpad waylaying crusaders, in conference with Hitler or behind the steering wheel of JFK's Lincoln limousine in Dallas.†

'Altamont' named after the Stones' disastrous free concert near San Francisco in 1969 (where a fan perished with multiple knife wounds) was one of the selections on *666*, a double-concept album by Aphrodite's Child, a Greek combo that was to spawn two solo attractions in Vangelis and Demis Roussos. While these

* Of which two versions (one in-concert) were officially released. It was covered on record by Sandie Shaw and revived in almost 'Monster Mash' fashion by Bryan Ferry in 1973.
† The Stones recorded a kind of sequel to 'Sympathy for the Devil' in 'Dancing with Mr D', first track on 1973's *Goat's Head Soup*. By coincidence, the engineer for the block-booked sessions became so ill with a digestive complaint that he was unable to finish. Producer Jimmy Miller was also infected but managed to complete the job – he never worked with the group again.

serious-minded young adults' grasp of English was admirable, they relied principally on complex instrumental passages, leaving *666*'s British guest speaker, John Forst, to pick the bones of meaning from an oblique metaphysical libretto about the Day of Doom, Babylon, the Four Horsemen of the Apocalypse, the Beast, and souls crying as the Earth trembles, the sea turns black, the air to poison, and the sun 'hotless' . . .*

666 and Scott Walker's *Scott 4*† each contained the title, 'The Seventh Seal'. Of the two, Scott's was by far the most accessible. Instead of Aphrodite's Child's fussy approximation of Japanese *koto* twanging behind Forst's act*o*rish recitation, Walker employed acoustic guitar, thudding snare drum on the off-beat, and a male voice choir going 'aaaaaah' to accommodate his straightforward account of the action in Ingmar Bergman's 1957 film, *The Seventh Seal*. This opens, like Scott's song, with the famous cliff-top scene of a knight in chainmail hunched over a chessboard as Death, with shadowed cowl, hourglass and scythe arrives for him. Scott narrates the metaphorical game between them, during which the knight unwittingly confides 'my life's a vain pursuit of meaningless miles'. The final move is made and Death, the inevitable victor, conducts the silhouettes of the hero and his entourage across a thundery dawn sky.

A town decimated by plague, a witch at the stake and barley as high as the hedgerows might be lyrical snapshots of mediaeval feudalism in which both the lowliest peasant and the Pope are united by religion and super-

---

* Carrying more lyrical *avoirdupois* but catching a similar if less intense drift, Colosseum's *Daughter of Time* was out in the same year as *666*.

† For which Scott reverted to his real surname of Engel.

stitious fear of what the Almighty's verdict might be on the day of reckoning. Translations into a modern context veer from the Doors' laboriously rhymed 'Riders on the Storm' – a sort of morose plea to make the best of transient life – to the Faustian 'Sinner's Dream' (1954) by Eugene Fox, mad with fright as Judgement Day approaches. Backed only by a sluggish, heavily reverberated guitar and outbursts of female sobbing, he promises to mend his ways, raising his voice Screamin' Jay Hawkins-style to a tormented shriek, then dropping to forbidding near-inaudibility.

Women, he implies, were among the main protagonists in his fall from grace. Various of Satan's concubines broomsticked into the charts, whether in 1966's 'Witches Brew' by Janie Jones at No. 46 or Redbone's 'Witch Queen of New Orleans' which got to No. 2 in 1971. Honourable flops included Them's 'Mystic Eyes' – seen 'down by the old graveyard' in an excerpt from a jam – and the Status Quo shuffle of 1981's 'In the Coven' from Dozy, Beaky, Mick and Tich minus Dave Dee. Had this been extant thirteen years earlier, with Dee rather than Dozy on lead vocal, it might have fared better commercially. With previous dramas ranging from tropical islands ('Zabadak!') to the high seas that wrecked the 'Antoinette', why not hellfire caves?

The hag-ridden hit most likely to trip off Mr Average's tongue is Hamburg's Rattles 1970 million-seller, 'The Witch'. This had been a domestic smash two years earlier just as the quartet was brought to its knees by compulsory army service and other external factors. The leader, Hans Hilderbrandt rallied by taking a tenacious backseat as producer, composer and general *éminence grise* to a new Rattles enlisted in Italy and fronted by a pulchritudinous Israeli singer with the stage name,

Edna. 'The Witch' was remade with English lyrics to soar into the UK Top Ten. The Rattles also entered the US *Hot 100*. They were, however, unable to secure a lasting place in foreign hearts, and soon returned to the West German circuit of engagements.

Flying by a more conventional mode of transport than a broomstick, the first-person narrator of 'I'm Mandy Fly Me' ends up in the drink via the nosediving of a passenger jet in the 1976 single from 10cc. This charming air hostess, not only saves him from the sharks but seems to walk on the waves to render the kiss of life 'just like the girl in Dr No' on top of providing – no, anticipating – every comfort during the flight. Unconscious, he is picked up by the coastguard but of her there is no sign. Studying her face on the airline's travel poster shortly afterwards, he debates whether it had all been a crazy dream but, if it had, how come he lived to sing the tale?*

A less altruistic mystery girl – 'Laurie' – saved the last dance for Dickey Lee, and had him rubbing his hands in anticipation of a tryst beneath the stars. Whether intimacy took place is unstated – probably not, as the weather was sufficiently inclement for her to borrow his sweater. After bidding her goodnight, the cold compels him to return to her house for the garment. Answering the door, her father wonders if Dickey's request is some sick prank as dear Laurie died exactly a year ago – and

---

* Four years earlier, the failure of 10cc's second 45, 'Johnny Don't Do It' had been blamed on the hit reissue of the Shangri-Las' 'Leader of the Pack' which also had a motorbike accident in it. The following year, the English group recorded 'Ships Don't Disappear in the Night (Do They?)', a ponderous musical discussion about whether events in horror fiction on film or in books can happen in real life.

on her birthday, too. Chastened but puzzled, the lad hastens to the cemetery where, sure enough, the sweater is draped across Laurie's tombstone. With understatement atypical of a plain-speaking son of Tennessee, he ponders that 'strange things happen in this world', like a professorial character in the concluding frame of a cartoon strip in *Creepy Worlds*.*

Before she popped off, did Laurie knit 'This Pullover' as worn by Jess Conrad 'until eternity'? And is there a launderette up there? So we near the bourne from which no traveller returns – you know, heaven, shangri-la, paradise, nirvana, Burl Ives' 'Big Rock Candy Mountain' with its lemonade springs and cigarette trees (not unlike Moses' 'Sugarcandy Mountain' in George Orwell's *Animal Farm*).

The valley of the 'White Buffalo' – which begins and ends with Red Indian babble – is where you'll go 'if your heart is good and true', sang New York City's C & W king, Bill Hayes†. No, you won't, reckoned Vaughn Monroe, it'll be 'My Isle of Golden Dreams'. Peter and Gordon, however, put their money on the 'Land of Oden', one thousand miles in the air where a single day lasts as long as it takes for a bird to wear away a mountain by sharpening its beak on it once every million years.

Are we really in for Pat Boone's 'Wonderful Time Up There'‡? It depends, I suppose, on your idea of fun.

* Lee was the originator of 'Patches', another sob-story but not the same one as the 1970 hit of the same name – composed by General Johnson of the Chairmen of the Board – by blind soulman Clarence Carter.
† Who recorded 'Message From James Dean' – about the hazards of careless driving – in 1956.
‡ Which was his second-highest UK chart placing. Alvin Stardust's born-again version ascended to No. 56 in 1981.

For some it was sitting in bohemian 'pads' listening beneath Che Guevara's bereted gaze to John Fahey. Prudently, *The Transfiguration of Blind Joe Death* had been packaged with a booklet – in seventeenth-century script – feventeenth-century fcript – containing a baffling and surreal account of a young Fahey's dealings with the sightless Joe, and a sleeve glutted with mortified symbolism with a track listing that included 'St Patrick's Hymn', 'I Am the Resurrection' and 'The Death of the Clayton Peacock'.*

Who the hell was this John Fahey anyway? Even if he couldn't get all his fingers going at once on the fretboard – and was a mesmerically ugly vocalist – Bob Dylan could shut Fahey down without effort as the single most reclusive and messianic effigy of hipness. Fans quoted Dylan's lyrics as if they were proverbs – such as 'there are no truths outside the gates of Eden'. When he recovered from his motorcycle crash, however, Bob's verses became less like hard work.

Little he penned after 1966 was as pared down and direct as 'Knockin' on Heaven's Door'†, a sombre three-chord chartbuster that sparkled amongst the incidental music realised by Dylan while playing an apposite role as 'Alias' in Sam Peckenpah's *Pat Garrett and Billy the Kid*. The most moving sequence in this idiosyncratically gory flick is when 'Knockin' on Heaven's Door'‡ sound-

* The death disc buff ought to be aware that earlier Fahey albums such as *Blind Joe Death*, *Death Chants*, *Breakdowns and Military Waltzes* and *Dance of Death* are all in more or less the same vein.
† As was Arthur Brown's one-line lyric to 1975's 'Is There Nothing Beyond God?'.
‡ Eric Clapton liked it enough to record it for a reggae-style 45 two years later. Ry Cooder recorded the traditional 'Billy the Kid' – the 'boy bandit king' who killed his first man at the age of twelve – for 1972's *Into the Purple Valley*.

tracks an elderly lawman smiling a lip-biting valediction at the fading image of his wife – 'Ma' – as he stands knee-deep in a horsepond at midday, mortally wounded by the Kid's bullets.

Many were surprised to learn in a 1986 interview that Charles Aznavour – mistakenly supposed to be utterly square – completely mesmerised Bob Dylan at a Carnegie Hall concert. Yet the artistic gap between the two was not unbreachable. For instance, if Bob knocked on heaven's door, Charles was on 'Le Chemin de l'Eternité' or – 'ow you say – 'The Road to Eternity' where 'I'll be free, no longer bound'* – just like those past the checkpoint to Dylan's 'Gates of Eden'. It would not, however, do the diminutive Frenchman justice to start a crash-course in his music with 'The Road to Eternity', crass album ballast in which he marches through the pearly gates to the blare of Billy Cotton brass, remembering, of course, to take off his shoes beforehand for fear 'they might leave footprints in the sky'.

* Also the sentiment expressed in Jon Hiseman's libretto to 'Downhill and Shadows', final vocal track on Colosseum's *Daughter of Time*. Its singer, Chris Farlowe would likewise service Jimmy Page's soundtrack to 1982's *Death Wish II*.

Chapter Eleven

Where All the Flowers Went

War is wrong. I mean, like, people get *killed*, you know.

And how has pop reacted to this? The easiest option – especially in the mid-1960s – was with one-size-fits-all protest songs which meant that you could make arm-sweeping dismissals without having to know any specific background about Wipers, Dunkirk, the nuclear arms race, east-west-black-white confrontations, Vietnam or anything else that had made eyes glaze over at the monotony of history and current affairs lessons at school. Beneath desk-top level, you could be stealing illicit squints at *War Picture Library*, *Record Mirror* or selected passages from *Lady Chatterley's Lover*.

That weekend, you might be shuffling about in the gloom past the burning spotlights in a local palais to, say, the Downliners Sect who, requested to play something smoochy, could oblige with the 1965 A-side, 'Bad Storm Coming' – a euphemism for impending nuclear holocaust – written by their Don Craine whilst a pupil at Gunnersbury Grammar. An undeserved flop, its contemplations induced a perverse aftertaste of enjoyable depression via the juxtaposition of minor key restraint with lines such as 'the land will crack and crumble' and 'what future can exist for you and me?'.

In the same situation, Manfred Mann may have slowed things down with 'With God on Our Side' from their 1965 EP, *The One in the Middle*. They brought an edition of *Ready Steady Go* to a standstill with this Bob Dylan number – the first of many they recorded. Its morning-assembly hymn quality was as arresting as its 'controversial' anti-war content that chronicled largely North American history from when 'the Indians died' up to when 'we forgave the Germans'.

During a 1963 residency at Hamburg's Star-Club, the Searchers had serviced dancers weary of the Twist with 'Where Have All the Flowers Gone' – a circular narrative like a serious 'There's a Hole in My Bucket' – which was an ideal forum for their trademark finger-picking of two electric guitars and distinctive melodic four-part harmonies, developed over hundreds of hours onstage. These characteristics were the richest legacies given by the Liverpudlians to their transatlantic cousins, the Byrds.

Once nicknamed 'America's tuning fork', Pete Seeger had been motivated to write 'Where Have All the Flowers Gone' by a passage in Mikhail Sholokhov's *And Quiet Flows the Don*. I've never read it either but it – and similar literature that failed to subscribe to the view that war is nature's pruning stick – did the rounds in New York's vibrant beatnik district, Greenwich Village, *circa* 1961 when the civil rights movement had fused with topical folk song to be labelled 'protest'. The prolific Seeger's singalong ditties – 'If I Had a Hammer', 'We Shall Overcome' and all the others – were among its party pieces, and Peter, Paul and Mary the house band. Therefore, as inevitable as Valentino's recording of 'Kashmiri Song' was the trio's of 'Where Have All the Flowers Gone'*. While their light commercial style was

* With 'Falling in Love Again' and 'Lili Marlene', it was also the opus most readily associated with the late film actress, Marlene Dietrich. In 1965, her German version – 'Sagt Mir Wo die Blumen Sind' – was revived by Joan Baez.

similar to that of Britain's Springfields – whose panda-eyed vocalist Dusty was to achieve spectacular solo success – Peter, Paul and Mary were instrumental in popularising material by hard-core folk performers who otherwise might never have accrued more than a cult following. They first intruded upon the UK Top Twenty, for example, with the then king of protest Dylan's plaintive 'Blowing In The Wind' with its punch-line about people getting killed in wars. They and their wholesome, twinkly-guitar sort also brought the likes of his 'A Hard Rain's A-Gonna Fall'* – about the effects of atomic fall-out – and Tom Paxton's 'hilarious' 'That's What I Learned in School?'† to a wider public who'd be ready to take their medicine neater as the actuality of the Vietnam war gripped around 1965, protest's golden year.

The hunt was on then for Dylan clones. These sprouted thickest in the States where a typical record company talent scout would be briefed to grab another pea from the same pod.

Dunhill Records got lucky after a fashion with professional Hollywood tunesmith P. F. Sloan who'd shrewdly switched from advertising jingles and surf output for such as Jan and Dean to protest with the album *Songs of Our Times* – the counterfeit Dylan period piece. Yet Sloan made it big only by proxy when Barry

* Rudely reawoken by Bryan Ferry in 1973 as a Top Ten single. However, on the boards, Ferry needed a written prompt for the fast-flowing, image-laden syllables of his 'Ha-ha-ha-ha-ha-hard Rain's A-Gonna Fall'.
† Which, when sung by Pete Seeger at a Carnegie Hall concert in 1963, capsized the audience with sardonic *bon mots* like 'soldiers seldom die' 'that war is not so bad'. It was included on *We Shall Overcome*, the LP souvenir of the event. Please steel yourself before listening, lest you verily become injured with thigh-slapping mirth.

McGuire, a gruff ex-New Christy Minstrel with a sartorial predilection for jackboots, topped the US *Hot 100* with his all-purpose, anti-everything 'Eve of Destruction' in which 'even the Jordan river has bodies floating' (to rhyme with 'what's that gun you're toting'). Though derided as 'phoney' by Mick Jagger, it struck the right chord because protest was all the rage in 1965. Also unfurling from an introductory guitar jangle and doomy thuds of timpani, 'it's a great sound', enthused singing undergraduate Jonathan King, 'Since when has pop music been a vehicle for sincerity?' He should know. Barry himself protested that 'it's not exactly a protest song. It's merely a song about current events' – like the Watts riots which got the record the elbow on all Los Angeles stations because King Mob was more likely to take heed of McGuire than informed opinion in a newspaper. There again, why should any one of Barry's young minds 'old enough to kill but not for voting' matter to a politician in office any more than it did to the Congressman who told Eddie Cochran, 'Sorry, son, but you're too young to vote' in 'Summertime Blues'?

McGuire's follow-up, Sloan's 'Upon a Painted Ocean', didn't matter to very many – though, if released first, it might have been the hit rather than 'Eve of Destruction'*. Nevertheless, protest had set in motion the restoration of North America as the storm centre of pop. From Britain, a crumpled Scot named Donovan began a virtual residency on *Ready Steady Go* as a more beatific disciple of Godhead Dylan. His one great gesture in the protest direction was with the *Universal Soldier* EP which, like *The One in the Middle*, sold enough to enter the

---

* Which was revived with no lyrical updating by the Pretty Things in 1987.

singles list. One more naive – if the least opportunist – addition to 1965's pile of anti-war tracts, its title number was written by Buffy Sainte-Marie, another Greenwich Village sage, and was attended by a promotional film with Donovan wandering round World War II battle sites in France. Printed howls of rage on *The Times* letters page from a few retired admirals and brigadiers about this scruffy young pacifist who'd escaped national service was but more grist to the publicity mill. In the States, as well as a cover of Donovan's cover by Glen Campbell, Jan of Jan and Dean came up with an 'answer' in 'The Universal Coward'.

The American War of Independence recruiting song, 'When Johnny Comes Marching Home Again'* had long been warped to suit the anti-war movement as 'Johnny I Hardly Knew Ye'. A description of a youth returning from the Pacific theatre as a limbless, 'eyeless, noseless, chickenless egg' after 'the enemy nearly slew you', it reared up again in 1966 when revived by two Irish acts, the Feis Eirelann choir and the Clancy Brothers and Tommy Makem. A touch of the Ould Sod is prevalent too in Scott Walker's 'Hero of the War' when, to a neo-Bo Diddley rhythm, 'Mrs Reilly' – widowed in the previous war – shows off her mutilated soldier son's medals to the neighbours, though the proverbial girl-next-door is nowhere to be found.

Sparing us the uncomfortable details of reality until the last verse, the Yardbirds used the metaphor of toys for 1967's war-fevered 'Little Soldier Boy' who fell from the mantelpiece into the fire 'after one last triumphant

---

* Recorded by artists as disparate as Glenn Miller and Adam Faith – who tramped into the UK Top Five with it in 1960. His amended chorus contained the line, 'we'll give him a swinging welcome then, oh yeah, oh yeah'.

cry'. That same year, Tim Buckley employed bomb sound effects when looking at 'the war inside your mind' for 'No Man Can Find the War' on his début album.*

Even though it was a subject too impersonal for most drip-rockers†, 1970 proved a silver age for pieces about war in general for former performers and clientele of the celebrated Ealing blues club of the early 1960s – whether Colosseum with their bitty 'Three Score and Ten Amen' ('they take the young and teach them death but call it bravery') or the Rolling Stones and 'Gimme Shelter'‡.

Non-specific wars in pop were thin on the ground in the 1980s. Mary Black's 'My Youngest Son Came Home Today' ('in a box of polished pine') trod familiar ground while The Dancing Did's rat-a-tat-tatting 'The Lost Platoon' was a kind of pluralised Universal Soldier in that the said body was present at every armed conflict since time immemorial – 'up Roman roads, down Saxon tracks . . . through Puritan towns'. Messerschmitts zoom overhead, 'torsos lie in cathedrals', and, for good measure, the Dancing Did chucked in strident snatches of 'Lillibulero' which, attributed to Purcell, was the march whistled and sung by the Prince of Orange's forces as they dethroned James II in 1688.

Jumping back through the past, we're up against the

* At a party on 24 June 1975, twenty-eight-year-old Buckley mistook a mixture of heroin and morphine for less harmful cocaine. The next day, he was found dead in his Santa Monica home.

† Although James Taylor penned 'Soldiers', which wasn't too bad, I suppose – but it was improved upon by the Keeper's Gate Band as part of a 1984 medley with 'When Johnny Comes Marching Home Again' and Tim Brooks' 'Far From Home' ('with every man an enemy').

‡ Which provoked versions by Merry Clayton – who'd duetted with Mick Jagger on the original – and also Grand Funk Railroad. The Stones' instrumental introit resurfaced in an ITV commercial for an automobile breakdown and relay service.

sweeping cavaliers-and-roundheads violins of 'Soldier's Song' which, in 1980, gave the Hollies their first sniff at the charts in many a long year.

'The Battle of New Orleans' was celebrated with a hillbilly fiddle tune to which singer Jimmy Driftwood added words for a well-received performance at 1959's Newport Folk Festival. It was then seized and recorded for the pop market by Johnny Horton and, over the water, by Lonnie Donegan who weathered charges of disloyalty for profiteering from the scrap in which – as he rubbed it in during the introductory dialogue – we 'blooming British' 'didn't do no good no how'.

For all his gorblimey chirpiness, Donegan had been born a Scot. So, more obviously, had been wee Andy Stewart who, until a freak hit wth a reissued 'Donald, Where's Your Troosers' in 1989, scored but once in the Top Twenty – with 1960's 'A Scottish Soldier'. Like Driftwood, he'd grafted lyrics on to a traditional melody, 'Green Hills of Tyrol'. To tear-jerking effect, a warrior in the late evening of his life accepts that a corner of a foreign field will be forever Scotland, and so bids the regimental piper to blow a pibroch refrain for him back home. Striking while the iron was lukewarm, Andy was back in the hit parade to lesser effect a few months later with 'The Battle Is O'er' – after 'some fell in their hour of glory'.

There were plenty more poor fools like that in the American Civil War of 1861. When the cannon smoke cleared, 'it took days to count the dead' in Johnny Horton's 'Johnny Reb' but, if his colleagues' high opinion of his pluck meant more to him than the ultimate Confederate defeat, then Reb 'didn't die in vain'. In a wider sense, neither did the martyred abolitionist whose incitement of Negro slaves to down tools led to the war in the first place. In his honour, Germany's Lords set 'John Brown's Body' to a perky pseudo-reggae jerk with leitmotifs from 'The Star-Spangled Banner' and Tchaikovsky's *1812* plus a side-serving of explosions and gunshot whinnying. Mouldering in his grave? I expect Brown was revolving in it.*

The futility of it all was expressed through small lives – and deaths. Because 'a cannonball don't pay no mind', sang Tom Jones, only one of 'Two Brothers' ('one wore blue, one wore grey') came back. In an exact replica of Johnny Cash's lowdown growl, P. J. Proby – backed by a nascent Led Zeppelin – was a rifleman pondering that 'Today I Killed a Man I Didn't Know'. From Nottingham, the lace-making county town that lent them their name, Paper Lace's victory in *Opportunity Knocks*, the ITV talent contest series, was accomplished with another Civil War saga, 'Billy Don't Be a Hero' – called to arms, a Southern boy is begged by his intended to reconsider – their passport to a chartbuster. Hopes of duplicating this feat in a potentially more receptive North America, however, were dashed via a sly cover – with some fine-tuning lyrically from P. F. Sloan's erstwhile partner, Steve Barri – by the obscure Bo Donaldson and the Heywoods.

The Civil War was a fount of many more such sagas about women bearing the harder burden while their men go gallivanting off when duty calls. The most potent of these was Cindy Walker's blood-and-thunder 'Distant Drums' with the telling line, 'love me now for now is all the time there may be'. Relegated to a 1963 flip-side by

* Sung to 'The Battle Hymn of the American Republic', 'John Brown's Body' has been disseminated in many forms. One of the most popular has been the barrack-room ballad 'He Jumped Without a Parachute from Forty Thousand Feet'.

Roy Orbison, it was a posthumous UK No. 1 for Jim Reeves three years later.* The bloodiest clash of the whole war was 'In the Hills of Sholoh' as lilted by Barry McGuire (when still a New Christy Minstrel). Common to this and 1967's 'Suzannah's Still Alive' by Dave Davies is a lady ritually awaiting her man's return years after he's been missing, presumed dead.

Onward to the war-to-end-all-wars, and we might be viewing Florida's Royal Guardsmen's aerial dogfight of 'Snoopy Versus the Red Baron', i.e., Charles Schulz's cartoon mutt and Maurice von Richthofen†, the Fokker E-2 ace. In the Great War's trenches, there was less avenue for even the weakest humour as exemplified in 1969's chilling 'Butcher's Tale' by the Zombies, and Dave Clark and Friends' 'Officer McKirk'.

As if the British government hadn't enough on its plate, the Easter uprising in 1916 began the Troubles in Ireland which have continued, on and off, ever since. Hardly any music commenting on the situation has been supportive of England's stance. The very essence of it was distilled by the Clancy Brothers and Tommy Makem on the rowdy Dublin concert album *Freedom's Sons*. The theme is stated in the opening 'Outlawed Raparee' – 'I'm England's foe! I'm Ireland's friend!' – and the rapt audience is further charged with the rightness of the good old cause with the likes of bellicose

* In 1968, a version by Tex Ritter was released.
† Who brought down over eighty Allied aeroplanes in a single year. He met his match, however, in April 1918 when he was killed in action. He would have been even less flattered by the Royal Guardsmen's bubblegum commemoration in 1966 – and their predictable 'Return of the Red Baron' follow-up – than by the unpleasing portrayal of him in the film *The Blue Max*, on general release the same year.

'Green in the Green' (alias 'The Merry Ploughboy'*) and the incorporation of a reading from W. B. Yeats' 'Easter 1916' in a medley acknowledging the 50th jubilee of the occasion.

Mostly, the message was administered with boisterous, dare I say harmless, humour. Dating from 1939, even 'The Old Alarm Clock' with its talk of gelignite 'to make the people dance' might drag a puffy smile from the most xenophobic loyalist when emitted from the corncrake-toned vocal chords of the Dubliners' Ronnie Drew – and it was also the way Dominic Behan told 'em in 'The Patriot Game' (derived from the traditional 'The Merry Month of May') where one fighting 'John Bull's tyranny' puts a good face on the realisation that 'my body's all holes'.

It would've been hard for either the Dubliners or the Clancy boys to extract much hilarity from Belfast punk quartet, Stiff Little Fingers' 'Suspect Device' or 'Alternative Ulster'. As the Dubliners would combine with the Pogues for a Top Ten single in 1987, this might not be as ridiculous as it appears. Nevertheless, more typical fare for the older outfits was 'Roddy Mac Corley' where he 'goes to die on the bridge of Toon today'. Forever on BBC television's Welsh language pop programme, *Disc a Dawn*, the dour Hennessys demonstrated solidarity with fellow Celts by waxing 'Roddy Mac Corley' *and* 'Hoist Down the Flag', a litany of other republicans executed by the army.

Many young Irish resolved matters by renouncing allegiance to both the Emerald Isle and Great Britain, and emigrating to the States – even if national service

---

* As it was when recorded by the Dubliners – though it was 'The Jolly Ploughboy' when done by the Tinkers.

was compulsory for all its male citizens, naturalised or not. In World War II, exiled Irishmen found themselves on the same side as the English anyway.

US servicemen who were also musicians might be with luck attached to regimental bands and choirs whose presence in the turmoil of battle was not required. The cream of these would amalgamate as the United States Army Chorus and Band to churn out official songs pertinent to particular military sub-groups – using the same tune with modified lyrics. A prime example is that written for the chemical corps which argues that 'every other corps is tops in its own way but the chemical corps is where we want to stay' – you know, manufacturing, say, a new brand of nerve gas to make the enemy sicker quicker.

Nazi Germany too had signature tunes like 'Wenn die SS und die SA Aufmarschiert' ('When the SS and SA March Away') for each of its base and combat divisions as well as singalong oompah exultancies directed at bolstering national pride and the fixed idea of conquest. 'Heil Hitler Dir' ('Hail Hitler to Thee'), the disturbingly stirring 'Horst Wessel Lied'* and, for the children, 'Die Jugend Marschiert' ('Youth on the March') were all included, along with speeches by the twentieth-century Attila himself, and members of his high command pleading 'Not Guilty' at Nuremberg on *Hitler's Inferno*, 'words and music of Nazi Germany', issued on North America's

* Supposedly a staunch National Socialist who died in heroic circumstances, Wessel was actually a pimp (and songwriter) shot in the mouth for stealing another's mistress. During the five weeks he lay dying, his fictional life story was serialised in a national newspaper and one of his compositions, 'Die Fahne Hoch' ('Raise The Banner') – which predicted that 'soon Hitler banners will wave over the barricades' – was adopted to conclude party meetings before coming into general use.

Audio Rarities label. The Fatherland's own Dokumenta-Serie company had big-selling smashes on its hands in the 1970s with the spoken word *Adolf Hitler* and four more of the Führer's solo albums. To which South American address were the royalties sent, I wonder?

Hitler's war had inspired both mainstream and avant-garde music for orchestra. Too stubbornly chromatic and extreme of pitch to be even remotely connected to pop – despite some novel sonic effects – the post-serialist Krzysztof Penderecki's powerful and unpretentious 'Threnody for the Victims of Hiroshima' (1960) must, nevertheless, be mentioned because it may well have influenced Penderecki admirers like Frank Zappa, Steve Winwood, and Robbie Robertson, the leader of the Band.

David Bowie's 'Warszawa' of 1977 exuded a ponderous outpouring of modern desolation concerning the after-math. Singing in an imaginary tongue over a stately organ-dominated track, the piece was clinically devised with Brian Eno to Bowie's 'emotive, almost religious' specifications.

As unlikely to get everyone out on the dance floor, Throbbing Gristle's 'Zyclon B Zombie'* was a formless electronic scream-up – not that far removed from the opening bars of Penderecki's threnody – released as a B-side postscript to this late 1970s *nouvelle vague* combo's début album, *Second Annual Report*, emblazoned with the ticker 'Nothing Short of Total War',† and subtitled *Music From the Death Factory*.

---

* Zyclon was a type of gas discharged to implement the Final Solution.

† Front man Genesis P. Orridge sported a T-shirt with the legend 'Nuclear War Now!' printed on it. Throbbing Gristle's second LP, *D0A The Third and Final Report* contained 'Death Threats' which incorporated unpleasant messages left on the group's Ansafone.

Other attempts to give tongue to the genocidal atrocities included 1967's 'Auschwitz' by Equipe 84 and 'Dachau Blues' ('those poor Jews') from Captain Beefheart and his Magic Band. However, the motive behind the two versions – sung respectively by Johnny Rotten and Great Train Robber Ronald Biggs – of the Sex Pistols' 'Belsen Was a Gas' was principally to touch up the group's outrageous reputation as they slid into self-parody.

Though German propaganda stressed that concentration camps were introduced by the British during the Boer War, there were, advisedly, few pieces criticising the victors' conduct while overrunning the Fatherland. The means whereby Japan's surrender was attained – notably the mushroom-shaped shadow cast across the country on 6 August 1945 – were, however, the subject of slow-burning 'Memories of Hiroshima', an excerpt from the soundtrack to 1973's *Man From the East* – a tableau of Nippon history as seen through the eyes of a beggar – by Stomu Yamash'ta's Red Buddha Theatre. Apart from its intrusive 'rock' electric guitar squitterings, 'Memories of Hiroshima' is as moving in its way as 'Warszawa'.

The sinking of the Reich's mightiest battleship by the British fleet in 1941 was chronicled in 1960's stiff upper-lip movie, *Sink the Bismarck!*, which, in turn, enthralled Johnny Horton – or so it said on the record label – who, within weeks of seeing it, had co-written and recorded a 45 of the same title. The lyrics were bombastic and convoluted but the square-bashing snare rolls, the barking non-melody and Johnny's hayseed Texan drawl cut through the song's shortcomings, and listeners are transported to the North Sea too, sure rounded by oily waves with shells 'as big as trees' whizzing past their ears 'on that fatal day'.*

Another countrified Johnny – Cash – accorded a tattered grandeur to a Red Indian marine in the cautionary 'Ballad of Ira Hayes'. As the underdog among but a handful of survivors of another Second World War shoot-out on the azure main, Hayes almost believed he *was* a hero as great as Lysander when he received the lion's share of admiration back home. For a while, everyone clamoured to hear him retell his story but when they tired of it, he hit the bottle until the night when 'two inches in a lonely ditch was a grave for Ira Hayes'.

At least he'd been in a sufficiently unfit state to be exempted from the Korean stalemate in the early 1950s. *M.A.S.H.*, 1970's blood-soaked film comedy from a Mobile Army Surgical Hospital out there lived on via subsequent television series – and relentless Radio One plugging by presenter Noel Edmonds made a 'sleeper' UK No. 1 in 1980 of its 'Theme from M.A.S.H. (Suicide is Painless)'† by Mash, an act with no existence beyond the studio. In one ear and out the other, the disc's success had less to do with any intrinsic quality than the popularity of the show which was screened on BBC2 at the same time as *The Nine O'Clock News* on the other Corporation channel.

After Korea, another global conflict – the Cold War – intensified but stopped short of air-clearing military aggression. The mobilisation of nuclear war-heads 'just

* Horton was married to Hank Williams' widow who would mourn once again after Johnny was killed in an automobile collision in Milano, Texas, on Guy Fawkes Night 1960.
† Co-written by Michael, son of Robert Altman, the movie's director.

in case' spurred the writing of many earnest 'folk songs' in the early 1960s. North America had more than its fill of these from the Pete Seegers and Tom Paxtons but few impressed British record company talent scouts, however often they were cantillated *omnes fortissimo* on Ban the Bomb marches. Whither John Brunner's 'The H-Bomb's Thunder' and just plain 'H-Bomb' (to the tune of skiffle standard 'Freight Train'), Fred Dallas' 'Strontium 90' ('the only party that gets my vote/says "Ban the Bomb!" on its election note'), Ewan McColl's 'Join in the Line' and 'The Sun Is Burning' by those stalwarts of the Midlands, the Ian Campbell Folk Group?

That's the difficulty with topical ditties: what becomes of them when they are no longer topical or the topic gets tedious? Besides, the lumpen proletariat's teenage scions – the record industry's most vital consumer group – weren't that bothered about Living in the Shadow of the Bomb, particularly after national service was abolished.

If you were a Campaign for Nuclear Disarmament (CND) sympathiser, you'd probably settle for the Searchers who, as well as 'Where Have All the Flowers Gone', also recorded Malvina Reynolds'* 'What Have They Done to the Rain'† which, without quite spelling it out, dealt with ecological damage from nuclear fission. Offending Searchers purists with its use of strings and bongos, it struggled to an abysmal No. 13 in the charts, a true comedown after three chart-toppers the previous year.

---

* This elderly songwriter was also responsible for Tom Paxton's 'Little Boxes' (also recorded by Pete Seeger) – as 'rib-tickling' as 'That's What I Learned In School'.
† Joan Baez's version of 'What Have They Done to the Rain' was more likely to have served as a useful 1964 demo for the Searchers than that of the composer.

The Searchers' last Top Fifty entry was in 1966 with 'Have You Ever Loved Somebody', a cover of an album track by the Hollies who'd addressed the nuclear issue in 1965's 'Too Many People' which ended with a field recording of an actual H-bomb explosion. Furthermore, the image of Tom Jones was superimposed less altruistically over a photograph of an explosion for the cover of 1966's *A-Tom-ic Jones*. Get it?

Sounds of modern warfare and, fingered on an electric guitar, several bars of 'The Last Post' punctuated the Byrds' 'Draft Morning'. This reaction to the conscription of US youth to do their bit against the Vietcong was but the thin end of a wedge of pop songs that voiced growing disillusionment and a blatant opposition beyond conscientious objection to the Union's intervention in the war. It started, as you'd expect, with long-haired weirdos who wouldn't last a week in the barracks at home, let alone Pnom Penh. A Fugs LP of 1965, for instance, was blessed with both Tuli Kupferberg's slogan-ridden 'Kill for Peace', and sleeve notes by *vers libre* bard and part-time Fug Allen Ginsberg, who, invoking the Bible, carried on about 'the madness of our white-haired government', 'the whole nasty Military Secret' and suchlike. While resident in New York the Mothers of Invention enlivened one of their regular extravaganzas at that city's Garrick Theatre by inviting three uniformed marines up on stage to 'show the folks in the audience what you guys do for a living', handing them a huge doll with the instruction to 'pretend that this is a "gook" (i.e., Vietnamese) baby'. They responded by tearing it apart.

The Fugs and the Mothers were hampered by too many marketing problems – mostly to do with physical appearance and uncompromising lyrics – to be considered teen idols but those that could began coming up with anti-war statements – musical and otherwise. 'Epstein always tried to waffle on at us about saying nothing about Vietnam', John Lennon would later confide to a journalist's tape recorder, 'So there came a time when George and I said, "Listen, when they ask next time, we're going to say we don't like the war and we think they should get out".' At Beatle press conferences he defended the 'butcher sleeve' with the unfunny quip, 'Anyway, it's as valid as Vietnam'.

Even the Monkees' 'Last Train to Clarksville' was thought by some to concern a drafted lover off to southeast Asia ('and I don't know when I'm ever coming home'), bidding farewell to his lass on a railway platform. There was, however, no ambiguity about the Saigon Saucers' 'Howdy Doody Doctor Death' which, in a swirl of buzzsaw-toned guitars, greets and blames President Johnson whose ordinances, it claims, were at the root of whatever 'blowed my mind out in the ditch' in Saigon where there's 'no Beatles . . . no Dylan . . . no nobody'.

Among more coherent (and lucrative) examples are 'The I-Feel-Like-I'm-Fixin'-to-Die Rag' from Country Joe and the Fish, Eric Burdon's 'Sky Pilot' (slang for a regimental chaplain), Dozy, Beaky, Mich and Tich's 'For the Use of Your Son', Freda Payne's 'Bring the Boys Home', 'Talking Vietnam Pot Luck Blues' by Tom Paxton or, when sung *en masse* outside the White House during the Vietnam moratorium, the Kinks' ballad, 'Every Mother's Son'.* The Rolling Stones' much-

* The Doors' 'Unknown Soldier' is not listed because Jim Morrison assured an interviewer that, despite a promotional film that concludes with his 'death' before a firing squad, the subject was one of the usual millions of sperms that perish during ejaculation.

banned 'Street Fighting Man' was put in the same context with the knowledge that Mick Jagger had joined together with militant protesters outside London's US embassy.

From a comparatively safe billet in Germany, some US soldiers with ragged nerves formed the Monks. They might have wound up in the glasshouse had they not been discharged weeks before the release of a 1966 LP, *Black Monk Time* – because highlights like 'I Hate You' and 'Shut Up' pale beside the title track which states how much the group loathe the army and the killing in Vietnam in the midst of drivel about *Goldfinger* and other ravings nuttier than those in 'Howdy Doody Doctor Death'.

Established artists stepped out of conservative public character to pitch in too. Hence, another graduate of the New Christy Minstrels, Kenny Rogers – with his First Edition – made the frustrated paraplegic who'd done his 'patriotic chore' in the mawkish but, apparently, true story-in-song, 'Ruby Don't Take Your Love to Town'* a product not of Korea (as C & W composer Mel Tillis had intended) but Vietnam in 1969. The rawer country of the self-referential 'Man in Black' has Johnny Cash groaning that 'each week we lose one hundred fine young men'. Virtually his next-door-neighbour, Roy Orbison brightened Christmas 1966 with 'There Won't Be Many Coming Home'. It had been composed for the Big O's starring role in *The Fastest Guitar Alive* before this 1966 movie was remodelled from a taut historical yarn centred on Robert E. Lee's surrender at Appomattox in 1865

---

* Though merely threatening it in the song, the real-life cripple, unable to tolerate Ruby's suspected adultery any more, really did 'get my gun and put her in the ground'.

into a 'rollicking western comedy-drama'. However, briefly, Orbison earned the approbation of the blossoming drop-out sub-culture as his accidental donation to the anti-war effort was seen as a rebuttal of RCA's fastest-selling disc of 1966, 'The Ballad of the Green Berets' – also at a slow march tempo – by Roy's fellow Texan, Staff Sergeant Barry Sadler. No conniving Bilko, Sadler made you feel proud to be American when, standing smartly to attention in full uniform, he piped it out in a strong tenor on *American Bandstand*. The Ultimate Camp or what?

This paragon had been a glutton for punishment. After four years in the air force (with 'fearless men who jump and die'), he transferred to the army in 1963. With only three in every hundred applicants passing the qualifying test, Barry's Green Beret signifying his office as a combat medic was hard-won. On jungle patrol in Vietnam, so it was said, he tumbled into a man-trap where his leg was impaled upon a sharp and poisoned bamboo stake. He performed first aid on himself between bouts of fainting until a stretcher arrived to carry him back to base.

The laceration was severe enough to bring his combat duties to an end but, an orthodox and ruggedly handsome veteran not yet thirty, his picture adorned the jackets of chin-up publications recounting the deeds of our lads in the front line. One of these was the best-selling *The Green Berets*. Its author, Robin Moore, submitted some lyrics to Sadler, who RCA had discovered was an amateur songwriter. Together, they came up with 'The Ballad of the Green Berets', a jingoistic piece that extolled the virtue of dying 'for those oppressed' (by, presumably, the Vietcong), and citing one proud fighting man who, before being killed in action, requested his young wife to ensure that their son follows in his footsteps as 'one of America's best', i.e., 'have him win the Green Bereeeeeet!'.

If rather a one-trick-pony, our humble hero was, nevertheless, worth contracting due to the prevailing zeal for smashing the Commies that paralleled the anti-war faction in 1966. Sure as fate, within a fortnight of issue, the 'Ballad of the Green Berets' was a US No. 1; a lieutenant colonel was assigned by the Army to serve as the new star's booking agent, and a Sadler album was rushed out to cash-in quick. Selections included 'Badge of Courage', 'Letter from Vietnam' and 'Salute to the Nurses'. Then came at least a dozen round-the-world covers of the hit – including a German version by Freddy Quinn which stayed at the top even longer than the original did in the States. Next, a Private Charles Bowen was found to record 'Christmas in Vietnam' which just missed a December sell-in already clogged with the likes of Ric King's 'Hymn to a Returning Soldier' and 'An Open Letter to My Teenage Son' from Victor Lundberg as one still over there. None sold all that well but there were a lot of them.

The other side of the same coin showed in 1971's 'Battle Hymn of Lieutenant Calley' by Terry Nelson. It went on sale ten days prior to the verdict on Lieutenant William L. Calley Jnr, who was being court-martialled for the premeditated machine-gunning to death in 1968 of over one hundred South Vietnamese civilians at Mylai in 1968. Nelson and his investors' prayers that Calley *wouldn't* be acquitted were answered, and the 45 shot into the US Top Twenty. To the tune of 'John Brown's Body', it strove to vindicate the officer on the grounds that he and his squad were simply obeying orders, 'even though they made me out a villain, my truth was marching on'. At least a million music lovers – largely from the Deep South – agreed.

Old wounds were reopened in 1985 too when studio re-mix expert Paul Hardcastle crowned his recording career with a UK chart-topper, 'Nineteen', a title based on the average age of US combatants in Vietnam. Not an endorser of the lost value of just standing up and singing, Paul produced a sound collage loaded with all the latest state-of-the-art techniques – scratching, sampling, 'twanging plank' synthesised bass and a drum-machined disco beat – with edits from period news bulletins and the recurrent 'n-n-n-n-nineteen' tape loop the most prominent human elements.

Better to be well out of date than latch on to last year's thing – or, if last year didn't have a thing, the previous year's – which is why Hardcastle homed in on Vietnam rather than the Falklands. At half-time during the twelve-week crisis following Argentina's invasion of the British-held islands, punk outfit Crass demonstrated that protest was alive and kicking with *Yes Sir I Will*, an album title taken from a Royal Navy seaman's reply to Giving Your All for a Noble Cause from some princely personage on a walkabout round the battleship.

Unlike Crass, Robert Wyatt was not trying to out-gross the Sex Pistols when he slipped into the UK Top Thirty with 'Shipbuilding'. In the song an unemployed shipbuilder longs for the shipyards to open, even though he deplores the purpose of the war vessels – destined for the Falklands conflict – that form his livelihood. With Robert's 'ordinary bloke' voice in mind, the melody and chord structure of 'Shipbuilding' was the work of former Deaf School guitarist Clive Langer – 'and I went "la la la" and put it down on tape, played it to Elvis (Costello) who was knocked out with it. So he wrote it . . . you know, "Is it worth it?" – the casual way in which Robert Wyatt would write. He (Elvis) called me up. Said, "I think I've written the best lyric I've ever written". I said, "Well, it's the best tune I've ever written so let's play it to Robert". And Robert went for it – the saddest, most brilliant thing I've ever been involved with'. A Costello version of 'Shipbuilding' was selected for 1983's *Punch the Clock* (co-produced by Langer).

A few years later, Paul McCartney sought Costello as a songwriter partner. The ex-Beatle's commercial apotheosis during the 1980s had been with 1983's Yuletide No. 1, 'Pipes of Peace' which had been accompanied by a video re-enacting the mythical and cordial seasonal encounter in No Man's Land between British and German soldiers in World War I.

Outside Harrods on the very December day that 'Pipes of Peace' made its chart début, an IRA bomb killed six and maimed many more. No one wrote a song about that but earlier instances of civil unrest involving fatalities had led certain artists to put pen to paper or otherwise articulate disquiet. On New Year's Day 1970, Jimi Hendrix dedicated a performance of 'Machine Gun' to 'the soldiers fighting in Chicago, Milwaukee, New York and Vietnam'. As racial tension smouldered into open riot in the depressed Watts suburb of Los Angeles during 1965's humid 'Eve of Destruction' August, Frank Zappa in 'Trouble Comin' Every Day'* synthesised his observations of competing media coverage as the reek of burning seeped as far as the city centre. On the album recording with his Mothers of Invention, Frank chose an

---

* This number was savagely cut from six minutes to just under three for the 1966 pressing of *Freak Out* in Britain. In the late 1970s, Mick Farren and his Social Deviants released an arrangement of 'Trouble Comin' Every Day' with anglicised lyrics.

audacious burlesque of Mick Jagger for the lead vocal take but, with an accelerating tempo and nagging four-note guitar motif, the underlying anger was never so completely disguised that the verses could not be taken seriously.

With nothing to intimate that it was also in part a stylistic send-up, the group's 'Mom and Dad' from 1967's *We're Only in It for the Money** took a gentler tone with the 'plastic' adults indifferent to the police turning their shooting irons on some drug-crazed hippies in grubby floral tat idling in a public park – until the revelation that their own daughter was among them.

That was for nothing. Wait until the lazy good-for-nothings did something – as National Guardsmen in battledress did by opening fire on demonstrating students at Ohio's Kent State University on 4 May 1970.† That four protesters lay dead afterwards did not deter further campus disturbances – including one at a Mississippi college where two more teenagers were killed – or as Mike Love, rewriting the words of the Robins' 'Riot in Cell Block Number Nine' for his Beach Boys as 'Student Demonstration Time' put it, where 'four martyrs earned the new degree: the Bachelor of Bullets'. Well, his heart was in the right place – as were those of

---

* On the same LP, the Mothers sang of Californian concentration camps for hippies in 'Concentration Moon' (with the hook-line 'Cop kill a creep! Pow pow pow!'), and advised reading Franz Kafka's *In the Penal Colony* prior to hearing the album's finale, the challenging 'Chrome-Plated Megaphone of Destiny'.

† Among whom was future Pretender Chrissie Hynde. Her commendable involvement in environmental issues and animal liberation led to unlooked-for publicity in 1989 when an off-the-cuff remark was interpreted by the tabloid press as her incitement to firebomb McDonald's burger chain.

Crosby, Stills, Nash and Young who got their angry 'Ohio' behind the counters by 12 May.

They had less need of poetic licence than David Bowie did in 1973's 'Panic in Detroit', heavy with guitar sustain and lyrical snapshots of violence by the 'National People's Gang' – White Panthers? – and an aftermath when 'a trickle of strangers were all that were left alive'.

Today, no matter how unofficial or parochial, war is still wrong but there has been little pop music inspired through watching, say, Mrs Thatcher's poll tax turmoils on *Newsnight*; the helicopter's-eye-view of further burning and looting in Los Angeles in 1992; or more of Ireland, bloody Ireland – scenes that now horrify viewers about as much as a gunfight in a spaghetti western.

Chapter Twelve

Dead End Kids

Let's consider the death disc's role as an avenue for sociological comment – or, at least, as a chronicle of current affairs. We'll begin by going over to the sports desk.

Boxing wasn't a hip sport to like in the early 1960s. A glance at the bestial faces watching the fun told you that it ministered to the lowest form of sensual pleasure. Not only that but it was downright hazardous for the participants. A death on the canvas prompted Bob Dylan to write 1963's 'Who Killed Davey Moore'. In itself, it wasn't much of a song but, in the immediate aftershock of Moore's battering by an opponent from Cuba 'where boxing ain't allowed at all', it carried ovation-earning punch when Pete Seeger smashed into it at his recorded Carnegie Hall show. He didn't miss a trick.

While the customers were still reeling from 'Who Killed Norma Jean', next up was the Dylan number. In the song, Davey Moore's manager, his opponent and the referee, who wouldn't stop the fight because 'the crowd would've booed at not getting their money's worth', each absolve themselves from blame.

At least it kept them off the streets. There are worse ways of relaxing after work. Canadian rock 'n' roller-turned folk balladeer Ronnie Hawkins' 'Ballad of Caryl Chessman' concerned a multiple rapist sentenced to the

240

as chamber in San Quentin where, in the death cell, he whiled away eleven years and nine stays of execution.

Generally, when the electric chair is activated, its urge causes lights throughout the building to flicker and dim, a phenomenon noted by the convicts – and Reading's El Seven in 'Turn Out the Light'. After the *coup de grâce*, the fun doesn't necessarily stop for the condemned prisoner who may have requested in advance that certain organs be surgically removed for scientific research or transplant – as were murderer 'Gary Gilmore's Eyes' – which provided the title and lyrical backbone of the only UK Top Twenty entry for punk outfit, the Adverts.

In 1969, the Rolling Stones incorporated the fragmented dialogue from the police-station confessions of Alberto de Salvo, the Boston Strangler, in the slow motion middle section of 'Midnight Rambler' who was, nevertheless, 'not one of those' as he favoured a knife for his deadly doings. Neither was he like the wielder of 'Maxwell's Silver Hammer', Paul McCartney's wordy if infantile 'granny music' on *Abbey Road*, the Beatles' finale. To a jaunty, see-saw rhythm, medical undergraduate Maxwell Edison bumps off his date, a reproving teacher and the judge about to sentence him.

Fictitious or otherwise, the crimes of Chessman, the Rambler and Maxwell were probably calculated, but, sometimes the mind cables snap, and the deed is entirely spontaneous. It appears, for example, that everyone in Berkshire had known somebody who died when a Michael Ryan went berserk with a firearm in the streets of Hungerford in 1988. Afterwards, just what the bereaved families needed was a fund-raising outdoor pop concert. Fortunately, its organisers thought better of it.

In 1971, David Bowie's 'Running Gun Blues' described a demobbed sniper so incapable of adjusting to Civvy Street after the horrors of Vietnam that he suffers episodes of homicidal dementia – and his random victims – 'twenty-three down since Friday' – suffer too.

The similar tendencies of ex-marine Charles Whitman were braked until his father walked out on his mother. Blaming himself for the domestic misery his parents had endured for the proverbial sake of the children, the twenty-five-year-old Texan sought psychiatric help in hopes of quelling his bottled-up passion by verbalising it on the couch. For a while, he was successful but, on August 1966, he ran amok with a high-powered rifle. His story was told by another son of Texas, the blind C & W composer Leon Payne, in the 1974 monologue 'Psycho'. Almost-but-not-quite-comic in its diseased and peculiarly intimate attention to morbid trifles, it runs through four of the fifteen human killings – an ex-wife, her boyfriend, Whitman's brother and a child – and that of a dog before the Roald Dahl-ish twist-in-the-tale, 'Mama, why don't you get up' – a reference to the first person he shot, now unable to hear her boy's 'you better let 'em lock me up' plea in the chorus.*

Whitman and Ryan alone might have understood the attitude of the girl in 'I Don't Like Mondays' by the Boomtown Rats – which scaled the summit of the UK charts in 1979. On a promotional visit to the States, the group's vocalist Bob Geldof, a former journalist, had been intrigued by an item of news coming over the wire services. Apparently, an adolescent Californian named Brenda Spencer had returned to school after the weekend

---

* Whitman also injured thirty-one before he himself was gunned down by police in a tower at the University of Texas. He left behind a long letter that contained a request for an autopsy to prove he was insane. 'Psycho' was revived by Elvis Costello as a 1981 B-side when recorded in concert at Hollywood's Palamino Club.

with a pistol in her satchel. Before the first lesson, she'd emptied every chamber, ending the lives of several – including the headmaster – of those unlucky enough to be in sight during a playground rampage sparked off, so the malevolent little madam explained when apprehended, because 'I don't like Mondays'. Startled as much by this remark as the bloodbath, Bob had an idea for a song.

It's not improbable that Brenda was a few pfennig short of a Deutschmark – but so was Adam and the Ants' 'Killer in the Home' dangerously obsessed with Geronimo, Red Indian scourge of half a continent. Upbringing might have had a lot to do with it. It certainly explains the behaviour of the Lost Weekend's 'Young Man with a Gun' whose father 'took me hunting when we killed things just for fun'.

He got no further than the Chicago youth who'd been another little hungry mouth to feed' in Elvis Presley's 'In the Ghetto', aswarm with children and vermin. In one of the King's isolated excursions into social comment – and, in 1969, his biggest hit in ages – heavy-hearted *legato* strings underline the hopelessness of an environment of few illusions from where, in one grand but foolish gesture, a lad defies the preordained fate of either dead-end job or prison. In a stolen vehicle, he is cornered by squad cars. Instead of raising his arms in surrender, he runs off with a gun in his hand, knowing that the cops aren't likely to listen to what he might have to say before opening fire. As he lies face down on the pavement, 'his Mama cried'.

A Chicago gangland massacre in the 1920s and Britain's Great Train Robbery were juxtaposed in 'Just for Money', Paul Hardcastle's follow-up to 'Nineteen'. More of the same in terms of production and arrangement,

'Just for Money' featured repeated phrases by Sir Laurence Olivier and Bob Hoskins ('just fink what you could do with it'). When thus tempted, Ronald Biggs escaped from a hand-to-mouth existence in London's East End to what turned out to be a hand-to-mouth existence in Brazil, albeit as something of a tourist attraction. As well as 'Belsen Was a Gas', he recorded the Top Ten A-side 'No One Is Innocent (a Punk Prayer)', with the remnants of the Sex Pistols. An alternative title had been 'Cosh the Driver' but this had been discarded, possibly because the man assaulted by Biggs on 8 August 1963 had died with his reflexes and mental co-ordination impaired.

Moral opprobrium also occurred on Ferlin Husky's 'The Drunken Driver'. As he released satirical recordings as 'Simon Crum', could it have been that this country singer was undergoing an identity crisis? In a voice like a dotard with a hernia, Ferlin recited a scarcely credible account of what caused 'two dear liddle children to be sleepin' beneath the clay'. While strolling down the highway they'd been lost in a reverie about their late mother when their father – who had deserted them – 'hollered a drunken sound' at the wheel of his speeding car as he hurtled into them. His senses returned swiftly enough when he halted to inspect the damage. The daughter had died instantly, and his son had been hurled into a ditch where he remained alive just long enough to recognise Dad and ask piteously why they had to meet again this way.

In the original words of the Crickets' 'I'm Looking For Someone To Love' 'drunken man/street car/foot slip there you are' were altered on the sheet music by the censor.

But it isn't always driving that kills the drunk – sometimes he *dances* himself to death. Charles Aznavour is propping up the bar in 'Two Guitars', spewing out dismal platitudes of 'we're all the same when we go' bent. The saloon band's tango gathers tempo, his sozzled torpor dispels and he becomes active and restless – 'if the end should come today, let me take the gamble'. The music is now *allegro con fuoco*, and he's off – a hostage to the beat until he drops exhausted or dead.

Was there anything in the Ten Commandments about not boozing? No, there wasn't! Therefore, Aznavour's lousy drinker – if that's all he was – was surer of salvation than the Yardbirds' 'Ten Little Indians' who each transgressed one of God's holy laws as the song ticked off coveting your neighbour's wife, theft, lying, murder, matricide, not saying your prayers, taking the Lord's name in vain *et al*. Composed by Nilsson, this resort to cover material rather than writing their own songs was the group's final despairing throw before folding after a showdown at Luton Technical College in 1968.

The Yardbirds had once been eliminated from the heats of the 1966 San Remo Song Festival. A less miscast entrant, Gene Pitney put up a more polished show. With his distinctive nasal tenor, Gene had 'arrived' in 1961 with Dmitri Tiomkin's million-selling theme song to *Town without Pity* in which, through the oratory skills of their barrister, four GIs on occupation duty in Germany are cleared of raping a local girl who is so traumatised by the experience that she commits suicide. Matching Roy Orbison's reputation as a merchant of misery, Pitney repeated his triumph the following year with the main title of *The Man Who Shot Liberty Valance*. Perpetuating the gloomy atmosphere the second-person principal character in Dylan's haggard 'Ballad of Hollis Brown' regretted begetting offspring as, in his grinding poverty, he sees his 'baby's eyes look crazy there a-tugging at your sleeve'. With a scolding wife and five more children starving on a drought-ruined smallholding, he spends his last dollar on seven shotgun shells to finish the agony quickly rather than let the family die by inches. This most harrowing of all Dylan's early tracts closed with a suggestion of a backwoods reincarnation: 'someway in the distance, there's seven new people born'.

On the same LP, Bob delivered musical lectures on more specific topics. However, 'A Pawn in Their Game' did not waste time telling the listener what could be read in newspapers about the murder and burial in concrete of black Medgar Evers by Ku-Klux-Klansmen in Mississippi on 12 June 1963. That was the more pedantic approach of the Pete Seegers and Tom Paxtons. Instead, Dylan got it all out of the way in the first line – 'a bullet from the back of a bush took Medgar Evers' blood' – thus leaving space to discuss its implications. Likewise, 'William Zanzinger killed poor Hattie Carroll' kick-starts 'The Lonesome Death of Hattie Carroll', a swipe at there being one law for the rich, thus guaranteeing a light sentence for wealthy Zanzinger. Smothering it in imagery, Bob reiterated this complaint here and there in 1965's 'It's Alright Ma (I'm Only Bleeding)' which closes with Dylan's fear of being guillotined should his radical ideas become known to the mysterious 'they'.

If money sometimes keeps your neck out of a noose, it doesn't necessarily bring happiness, so I'm told. Look at the Pretty Things' 'Death of a Socialite'. Look at Paul Simon's 'Richard Cory'. The last-named well-heeled gadfly owned half a town, was conducted to the best table in restaurants, and his every public appearance was worth a photograph and a write-up in high-society journals. Still, a worker in one of his factories didn't envy him, for, tired of flattery without friendship, Cory 'put a bullet through his head'.

'Richard Cory' was most effectively overhauled in mean R & B mode by Them, one of the British Invasion groups that had shaken the wistfulness from Simon and confirmed Dylan's resolve to hire a backing rock 'n' roll combo.

Pop's gingerbread castle hour in 1967 had an underside as cruel as Richard Cory's. In Keith West's 'Excerpt from *A Teenage Opera*', a village community thumps impatient cutlery on breakfast tables when lonely eighty-two-year-old Grocer Jack misses his round for the excellent reason that his weak heart has finally packed up. Reproaching themselves for not showing the old man more affection and respect' when he was alive, the adults offer the consolation of a bouquet-laden send-off while a bewildered kiddie chorus enquires of the coffin, 'Grocer Jack, is it true what Mummy says, you won't come back?'*

From Mummys to Mothers. The Mothers of Invention's 'I'm Not Satisfied' from 1966's *Freak Out!* dealt with another sort of outsider, possibly a beggar, obliged 'to roam from door to door'. Otherwise, he's a silent, apathetic observer, bereft of human companionship and even opportunities for conversation. 'I don't like the way life has been abusing me', he grouses. When it becomes

Though the existence of the rest of the work (co-written with pianist Mark Wirtz) was denied by West later, 'Sam' and two further A-sides by Wirtz alone continued the narrative style set by the saga of Grocer Jack. Nevertheless, though Cliff Richard was mooted for a major role, the opera – if it was ever completed – was neither seen on the public stage nor heard on a cast album release.

intolerable, he has, it seems, but one option: 'maybe I'll just kill myself/I just don't care no more'.

What might have been a biting indictment of the World in Which We Live was dampened by Frank Zappa's sleeve notes assuring browsers that 'I'm Not Satisfied' 'is OK and safe and was designed that way on purpose' – and the Mothers' projection of themselves as freaks leading Joe Average to believe that everything they recorded was somehow parodic. On *Absolutely Free*, the LP that came after *Freak Out!*, a key opus is 'Uncle Bernie's Farm', a song suited perfectly to the misbegotten chorale bawling the message 'murder and destruction scream the toys in every store'. Its specific targets were the stepping-up in December of the hard sell of the sorts of toys that pander to children's inherent sadism and morbid inquisitiveness. This is summarised by a spoken passage delivered with all the possessive venom of a six-year-old about 'this car and when it hits the wall, you can see the guy dying inside. Got the little plastic puddles of blood, plastic intestine stuck back in his stomach . . . '

The Mothers' blood brothers, the Fugs' obnoxious redneck spoof, 'Johnny Pissoff Meets the Red Angel' extended the Deep South's old right-wing bigotries to 1968's draft-card burners and 'peace queers' during a period when a Houston radio station was twice fire bombed by some good ol' boys who begged to differ over its anti-Vietnam war bias. To Pissoff's brutish foul-mouthed stereotype, the Fugs added some disgusting details, e.g., 'today I cut some frogs' legs off and left them by the pond', before the lengthy coda where the Red Angel as the unheeded personification of the hard man's conscience intimates that he'll never get to heaven 'with a violent heart'.

*

248

Godfather of Soul and catalyst in calming race riots, James Brown exerted his quasi-monarchical influence to block drugs trafficking in black areas with 1972's admonitory 'King Heroin', a graceful but hard-hitting rap from days before the form evolved into an excuse for gross braggadocio. Born of a dream, Brown's recitation over an unobtrusive riff lists the unsavoury aspects of addiction, how it can 'put a gun in your hand and make you a killer' and 'make the most virile of men forget their sex', before signing off with 'the white horse of heroin will ride you to hell until you are dead, dead, dead' (agonised shriek on fade-out).*

Extremes of the mental distortions of hallucinogenics were implicated in the Small Faces†' effervescent 'Itchycoo Park' (with its 'it's all too beautiful' chorus) and the Move's horrific 'Night of Fear'/'Disturbance'. Preferring ale to acid, this Birmingham outfit's warning came too late for the puncture-veined chappie who was putting his affairs in order in Love's 'Signed D.C.' This doleful ballad unfolded as DC's last letter before an inevitable and pathetic death which he blames both on his own weakness – and the predatory narcotics dealer who got him hooked in the first place. Such scum deserve to be shot on sight, declared bikers' band Steppenwolf when they grabbed by the scruff of the neck and wrung the life from Hoyt Axton's 'The Pusher' whose trade created addicts 'with tombstones in their eyes'.

* Yet, on 17 December 1988, Brown was sentenced by a South Carolina judge to six years imprisonment on charges that included possession of dangerous drugs.
† The Cockney quartet's ace face, Steve Marriott, perished in a fire in his Essex home on 20 April 1991. Many famous friends attended the funeral where the Small Faces' 'All or Nothing' 45 was spun as Steve's requiem.

In the very first verse, Axton confessed that he had 'smoked a lot of grass'. Marianne Faithfull, however, went a lot further when, as her wretched heroin odyssey found its sea-legs *circa* 1968, she offered Mick Jagger and Keith Richards some lyrics as they tinkered with a slow but captivating melody. With Jagger on acoustic guitar, she recorded the resulting 'Sister Morphine' as the B-side of her final 1960s single. Smelling of hospitals, the song pictures a fragile junkie on a ward mattress after her arrival to the agitated clang of an ambulance bell. While the surroundings fill her with nightmare reflections – 'why does the doctor have no face?', 'tomorrow I'll be dead . . . clean, white sheets stained red' – a sense of longing for an antidote also permeates the atmosphere. Grippingly shorn of former mezzo-soprano purity, chain-smoking Marianne's detached vibrato is that of a woman profoundly changed from the convent girl whose party dress Mick Jagger had splashed with wine in 1964.

On the orders of a fretting executive who'd bothered listening to it, 'Sister Morphine' was withdrawn from circulation and no further copies manufactured. Not only was it, in his misinformed view, 'drug music' but the image of the artist – and, indirectly, that of the record company – had been tarnished too much already by her frank opinions on free love, her cohabitation with Jagger, and the identification by innuendo of her as the 'nude girl' in the famous Rolling Stones drugs bust. When 'Sister Morphine' appeared on the Stones' *Sticky Fingers* two years later, it was still considered sufficiently venal for the substitution of another number on the Spanish pressing.*

* Prescribed drugs had already come under the Rolling Stones' scrutiny in 1966's 'Mother's Little Helper' – concerning habit-forming

More obviously a censure of hard drugs – a hip Hilaire Belloc poem when compared to the libretto of 'Sister Morphine' – Canned Heat's 'Amphetamine Annie' with its unison 'speed kills' punch-line had been passed as fit for the radio because by 'shovelling down snow', Annie finished up 'awfully dead'.

In 1972, 'junkies laying on the floor dying were among occupants of 'L.A. County Jail '59', a track on an eponymous album by Geronimo Black, a combo formed by some ex-Mothers of Invention. Stacked on shop shelves, the sleeve of *Geronimo Black* yellowed while, that same year, Curtis Mayfield scored his biggest hit with 'Freddie's Dead' from the 'fast, flashy and funky' film *Superfly* which, deplorably, made comedy folk-heroes of a happy-go-lucky pair of thuggish New York cocaine pedlars.

The streets of London weren't safe either. On his way home, a gentleman was accosted by hoodlums 'Down in the Tube Station at Midnight' by the Jam. 'My life swam around me', he noticed whilst writhing around on the scuffed platform, trying to protect his head and genitalia.

Barging into the Speakeasy one evening, Sid Vicious almost succeeded in picking a pointless fight with the Jam's Paul Weller. Though he wondered why, Sid had been granted a co-writing credit for his Sex Pistols' 'Bodies', the withering blast that told of Polly of Birmingham's abortion*, the 'fucking bloody mess' that so

---

tablets which hasten a frantic housewife's 'busy dying day'. It was covered by the late British R & B vocalist Gene Latter (who'd been accorded a modicum of publicity by alleging that Jagger had stolen his stage act).
* 'Carry the Blame' by the River City People is, apparently, about abortion too.

degraded her as a human being that she was reputed to have been seen in public with the foetus strapped to her side in a plastic bag. It isn't saying much but 'Bodies' was, perhaps, the most socially committed piece on 1977's *Never Mind the Bollocks*. However, its effect was spoiled for those who read guitarist Steve Jones' admission in the *New Musical Express* that, yes, he knew Polly. Actually, he knew her well enough to have given her a knee-trembler in an alley behind London's Marquee club.

Chapter Thirteen

Rameses II is Dead, My Love

Like Dave Dee, Dozy, Beaky, Mick and Tich before them, Adam and the Ants were gainfully employed in the early 1980s with sure-fire hit singles each of which concentrated on a different period of romanticised antiquity, thus giving plenty of scope for associated videos that accommodated gorgeous costume drama. Their chart career began the year before when they ditched punk garb for a new look – a hybrid of swash-buckling pirate and Red Indian – in keeping with the album, *Kings of the Wild Frontier*.

As you'd expect from tracks linked conceptually to sea-rovers and barbarians who enjoy inflicting pain for its own sake, violent death was a constant possibility. One minute dodging bullets in *'Los Rancheros'*, next as prey for 'the murder-happy characters' in 'Making History', then being hanged from the gallows 'to see if they could dance' by Blackbeard ('so damnable a fiend from hell') in 'Jolly Roger': it was Gilbert and Sullivan boiled down to four-chord guitar distortion.

The group's gravitation towards historical themes had been present even in their punk genesis – notably in 1979's 'Cleopatra' which discusses the oral sexual prowess and tenacity of the Egyptian queen, a 'wide-mouthed girl', apparently, given a 'weak, distorted image' in 1960's expensive silver screen spectacle with Elizabeth

Taylor in the title role, and her future husband, Richard Burton as Mark Antony.

One of Cleopatra's royal ancestors was the subject of a doubtful tribute in 'Rameses II is Dead (My Love)' by the Fugs. Couched in a cracker-barrel C & W waltz fattened with strings, blue yodels and multi-tracked choir, composer Ed Sanders' affected Tennessean drawl might confuse the ignorant as to which Memphis the Pharaoh's splendid funeral bier left 'with a coffin of gold and the pretty pale carvings' as his soul travelled to its heavenly reward – possibly for his victories against the Hittites – when led by Ptah 'to Nut's celest'l shores'.

From ancient Greece (sometimes via Roman literature) came 1984's patricidal 'Oedipus Rex' from King Kurt – and, seventeen years earlier, 'From the Underworld' by the Herd. A crack at artistic respectability by the Dave Dee outfit's writers Alan Blaikley and Ken Howard, it strove to preserve, said Ken, 'many of the original allusions' in Virgil's *Orpheus in the Underworld* (and John Milton's *L'Allegro*) even if these went above the heads of the majority of the Herd's *Rave*-subscribing schoolgirl admirers. Some, however, might have been cognisant with the fable of Eurydice, beloved wife of Orpheus, who was consigned on her death to the infernal regions. Following her there, Orpheus persuaded Pluto, ruler of the Underworld, to release Eurydice on the condition that he led the way back to the surface without looking back at her. But a footstep away from journey's end, he involuntarily turned and all was lost ('never again can I reclaim you'). Yet the funereal bell introit – 'dungggggg!' – overhanging chords on trendy fuzz-box guitar, word-less male chorus and bright trumpet *obligato* made 'From the Underworld', for all its self-consciously 'poetic' lyrics, every bit as gimmicky as a Dave Dee 45, and it took just a few television appearances by the Herd with their tight-trousered, boyishly handsome singer, Peter Frampton – soon to be *Rave* magazine's 'Face of '68' – to hoist it into the Top Ten.

A millennium or two after the imaginary Orpheus, the exploits of our own Robin Hood remain open to debate. His only connection with death on vinyl, however, is in 'Riddle De Diddle De Day', a 78 r.p.m. single that unites the verses of commentary sung by Elton Hayes as 'Alan A Dale' throughout Walt Disney's *The Story of Robin Hood and His Merrie Men*. It didn't do much for me but a hamlet of peasants fell about with laughter with Elton's 'Now Robin Hood doth hunt the deer that in the woodlands prance/but oft times shoots the Sheriff's men – by sorrowful mischance'. Not above half, I don't think.

Pressing ever onwards towards our Coca-Cola century, we arrive in France in time to catch Joan of Arc at the stake. 'Maid of Orleans' was a 1982 arrangement by Orchestral Manoeuvres in the Dark of their previous British hit parade strike, plain 'Joan of Arc' that featured a synthesiser riff and snare drum rataplan with impressionist and perfunctory lyrics.*

Parts of France were still under British control in the reign of Henry VIII who, in 1537, had been in the same dilemma as Pat Campbell with the life of either his wife – Jane Seymour – or unborn son in jeopardy. The much-married Tudor monarch, however, was above bargaining with God – and his missus understood his attitude completely. With the Wars of the Roses not a distant memory, the family either had to produce an heir or risk

* This Liverpool-based combo first penetrated the Top Ten in 1980 with 'Enola Gay', a pleasantry concerning the aircraft that dropped the atom bomb on Hiroshima.

deposition. Therefore, the utterance 'open my right side and find my baby' slips from the agonised royal in 'The Death of Queen Jane', penned by a David Sproule and recorded by Joan Baez in 1964 and the Keeper's Gate Band twenty years later.

In more robust health than Jane when he died, Hanoverian highwayman Dick Turpin was also the source of more ballads than she. In most of them, his remarkable overnight ride from London to York on Black Bess is mentioned. Yet his crimes, however justified, never pay and, betrayed – usually by 'cowardly informers' – but unafraid, he keeps his historical appointment with the gallows, 'for a game cock must hang at last', concludes the traditional 'Turpin Hero'. So it was in 1965 that he had a near-hit in the UK charts with 'The Ballad of Dick Turpin'* by Brian Gregory (not the Cramp) from a seldom-seen Walt Disney movie, *The Legend of Dick Turpin*.

The last years of Rasputin also inspired a film – 1932's *Rasputin the Mad Monk* – but this malign *éminence grise* from Tsarist Russia exerted a more powerful influence on 1978's British charts when Boney M's 'Rasputin' shuffled to No. 2. Like Adam Ant's 'Cleopatra' and King Kurt's 'Oedipus Rex', it dealt principally with its subject's love life.

Other twentieth-century bogymen chronicled on record include the Italian-American gangster whose 'guns don't argue' in the bludgeoning neo-instrumental 'Al Capone' by Jamaican bluebeat pioneer, Prince Buster. Hitler too was covered in the Boomtown Rats' 'Love Song of Eva Braun'.

* Recorded under the supervision of Harry Robinson, the brains behind Lord Rockingham's XI.

When the United States first entered World War II, some civilian Yanks were so overwhelmed with the notion of caning the Hun that they threw symbolic stones at dachshunds. Lingering in a few of those cowards' memories might have been the distressing story of Mary Provost, 'mysterious angel of the silent screen' as Nick Lowe put it in a 1977 song that need not have been written about how 'the cops burst into her loneliness' weeks after her suicide in 'the cheap hotel up on Hollywood West'. Instead of finding a faded beauty looking pensive on a snow-white eiderdown, the police vomited at the gory mash on the floor, half-devoured by the pet dachshund that self-fixated Mary had neglected to consider as she 'got ready for that last big sleep'.

Worse things happen at sea. Bronislau Kaper's incidental music to 1962's *Mutiny on the Bounty* corrupts its 'Follow Me' love song to frame 'Christian's Death' on Pitcairn Island – and a vanished submarine was the subject of the following year's 'The Thresher', a 45 by Abner Jay. Tearing a chapter or two from Johnny Kidd's book, Dave Dee, Dozy, Beaky, Mick and Tich were kitted out in Captain Pugwash gear with a galleon backdrop as the publicity angle on 1968's 'Wreck of the *Antoinette*'. This merchant vessel swung her bows into the winds in order to keep the lady whose name she bore in the manner to which she'd become accustomed. Predictably, the *Antoinette* went down with her crew after a night storm flooded the deck – an eventuality telegraphed by Dave in his murky 'full fathom five' introit.

A self-confessed 'frustrated actor', Dee had appeared on television that year as 'Caliban' in *The Tempest*, the Shakespeare play that contained the song 'Full Fathom Five'. The Bard of Avon was not, however, credited when the same lyrics were set to a different tune in 'Full Fathoms Five' on Tim Hollier's *Message to a Harlequin*, another chunk of musical driftwood from brine-washed 1968.

With music from Matthew Fisher and an assembly-line impressionistic libretto by Keith Reid, Procol Harum cornered 'The Wreck of the *Hesperus*' on an album hinged on their equally epic 'A Salty Dog' (who sailed 'where ships come home to die'). Come 1976, and Gordon Lightfoot commemorated 'The Wreck of the *Edmund Fitzgerald*' which sinks with all hands when 'the witch of November came stealing' – and, at the memorial service in Detroit, an organ wheezed the 'Maritime Sailor's Cathedral' as the bell chimed once for each of the twenty-nine seamen who perished. Consuming nearly half an hour's needle-time, Gavin Bryars' 'The Sinking of the *Titanic*' developed from the three turgid hymns* that a string band was gamely creaking out as the liner up-ended after its collision with an iceberg off Cape Race on 14 April 1912. These are interspersed with dialogue from a survivor and the tinkling of an Edwardian music-box. As there was no report that the ensemble ever stopped playing, producer Brian Eno creates an illusion of the music descending with the ship to the depths of the ocean.

Up in the sky, Duncan Browne's 'The Death of Neil' was caused by the inventor of a flying machine steering it into the sun. The less whimsical 'Julie' by the Captains of Industry was a wasp-waisted jet-setter 'breaking hearts at altitudes too high for other girls' – a possible euphemism for the Mile High Club. During one flight,

* One of these was believed to be the rather tactless 'Nearer My God to Thee' – which might have led to unnecessary panic.

her sexual athleticism goes horribly wrong and she is condemned to 'eternal silence', oblivious to her luxurious surroundings including the four-poster on which she lies in a coma.

We gaze far into the cosmos for David Bowie's 'Space Oddity', a pertinent vinyl artefact of the year when Neil Armstrong took his small step. With 'New York Mining Disaster 1941' its inspirational root, this 'mini solo opera' – as one reviewer described it – is centred on astronaut Major Tom's decision to disconnect his craft's links with a foul and distant Earth – and drift away, presumably to a lonely, airless demise.

Chapter Fourteen

Don't Jump off the Roof, Dad

Reader's Digest used to have a mail-order record wing trading in albums such as *Music for Reading*, *Music for Dining* and, yes, *Music for a Solemn Occasion*. 1963 brought *The Quiet Hour* spent with Patience Strong reading verse to holy organ accompaniment 'offering comfort and solace sorely needed in this hurrying, worrying world'. Not wishing to be left out, the silver screen's Master of Suspense, Alfred Hitchcock presented *Music to be Murdered By*, two years before *Psycho*. Pictured on the sleeve with a prop department axe through his head, the multi-chinned director introduced 'mood music in a jugular vein' in much the same idiosyncratic manner – 'good eeevening' – as he nutshelled *Psycho*, *The Birds*, *et al* in their trailer clips. Disappointingly, the album was merely cinema interlude music of the slushiest orchestral variety – albeit with titles like 'I Don't Stand a Ghost of a Chance with You' and 'I'll Never Smile Again' – apart from a goose-fleshed title track which crescendoed to a choking scream – and even that was no 'Night of the Vampire'.

Of the same instrumental vintage as the Moontrekkers' minor hit but as much of a confidence trick for horror enthusiasts as the Hitchcock effort was the Cannons' 'I Didn't Know the Gun Was Loaded' which, belying a promising title, was only a parody of Duane Eddy with twanging guitar, flatulent saxophone and rebel yells.

However, when the Beat Boom placed a greater emphasis on vocals, matters improved in the comedy line. Clacton's Dave Curtiss and the Tremors played it for giggles on the 1963 A-side, 'You Don't Love Me Any More'. Encapsulating the dilemma of many groups in that watershed year, the Tremors do a fair approximation of Merseybeat behind Dave's Cliff Richardisms as he sings of his 'suspicions that maybe, baby, you don't love me any more'. From sticking pins in his photo voodoo-style, his girlfriend moves on to pushing pies into his face, and eventually drives a truck through his front door. Hospitalised by her vindictive attentions, he is sufficiently thick-skinned to receive her during visiting time when she sneaks a lethal serum into his milk. Luckily for him, the ward doctor drinks it 'and he fell to the floor'.

By the run-out groove, you're left with the impression that, when discharged, the infatuated idiot will still be beseeching his murderous virago with flowers and boxes of chocolates. It seemed, however, that there was space in the charts for but one Freddie and the Dreamers*, and Dave's outfit reverted to 'sensible' numbers for subsequent releases.

There was also only one Peter Sellers†. As a recording artist, he'd scored his biggest smash by far with a 1960 duet with Sophia Loren, 'Goodness Gracious Me', which showcased his oft-mimicked Punjabi accent. On the B-side, 'Grandpa's Grave', he assumed the voice of a querulous elderly East Londoner. In a one-verse tempo change from quasi-martial singalong to racy

---

* Despite their clownish antics onstage, none of Freddie and his Dreamers' hits were with songs designed specifically to be funny.
† Who was taken by a heart attack in 1979.

Latin-American shuffle, he throws in his imitation of a bureaucrat who justifies a local council's decision to excavate the 'wretched fellow's grave' to build a sewer. On behalf of the deceased's indignant family, Peter-as-Everyman ponders 'what's the use of 'avin' a religion' in view of such desecration, just because 'some society gink wants a pipeline for the sink'. Darkly, he intimates that his disturbed grandparent will 'dress up in his sheets/ and 'aunt their country seats'.

Another whose records were an adjunct to earnings in a different sphere of showbusiness was Tommy Cooper. He grazed the British Top Forty in summer 1961 with 'Don't Jump off the Roof, Dad', much-requested on the BBC Light Programme's *Children's Favourites*. The raw song was spiced-up with Tommy's trademark manic cackle and, as if building up to some complicated trick, comic nervous procrastinations – 'Keep it going, boys. Nice and loud!' – to a piano-bass-drums session trio recycling the trilling ballroom-dancing class riff in waltz time until Cooper breaks into a less-than-euphonious baritone account of a harassed father who arrives home from the office to be bitten by his dog, irritated by misbehaving children and served an unappetising meal. We do not know whether his decision to commit suicide is reinforced or weakened when, just as he's about to fling himself from the rooftop of his home, the brats implore him not to crush Mum's freshly planted petunias by landing in the garden. Instead, they tell him to walk to a public park, 'and there you can jump in the lake'.

When he collapsed with a fatal seizure on stage at London's Her Majesty's Theatre before several million ITV viewers in 1988, Cooper was, arguably, Britain's best-loved comedian. Once that accolade might have been Benny Hill's before he started rehashing old ideas, and brutalising his art with the saucy inanities that made him the toast of North America. Yet 1991's compact disc reissue of his pre-'Ernie' output on record confirmed the opinion of the discerning psychedelic quarterly *Ptolemaic Terrascope* that here was 'one of the finest comic songwriters this country has ever produced'. On 1965's *Benny Hill Sings?*, he flirts with death in the pun-saturated 'The Garden of Love' where, unable to face the 'fuchsia' alone, a jilted horticulturist's weeping poisons his meticulously tended flowers. Benny's execrable 'Old Fiddler' 'played like a man possessed' until he 'unfortunately, fell down dead' but, beneath a full moon, some imagine that they can hear him scraping away in the glen where he was buried. Possibly the funniest Bob Dylan send-up ever recorded, the LP's 45, 'What a World' brushed aside P. F. Sloan's unconscious humour like chaff – especially in the last verse where the last human alive after the holocaust chose to live on the top of the Empire State Building. Overcome by loneliness, he jumped but 'as he passed the seventh floor, he heard the telephone ring'.

From 1965 the Shangri-Las' 'Leader of the Pack'* also sparked off a few spoofs. The most notorious was the all-male Detergents' 'Leader of the Laundromat' which whirled to No. 19 in the US *Hot 100*. In this case, *his* parents were the disapproving faction 'because our laundry always came back brown'. Whereas Betty's

---

* In 1979, 'Leader of the Pack' was revived by the incomparable Portsmouth Sinfonia (consisting mostly of musicians with unorthodox command of their instruments) with guest vocalists, the uncoordinated Sinfonettes – as intrinsically English as the Shangri-Las were American. Similarly, Julian Clary's stage act was enlivened by a version featuring Fanny the Wonder Dog.

Jimmy crashed his motorbike, the Detergents' washer-woman is run over by a runaway dustcart.

Well, that's the Yanks for you. Over here, we got by with the Downliners Sect's B-side, 'Leader of the Sect' which is dated by an impersonation of Snagglepuss, a mid-1960s cartoon tiger of Yiddish extraction, for the opening 'Don, is that Sarah's autoharp you're carrying?'*. To circumvent copyright difficulties, the combo then pile into a blues boogie nothing like the Shangri-Las tune, as if performing at the very venue in the song where Don (Craine) refuses to go steady with Sarah who, blinded with tears, dashes into the path of a 'souped-up bass guitar' (!?). Out of respect, Don for once removes his perpetual 'headcoat' (i.e., deerstalker).

The clannish libretto of 'Leader of the Sect' was forgivable if only because most radio disc jockeys were not expected to listen to it anyway. Few bothered either with the A-side – which happened to be an exhumation of 'Wreck of the Old '97'. Making another depressingly familiar trek to the bargain bin, the next 45, 'I Got Mine', was coupled with 'Waiting in Heaven Some-where', a respectful take-off of Hank Williams' 'When God Comes to Gather His Jewels'†. A soldier wounded in the front line of battle is fast slipping away. Neverthe-less, he finds it in him to smile at death because his lost love is 'waiting in heaven somewhere . . . just round the bend'.

A variation on the piano riff of Elvis Presley's 'All Shook Up' lies at the heart of the Bonzo Dog Doo-Dah

* The Sect were probably the first – and, well before Pinkerton's (Assorted) Colours acquired one, the only – beat group to use an autoharp.
† Released in 1946, it was mistitled 'When God Comes and Fathers His Jewels' on initial pressings.

Band's 'Death Cab for Cutie' ('starring God') which, in 1967, accompanied a stripper's cavortings in the Beatles' interesting-but-boring television spectacular, *Magical Mystery Tour*. Quite negating his yellow Custer tresses, moustache and octagonal specs, vocalist Viv Stanshall proved a marvellous Presley mimic and the saving grace of a narrative which concerned a floozy neglecting her boyfriend in order to paint the town red. En route in a taxi, her coquettishness distracted the driver ('curves can kill') just as traffic lights on Highway 31 turned red – and 'they both wound up dead'.

The nearest to a companion piece on the same album is 'Big Shot', a Raymond Chandler-esque monologue from a New York speakeasy with side-servings of machine-gun noises and foggy, slip-slapping wharfs. Curiously, its saxophone solo anticipated the wild improvisational excursions and the buzz rather than honk achieved on the Mothers of Invention's *Uncle Meat*. This was recorded in 1968 simultaneously with its predecessor, *Cruising with Ruben and the Jets*, an exercise in collaging clichés of the shooby-doo-wah school of rock 'n' roll, born of 1950s teenagers harmonising for their own amusement. However, the group came clean with two minutes of fierce state-of-the-art jamming as a coda to a closing track with a title, 'Stuff up the Cracks', referring to the prevention of air coming in as a boy unlucky in love sticks his head in a gas oven and turns on the jets.

Nobody utilised an antiquated *alter ego* on the same scale as the Mothers but the late 1960s also brought a Fleetwood Mac flip-side, 'Someone's Gonna Get Their Head Kicked in Tonight' by 'Earl Vince and the Valiants', and mixed-media aggregation, the Liverpool Scene, came up with 'Bobby and the Helmets', a legendary 1950s combo who perished – like Buddy Holly and the other two – in a crash landing.

Though Alberto y Los Trios Paranoias emerged from the north too, these were more pub-rock successors to the Bonzos than the Liverpool Scene. In 1979, they issued *Snuff Rock*, an EP whose title was spray-canned on walls along main thoroughfares in central London. Standing more plays than *Music to be Murdered By*, it propagated in jest an ultimate fad that might have supplied (and probably did) a plot for a video nasty. At the time, however, most thought it great fun – but not great enough to propel the outfit into the charts. Neither had the Top Fifty been in the mood for 'Little Dead Surfer Girl' ('whenever the tide comes in, so does Wanda') by Connecticut's Incredible Broadside Brass Bed Band.

This lot might have been trying to amuse but I've never been certain how you were meant to take Lord Executioner's 'We Mourn the Death of Sir Murchison Fletcher', a Trinidadian calypso ostensibly grieving for a highly placed civil servant whose intense – and possibly unwelcome – devotion to public affairs 'upset his mind'. Nevertheless, 'the whole population cried out in vain/that he will never come back again'. Frank Holder too is inexplicably jolly in the traditional Jamaican ditty, 'Murder in the Market'*, in which the lady who brained her violent husband with a frying pan could only plead that 'he had it coming'.

A disc jockey from pirate station Radio London saw an inadvertently funny side of the Sorrows' atmospheric 'Take a Heart' – pulsating tom-toms, unsettling guitar

---

* Retitled 'Stone Cold Dead' when selected by Nassau's Vincent Martin and the Bahamians for the 1957 *Island Woman* album.

interjections and Don Fardon's moody vocal – and could not resist inserting 'Ugh!', 'Messy!' and other inane quips between lines like 'first you take a heart/then you break a heart . . . then you give it back . . . '

Movie director Mel Brooks considered the Third Reich good for a laugh in his black comedy *The Producers*, worth watching for the purposely tasteless title song and choreography following the overture of the play-within-a-play, *Springtime for Hitler* ('winter for Poland and France'): Busby Berkeley meets Rodgers and Hammerstein in Nazi Germany.

In 1983, Mel laid down his 'cut!' megaphone, rose from his canvas-backed chair and stood before the cameras himself in field-grey uniform with actress wife Anne Bancroft (as Eva Braun) for his video of 'The Hitler Rap'. This self-composed opus (with Pete Wingfield) was an updating of jive-talkin' 'LSD' from *The Producers* as well as an imitation of Jack Benny's imitation of Hamlet imitating the Fuhrer in 1942's *To Be or Not to Be*. A Panzer march melts into a synthesised disco jitter which, interspersed with a girlie chorus and several bars of 'Deutschland uber Alles', allows Brooks to demonstrate an intriguingly flagrant contempt for historical context in his characterisation of the late dictator as a black hustler who, instead of committing suicide in a Berlin bunker, takes a 'one way ticket to Argentina' with 'Marty' Boorman and Eva after 'D-Day, the birth of the blues'.

While not strictly relevant to death discs, this discourse would not be complete without touching on two musical films. 1974's *Phantom of the Paradise* was an irreverent – and rather off-target – pop remake of *Phantom of the Opera*. Blighted by a middle-of-the-road soundtrack by its baby-faced male lead, US singer-songwriter Paul Williams, it hinged on the to-ings and fro-ings of the Death record company and its ceaseless search for likely talent.

The Rocky Horror Picture Show – written by Richard O'Brien, shaven-headed host of Channel Four's *Crystal Maze* games show – was screened at a cinema near you the following year. Some had gone to see it hundreds of times when it was staged in London earlier in the decade* – though it died a sudden and merciless death when exported to the States. It parodied the stock horror movie set in a castle sinister where a young couple go for help when their car breaks down on a stormy night. To lend a modern glam-rock touch, the main villain was a lipsticked androgyny named Frank N. Furter. Portly Texan hollerer Meat Loaf (as 'Eddy') and his pop anti-thesis, Beatle-fringed English piano-tinkler Bobby Crush – darling of pre-teens and elderly females – were among other *Rocky Horror* stalwarts on both stage and screen.

* And still do, whenever it is revived. Its fans have call and responses to the script, often getting there before the actors.

Epilogue

Selina Through the Windshield

Death Metal: if you've heard it once, you've heard it a million times over – so they say. Nevertheless, I found a television documentary about it quite absorbing – if only because of middle-aged Ozzy Osbourne's phlegmatic bemusement at this new strain of Heavy Metal which combined the frantic energy of punk with eardrum-bursting sonic assault and an extreme exaggeration of the more bloodstained lyrical preoccupations of Black Sabbath and Alice Cooper. As Bestial Vomit of Sore Throat explained, 'the lyrics are always about chopping people up and feasting on entrails, that type of thing'.

Among its brand leaders were Megadeth, Ipswich's Extreme Noise Terror, Carcass, South America's Morbid Angel*, Doom, Revulsion, Bathory†, Hellbastard and Nightmare Vision. Few other artists have had the nerve to cover, say, Napalm Death's 'Divine Death' – twenty seconds of squealing electronic distortion and gutteral utterances – Venom's 'Necrophiliac' ('I feel the urge, the growing need, to fuck this sinful

---

* Whose fans were dismayed if the bass player – a Sid Vicious admirer – didn't actually slash himself with a razor onstage as part of the act.
† A Swedish outfit who consternated even hardcore Death Metal enthusiasts by announcing that they intended to hack a lamb limb from limb during a 1989 series of British concerts. They were talked out of it.

corpse') or Unseen Terror serenades like 'Burnt Beyond Recognition', 'Charred Remains' or 'In a Shallow Grave'. A similarly unlikely choice for the cabaret circuit is *Reek of Putrefaction* by Carcass, with its sleeve design matching selections such as 'Regurgitation of Giblets' and 'Feast on Dismembered Carnage'.

Charmed, I'm sure. Yet certain Death Metal entertainers weren't above the same old publicity stroke that everyone from Presley to the Pistols had pulled – that they were nice lads when you got to know them. Pacifist and vegetarian Carcass, for example, consisted of two medical students and guitarist Bill Steer who was almost apologetic with his 'I'm intrigued by mass murderers and that, but I think people take all the gory lyrics with a pinch of salt'.

Did the same attitude prevail during New York performances in 1990 of *The Manson Family* by twenty-seven-year-old John Moran? Under the patronage of arch-minimalist Philip Glass (who also financed its release on compact disc), this so-called 'opera' was not immediately comprehensible but still managed to evoke a vague black nostalgia for the 1960s in its *mélange* of vignettes from the relevant Beatles numbers, extracts from Manson's court testimonies and taped anecdotes about domestic life on the ranch that the Family had commandeered to plan the Sharon Tate atrocity.

Another opera with a morbid theme was in the works in 1992 after Canadian composer James Powlik chanced to read an article in a local British newspaper about the death of Joan Abery from Berkshire who, following the sudden passing of her beau years before, elected to cake her face permanently in chalk-white makeup so that no man would look at her again – well not in *that* way. Apart from necessary excursions to shops, she never left her bungalow where it was said she encouraged and befriended rodent vermin, and slept in a garden nest of twigs and shrubs – rather like wild and pathetic Jill-All-Alone in the Edward German operetta, *Merrie England* (1902). Intrigued, Powlik – via constant recourse to cuttings from the *Reading Chronicle* – pieced together an as yet untitled but apparently final musical draft of Miss Abery's story for a cast of five. He is presently seeking a sponsor.

Best of luck to him. Perhaps it'll signal a return of the *decent* death disc instead of all this 'Regurgitation of Giblets' rubbish. If James Powlik hasn't got anything, maybe we need snippets of 'Tell Laura I Love Her' in a British Telecom commercial to spark it off. However, since the door slammed on the innocent era of Laura, Terry *et al*, output exploring the same area has been less 'pure': either burlesque or premeditated reconstruction.

Of the old school, we have Paul Evans who, absent from the charts since 1960, waited nearly another twenty years to enter the UK Top Ten with the lively 'Hello this Is Joanie (The Telephone Answering Machine Song)' – she can't take the call in person because she's dead – while another novelty – with shades of Stephen King's *Carrie* – appeared in 1984's 'The Homecoming Queen's Got a Gun' by Julie Brown. Two years earlier, Japan had clocked in with 'Ghosts', their highest chart entry yet, but otherwise you have to search B-sides and album tracks for any items tackling death with a serious degree of commitment, whether the Commercials' boy-girl duet, 'The Heroine Dies' in 1982 or Dave Berry's 'On the Waterfront' – a man continues to walk the shore and scour the waves a year after his girlfriend has drowned even though 'something washed up on the beach, and no one was sure it was you'.

The most ingenious example is from 1986 in the home-made mono passion of the Len Bright Combo's 'Selina through the Windshield'*: the marketing department of a hair-spray firm affirms the product's lasting hold by crashing a car containing model Selina who is reduced to a bloody pulp but, never mind, her stiffened hair still looked OK.

It's conceivable, I suppose, that 'Selina through the Windshield' – or the Smiths' 'Girlfriend in a Coma' – might be a harbinger of a new kind of death disc, inspired and stylish, that will relate to the forthcoming millennium in the same way that 'Leader of the Pack' did to the mid-1960s. Yet the clamber of a contemporary equivalent up the charts might not be quite the desired V-sign at everything I detest about 1990s pop. Even if technological advances in recording since the 1960s did not impinge upon rough-and-ready spontaneity and endearing imperfections, it would be impossible now to assume the necessary Shangri-La/Twinkle-type naivety to produce more than a premeditated reconstruction. Furthermore, the popularity of Rap and Heavy Metal begs the question: who wants proper songs anymore – least of all ones in the class of 'Johnny Remember Me', 'Leader of the Pack' or even 'Selina through the Windshield'?

Once I thought that a proliferation of death discs exposed periods of creative bankruptcy but, these days, the lack of them could be the first indication of the very death of pop itself – or at least, the sort of pop I loved. May it rest in pieces.

* It was penned by 'Wreckless' Eric Goulden who many – me for one – would rate as superior to Elvis Costello, John Otway and other more fêted songwriters of the same late 1970s vintage.

Index

277

278

279

285

287